LES Paul

L·E·S· Paul

AN AMERICAN ORIGINAL

Mary Alice Shaughnessy

WILLIAM MORROW AND COMPANY, INC.

NEW YORK

Shaughnessy, Mary Alice.
    Les Paul : an American original / by Mary Alice Shaughnessy.
        p.   cm.
    ISBN 0-688-08467-2
    1. Paul, Les.   2. Guitarists—United States—Biography.
I. Title.
ML419.P47S5   1993
781.64'092—dc20   92-35832
[B]   CIP
                                                                             MN

Printed in the United States of America

First Edition

1 2 3 4 5 6 7 8 9 10

BOOK DESIGN BY MICHAEL MENDELSOHN

To Brian and our
daughter, Ella, this book
is dedicated with love

Acknowledgments

First, I would like to thank my husband, Brian Nalepka, for his unflagging encouragement and support throughout the writing of this book. A musician as well as a music historian, he not only offered me acute observations and personal reflections about the dynamic era in which Les Paul evolved as an artist, but patiently read and reread the manuscript as it took shape and tendered first-rate suggestions along the way.

There are several other people who deserve special acknowledgment: Nancy Williamson, the chief-of-reporters at *People* magazine, who gave me enough on-the-job flexibility to undertake this project; Mitch Douglas, my agent at International Creative Management, whose continuing belief in me and my work spurred me on during my darkest hours; Jim Donahue, who fought to bring me into the Morrow stable; Sherry Arden and Margaret Talcott, my former editors; Elisa Petrini, whose wise editorial comments and enduring support made my efforts more fruitful; and Laurance Rosenzweig, my voice at Morrow.

I am also indebted to several friends and colleagues who read the entire manuscript and gave me invaluable insights and advice: Jane Sugden, Jeanne O'Connor, Walter Carter, Marge Runnion, Mark Joy, Mary Huzinec, M. E. Marcus, Richard Lieberson, Janet Diamond, Dan Callahan, Carson Taylor, and Peter Hammar. And I am grateful to Rita Messing and Leslie Strauss, both of whom provided moral support on numerous occasions. Thanks also to Renata Miller and Donna Brodie of the Writers Room, my home away from home. Then, of course, there are the scores of people who kindly shared their personal remembrances of Les Paul and/or their knowledge of the recording industry; they are given more detailed acknowledgments in the source notes section of the book.

Contents

LES Paul

Prologue

From the time he was thirteen or fourteen years old, Lester William Polfuss was known by the Waukesha, Wisconsin, locals as Red Hot Red. He was a funny-looking kid, long and skinny, with blazing red hair, jug ears and a crooked grin. Once he discovered he could earn a pocketful of change by playing his two-sided harmonica and Sears, Roebuck Troubador guitar, he seemed to turn up all over town: church socials, Rotary Club meetings, speakeasies, the café next to the movie house. Not only did he make good money, he had the pleasure of seeing people gather and hearing the applause.

Goerke's Corners in nearby Brookfield was one of his favorite haunts. Before being demolished to make way for Interstate 94, it was the crossroads to Milwaukee, Madison, and Waukesha. Gleaming white barns, grazing Guernseys, and mysterious-looking mounds said to be ancient Indian burial sites surrounded the small cluster of businesses near the bustling intersection.

The area's most popular landmark, though, was probably Virgil and Nona Beekman's barbecue stand. Beekman's didn't have table service. "Curb girls" raced from car to car to take orders for the couple's otherworldly barbecue beef, which was slowly cooked and basted over an open pit in the apple orchard behind the drive-in. For a few cents extra, Nona would serve one of her famous double-dip sandwiches, dunking both the top and the bottom of the bun in her spicy red sauce.

Always packed on warm summer nights, this parking lot was the perfect spot for young Lester to test one of his latest sound experiments. The gangly one-man street band had often entertained Beekman's regulars. Outfitted with his $4.50 guitar, harmonica brace, and rusty washtub drum that he played with his foot, he looked like a half-starved fugitive from vaudeville. Night after night, he had warbled his way through old-time tunes like "The Wreck of the Old 97" and "I Never See Maggie Alone," and the tips rolled in.

Everybody in the parking lot could hear his singing and harmonica playing through the carbon microphone he'd hooked up to his mother's radio speaker, but his guitar strumming was lost to all but a few in the closest cars. He couldn't stand the thought that the people in the back of the lot were hearing only half his act. So one day in the summer of 1929, he appropriated a speaker from his father's Kolster radio-phono set. "It was the radio my dad used to listen to all the Jack Dempsey fights, until I stole it to make my first electric guitar," Les said. "I'd have to return it if a fight was going to be on, or there would be a fight between me and my old man."

That night he taped the arm of the Kolster phono set to the top of his guitar, stuck the needle into the wood, and fed the sound through the phono input. Then he cranked the volume up as high as it would go. The speaker occasionally squealed with feedback, but the peculiar new sound attracted even more curious onlookers. They drifted over from the produce stand and gas station across the road, and Lester's tips tripled. Then and there he knew "the electric guitar spelled money."

Les would perform hundreds of other offbeat audio experiments over the next sixty years. Scores would fail—"My closets are full of inventions I tried that were stupid"—but a few would help reshape the way recording engineers and musicians work in the studio. Along the way, he became a hillbilly radio star, a highly regarded jazz guitarist, and an internationally known recording artist and entertainer. Ralph Gleason, the late dean of music critics, succinctly summed up the guitarist's career in *Rolling Stone:* "No one in the history of pop music has had a greater effect on the ultimate pop sound than Les Paul."

Chapter 1

WAUKESHA ROOTS

Les Paul descended from sturdy German stock. His paternal grand-father, August Polsfuss, was born on February 26, 1847, in Prussia, then a Baltic Sea kingdom on the brink of an abortive democratic revolution. Three months after his twenty-third birthday, August packed as many belongings as one small bag would hold and boarded the tall-masted ship that would take him on a six-week voyage to America, far from the civil wars and economic depressions that were devastating his homeland.

He landed in the port of Baltimore, Maryland, in June 1870 and eventually headed for Waukesha, Wisconsin, fifteen miles west of Milwaukee. Waukesha was a rapidly expanding village of nearly three thousand settlers, many of them German-speaking first-generation immigrants. August was stable, hardworking, and thrifty. Within five years of his arrival in America, he married a sweet-natured farm girl named Henrietta Degler and purchased a forty-five-acre spread in neighboring Pewaukee. By then, the famous dairy region was also becoming known as the "Saratoga of the West."

In 1869, Colonel Richard Dunbar, an Irish-born American railroad tycoon, had drunk from Waukesha's numerous springs and announced that the waters had cured his diabetes. He soon purchased his own spring and built an elaborate, multi-spired Victorian hotel. Through Dunbar's ardent sponsorship, Waukesha suddenly became a chic watering place. "From all over the country came hypochondriacs and the genuinely ill, men and women of fashion, quacks, confidence men and promoters. Some bathed, some drank, some scooped up the profits," notes the Federal Writers' Project history of Wisconsin.

One savvy Chicago entrepreneur built a commodious resort hotel and installed a side-wheel steamboat on Pewaukee Lake, not far from August Polsfuss's farm. Another constructed Waukesha's palatial Fountain Spring House, which quickly became the focal point of summer society. It offered separate billiard rooms for men and women, a bowling alley, croquet and tennis courts, a racetrack, and a dazzling ballroom. A stunning six-hundred-seat opera house symbolized the area's sudden cultural explosion.

An editorial in the *Waukesha Freeman* suggested that the natives believed "their visitors were inspired by some midsummer madness to come so far for what appeared so common and valueless to themselves." Indeed, the saying around Waukesha County was "We flush our toilets with the same water the kings drink."

August Polsfuss thrived in the midst of the playful rich. The free-spending summer inhabitants possessed enough of an appetite for his fresh dairy products to provide him a steadily rising income with which to buy more land and cattle and begin raising a family. In 1881, his first son, George William Polsfuss, was born.

That was the year Wenzel Stutz, Les's maternal grandfather, came from Germany with three little girls: Louisa, Tressa, and Frances. The thirty-nine-year-old widower married Elizabeth Myer around 1884 and had two more girls, Carrie and Evelyn (who later gave birth to Les). The Stutz family eventually settled in Pewaukee. But not for long. Elizabeth died shortly after Evelyn was born on March 30, 1888. Wenzel's two oldest daughters moved away, and he took the rest of his brood to live in a small house in the heart of Waukesha, which by then had grown to a thriving town of some six thousand year-round residents. During the summer months the population nearly doubled.

According to Evelyn, her father's family owned a profitable brewery in Germany. But he never managed to find a comfortable livelihood in America. Wenzel just barely supported his family with a succession of menial jobs, moving from one rented home to another. All his girls had to work. Even "little Eva," who loved to study, was forced to drop out of school in the seventh grade and take a job as a domestic.

Evelyn nevertheless nurtured fond memories of her childhood in the "Saratoga of the West." By day the streets of Waukesha were bright with ostrich plumes, taffeta gowns, and parasols. In the evening live orchestra music spilled from brilliantly lighted hotels. Evelyn often stood near a window on the veranda of the Fountain Spring House so she could watch the elegantly attired couples glide across the ballroom floor.

Dancing, in fact, was her favorite pastime. On warm summer nights she took the new electric railway out to the public dances at Waukesha Beach, on the southern shore of Pewaukee Lake. She was a boldly coquettish, thick-maned gamine, just an inch or two above five feet, with sparkling sky-blue eyes and a wit to match. A talented seamstress, she designed elaborate cinch-waisted dresses for herself that mimicked the high-fashion styles of the pampered Southern belles who made Waukesha their summer retreat. She never wanted for a partner.

The best dancing in Waukesha County, as far as Evelyn was concerned, was at Griffith's Grove, where the orchestra played such romantic melodies as "Kiss Me Again" and "Coax Me" under the moonlit summer sky. That's where she met George Polsfuss, a gregarious, twenty-five-year-old charmer who had a keen eye for pretty, vivacious girls. Evelyn later recalled that he made all of her previous suitors look like awkward boys. He didn't have to ask twice if she wanted to take a turn on the dance floor.

George was a well-built man of five feet ten inches. By all accounts he had a silky-smooth way with words and was one of the best storytellers in town. In no time at all, he wound his charms around Evelyn, as he did around nearly everyone. "He was full of fun," she remembered, "just like me."

And full of dreams as well. George had no intention of being just another hardworking Wisconsin farm boy. He was a delivery man for Rickert's general store when he and Evelyn started making the rounds of all the dance spots in Waukesha County, but he was constantly on the lookout for gimmicks, for deals, for possibilities.

"George was always ready to try everything," Evelyn later said. "Waukesha only had about ten thousand people when we met, but he used to say 'Before I get through with this town, it'll have fifty thousand.'" She wasn't sure how he was going to do it; she just knew he would. After all, this was the enterprising young man who had given her a fancy one-horse, canopied rig so she could make the five-mile run out to his family's Pewaukee farm as often as she liked.

Even though Evelyn's childhood had been one of impoverishment, winning her over was no small task. She had witnessed the struggle and failure her father had gone through, and she swore her life would be different. Evelyn wanted a man as ambitious and dynamic as she was, a man who was going to amount to something. She was the type of girl people described as "clever" in those days—sharp eyes, sharp wits, sharp tongue. An avid reader, she was full of opinions on everything from politics to the evils of white sugar, and she did not suffer fools gladly. "If she didn't like you, you'd know it in a hurry," said longtime family friend Harold Vinger. "Evelyn had what you'd call a withering glance."

She adored George Polsfuss's family, though. "They were the most gorgeous people in the world," she recalled. "They had cows, chickens, everything on that farm. His mother worked so hard. I used to help her iron. And can! I canned, canned, canned for her. George's older sister, Ida, was lovely too, a first-class seamstress, and his younger brother, Eddie, was a nice boy who always helped his father on the farm."

She was reluctant to discuss her own relations, usually dismissing questions about them with a wave of her hand. The close-knit Polsfusses were evidently the family she felt she had never had.

On March 28, 1907, less than eight months after their courtship began, Evelyn and George were married in Waukesha. He was twenty-five; she was two days shy of her nineteenth birthday. One of Evelyn's first major resolutions was to persuade George to drop the first s in their surname to make it easier to pronounce. He reluctantly agreed—from then on using the spelling Polfuss. But he never took the appropriate steps to make the change official, so Polsfuss remained the legal family name.

Life was comfortable for the newlyweds. They had plenty of help from George's parents, who sent them endless supplies of garden-fresh vegetables and fruits and meat from the Pewaukee farm. Evelyn was no longer forced to scrub floors for other people, so she vigorously applied herself to running her new household. She nipped at George's heels to do the same on his job at Rickert's, which sometimes made him think his new bride was getting entirely too bossy.

Except for the birth of their first son, Ralph, on September 7, 1908, the early years of their marriage were fairly uneventful. The Polfusses eventually moved into a snug two-bedroom apartment at 109 North Street, a few doors away from Evelyn's father. She loved her new home, which had natural oak woodwork, lots of interesting little nooks and crannies, and a giant picture window facing a tree-lined street that curved down toward the gentle Fox River. She polished every room to a high shine every day.

Ralph was a quiet, undemanding infant, so Evelyn had plenty of time to make the family's clothes and prepare the doughnuts and German pancakes for which she was famous. She was proud of the fact that she prepared only homegrown vegetables, never the store-bought kind. White sugar, white flour, and caffeine were strictly forbidden in her kitchen. Honey was the sweetener of choice. "The lighter the bread, the sooner you're dead," she used to say.

These were the happiest years of Evelyn's life, an ideal time to have a second child. Pregnant during the spring of 1915, she sang lilting German lullabies in low tones as she gently ran her fingers over her full, round belly. She dreamed of the little girl so desperately wanted. Instead, on June 9, she delivered a robust baby boy she and George named Lester William.

Any misgivings she'd had about having a second boy quickly disappeared. Ralph had been a lovely, quiet baby, but Lester was special. Evelyn marked him as having musical talent before he reached the age of three. She was astonished by the alacrity with which he learned to repeat the words and melodies of the songs she sang as she cleaned the house. She soon began telling friends and neighbors that she had been blessed with a little prodigy.

Evelyn loved to go downtown and show off Lester in his big green leather carriage with the gold trimming. One summer morning she twisted his red hair into ringlets that fell softly over his shoulders and dressed him in his best handmade outfit—a blue-and-white-striped cotton suit with a matching white collar and tie. She'd promised the girls at McCoy's department store that she'd bring him in for a visit. "He was so adorable-looking. I set him on the counter and he lifted his little pants and danced and sang some of the songs I taught him. He remembered all the words and never dropped a beat," Evelyn said, recalling one of the verses:

> I want a girl just like the girl
> That married dear old Dad.
> She was a pearl and the only girl
> That Daddy ever had.

The girls at the store were enchanted and begged Evelyn to let them play with her apple-cheeked lad a little longer.

In the meantime, Les's father was proving himself to be an astute and forward-thinking businessman, one of several important traits he would eventually pass on to his younger son. George had squirreled away enough cash by 1915 to start his own car-repair service, which he operated from the yard of his North Street home. He broke into the budding automotive industry at a time when most of his Waukesha neighbors were still driving horse-drawn carriages over hard-dirt roads. In 1900 there were only eight thousand motorcars in the entire country. That number had swelled to more than 1.2 million by the time George opened his garage. The speed of the transition to automobiles surprised nearly everyone in Waukesha but George. He was ready for this newest wave of progress.

By the fall of 1919, the Polfuss family had moved into a brand-new two-story wood-frame house that George built on the edge of Waukesha's business district. It was the last house on West St. Paul Avenue, and its windows overlooked a lush, rolling woodland of maples and pines, and the front porch faced the winding Fox River. There was even enough money to buy a Kimball player piano, a long-cherished dream for Les's mother. Evelyn quickly collected an impressive batch of piano rolls to keep up with all the popular tunes of the day and soon began taking lessons, hoping to teach her children to play someday.

While Evelyn managed the children and the house, George worked diligently at his trade. He began operating an auto livery out of the garage and is reputed to have started the town's first bus line. As the repair side of his business picked up, he recruited Evelyn to help out with the cab service, first as a dispatcher and later as a driver. They were one of the first couples in Waukesha to trade in their horse and buggy for an automobile, and that made her proud. It showed they were different—maybe a little smarter than everyone else in town. Evelyn loved to drive the two-door Willys-Knight Overland that she and George bought right off the boat from Detroit. When a call came in from a customer out at Waukesha Beach, she'd just load Lester into the front seat of the Overland for the twenty-minute ride north.

She also got a kick out of the furtive romantic interludes she witnessed from the front seat of her cab. Evelyn kept tabs on who was running around with whom in town. But she always kept her mouth shut. "All the husbands were such big sports with money, going to the sportin' houses. None of them were true to their women. The wives would call me up and ask, 'Where's my husband?' They ranted and raved and said, 'I'm going to have you arrested!' because they thought I knew what was what. But I never told one secret. That was part of the business."

Of course it was a different story when *her* husband started pulling the same stunts, along with the drinking and gambling. Prohibition hardly hindered George's late-night carousing with friends. If he didn't know where to get the best rotgut whiskey in the county, he'd make it. And he always made sure there was plenty to go around. "You'd go to his place, and he'd make you feel at ease," one of his longtime friends recalled. "He was a professional bullshitter. He'd tell these stories and you couldn't believe him a lot of the time. But he was always fun."

Tales of George's winnings and losses at craps and poker grew to legendary proportions in the little town of Waukesha. According to Les, his father once lost a full-size passenger bus that he'd picked up in a previous game. George didn't go home empty-handed that night, though. He won the Schlitz Hotel, a choice piece of real estate in the heart of Waukesha. But within a year, he'd gambled that away too. His extramarital affairs were also well known to his neighbors. "When it came to women," one said, "George was like our Lord. He loved 'em all. And he never made any attempt to hide it. He was all over town."

Evelyn tried to rein in her rowdy and ungovernable husband, but to no avail. George began staying away from home for longer and longer periods, which made chaos of both his family and professional life. Evelyn soon found herself trying single-handedly to keep the livery service going. "If a call came in the middle of the night from someone out at Pewaukee Lake, I got up and took 'em, even if I was tired," she later complained. "All the time, George was out with the boys. Or at least that's what he said."

When George came home at all, he was often drunk. Screaming fights became the norm in the Polfuss household. But to little Lester, George was like a lovable, footloose older brother, always full of dazzling surprises. One summer night he came stumbling through the front door with a big brass trombone. Spying his perplexed young son standing in the living room, he marched over to an open window to give the horn a blow. The slide flew out of his hands and crashed onto the driveway. Without hesitation, George hoisted one leg up on the sill and crawled out after it. Lester laughed and applauded his father's besotted performance.

Evelyn, on the other hand, simply couldn't abide her husband's unpredictable nonsense. Her world was turning upside down, and her outbursts of temper grew more and more intense. But there was no one to whom she could turn. Her eighty-year-old father was in no position to help, and she couldn't appeal to George's parents to make him come to his senses. In fact, the series of tragedies that began overwhelming her husband's family around 1920 might have been partly to blame for his increasingly erratic behavior. George's mother and father died within six months of each other, and his brother, Edward, who lived on the twenty-eight-acre farm adjacent to August's spread, succumbed to tuberculosis shortly thereafter.

Around this time Evelyn became drawn to the progressive politics that had been active in her home state for decades. A political party basing its beliefs largely on Marxist theories was active in Milwaukee as early as 1870. When Victor Berger emerged as its leader around 1894, he introduced the distinct modifications that became known as "Milwaukee Socialism."

Evelyn, who eventually became a passionate believer in Berger's political philosophy, was enraged when in 1919 the House of Representatives unseated the Socialist congressman from Wisconsin, even though he had been voted into office by a wide margin. This was the same year that an ambitious young Justice Department lawyer named J. Edgar Hoover helped deport Emma Goldman, Alexander Berkman, and two hundred others to Russia; the same year that John Reed was expelled from the Socialist party and helped organize the Communist Labor party.

Despite Milwaukee's progressive political atmosphere, the citizens of neighboring Waukesha remained rock-ribbed Republicans. Here the farmers, not the labor unions, controlled the vote, and they consistently voted according to their own economic interests. They considered those with leftist sympathies a disgrace to the flag. Evelyn nevertheless held steadfast to her political views. She didn't care what others thought. "There's no doubt about it," Les later said.

"She preached diehard communism. The *Daily Worker* was delivered to our door as soon as it came out. The meetings she'd go to sometimes ended up in fistfights."

Evelyn often lectured her boys at the dinner table about the evils of capitalism and religion. "My mother and brother would have terrible fights about it," Les recalled. "Ralph got so frustrated he once broke a plate and went running out of the house crying. He didn't want to listen to all that Marx and Trotsky stuff while he was trying to eat. He just couldn't take my mother's craziness."

Apparently George couldn't either. He fled the family's West St. Paul Avenue home around 1923 and temporarily went to live with his older sister, Ida. But not before he and Evelyn verbally bludgeoned each other one last time. Les thought they were arguing about who was going to gain custody of him. Yearning to follow his father out the door, he was crushed to discover that his parents were fighting over who was going to keep the sausage machine.

Evelyn never stopped hating George for humiliating and abandoning her. At thirty-five, she was left alone to raise Ralph and Les, then fifteen and eight. George's marriage to a Waukesha-born nurse named Mary Ann Liberty roughly a year after the divorce only deepened Evelyn's resentment. She did everything in her power to sever Les's and Ralph's ties with their father. If they wanted to see him, they had to sneak across the river to his new automobile dealership, which he built with proceeds from the estates of his late father and brother.

Evelyn's enduring bitterness toward George, however, only served to alienate her children. "My mother was terribly domineering," Les later commented. "I didn't blame my dad for leaving. I probably would have done it a lot sooner. He was a very lovable man, but mother would absolutely disown me if she caught me talking to him."

Over the years, Les tended to mythologize his father, from whom he had acquired some of his ability to charm and entertain. But his drive and reckless confidence seem to have been the contribution of his mother, who eventually began advertising him as a genius.

Chapter 2

THE BOY WITH THE "TERRIBLE FASCINATION"

Les was about eight years old when he felt his first real twinge of interest in music. He was standing in front of a window on the second floor of his mother's house, watching a road crew lay lengths of sewage pipe along West St. Paul Avenue. One of the ditchdiggers pulled a harmonica out of his lunch pail and began blowing one sweet-sounding tune after another. A few moments later Les flew out the front door and plopped himself down, cross-legged in the dirt, within a few feet of the stubble-chinned laborer.

"Whatcha wanna hear, kid?" the ditchdigger asked. "Wanna hear 'Yes, We Have No Bananas'? That's a good one, huh?"

Les simply stared, unable to muster an answer.

"Whatsamatter, kid? You don't feel so good?"

Still Les made no reply.

The old man shrugged his shoulders, told the pesky kid to get lost, and turned back to playing. A few more minutes passed before he realized that the sound of his harmonica had the boy completely mesmerized. Softening a bit, he slipped the battered mouth organ into Les's hands and told him to give it a try.

"I can't play," Les stammered.

25

"Don't *say* you can't," the old man insisted, "till you've *proved* you can't."

To this day, Les claims that the ditchdigger's exhortation became a governing principle in his life. At the time, though, he was simply thrilled to get his hands on the silver, leather-covered mouth organ. Persuading his mother to let him keep it was another matter. Evelyn couldn't bear the thought of her immaculate little Lester putting his lips on a harmonica that some dirt-encrusted ditchdigger had used. If Les wanted to keep it—which, of course, he did—he'd have to wait until she boiled it in a steaming pot of water.

Oddly enough, Evelyn's attempt to sterilize the instrument helped initiate the first of many sound experiments her son would conduct over the years. Les found that the waterlogged harmonica gave him a bubbling, bluesy sound that made him different from all the other kids in town. From that day forward, he got into the habit of soaking his mouth organ in a pail of water for a few hours before playing. Little did he know that this was a standard practice among veteran blues performers.

Les's penchant for practicing sometimes pushed Evelyn to the outer reaches of her patience. But she tolerated it because she had "seen Les was going to be the best." Sometimes she'd have to referee fights between him and his older brother, who threatened to box Les's ears if he didn't stop blowing. Ralph might as well have asked his little brother to stop breathing.

Within the year, Les felt confident enough to compete in a talent contest sponsored by the Parent-Teacher Association. His long hours of practice were apparently evident to the judges, who gave him first-place honors. The recognition fueled Les's determination to become the best player in Waukesha County. "Les almost broke me buying harmonicas," his mother later recalled, "and he insisted on having the best, not the ones from the dime store."

Les's newly discovered talent not only brought him the attention he craved, it also helped him get through Park Elementary School. His Waukesha friends remember him as an extremely outgoing, happy-go-lucky boy. He was clearly one of the brightest kids in his class. But he was often too preoccupied with his harmonica to spend time studying assigned subjects. "My teachers saw that I was a dreamer," he later claimed. "I wasn't interested in learning about the cotton gin. I was interested in music." Walking to school with him, said his cousin Orval Polsfuss, was sometimes a lonely and frustrating experience. Orval would try to carry on a conversation, but Les was usually too busy trying to figure out new ways to play some song he planned to perform for classmates during recess. He'd practice the same tune over and over again until he got it right.

Like his father, Les was fond of leading his friends into mischief, especially Claude Schultz, a scrawny younger kid who lived a couple of blocks away on Fairview Avenue. Wherever Les went, Claude followed. One morning he talked Claude into walking to school through the giant sewer pipe under the Barstow Street Bridge. The pair smelled so bad by the time they got to class that they were sent home. Their intense dislike for school, reflected in their report cards, got them both suspended at least once, and pretty soon they became regular truants. Claude's mother was certain that Les was at the root of her son's errant behavior. Whenever she saw the two boys together she called them "a couple of no good for nothin' rascals."

Even when Les and Claude were on their best behavior, things seemed to go dreadfully wrong, as on the windy Sunday afternoon they got fired from their newspaper job. After hawking all the papers they could at the Five Points intersection, the boys decided to move to a more heavily trafficked part of Waukesha. They loaded the remaining papers into a basket on the rear fender of Les's new bike, then Claude climbed onto the handlebars for the crosstown ride.

Les was peddling at a furious pace when he spotted a monoplane passing overhead. He had seen plenty of two-wingers buzzing across the Wisconsin sky, but this was an entirely new type of aircraft. Determined to get a better look, he tilted his head back and squinted into the sun. All of a sudden the bike slammed into the back of a parked car. He and Claude went flying, and a strong gust of wind quickly scattered their papers all over the street. Lester, famous even then for hanging on to a hard-earned buck, immediately dove for the loose change that had spilled from his pocket.

"To hell with the money," Claude hollered. "Let's get these papers before they blow away." The boys salvaged as many as they could, but "old man Maury canned us just the same."

Les's fertile imagination was easily excited. One warm spring afternoon he and Claude were playing by the railroad tracks along the Fox River when Les suddenly announced they were going to embark on an excursion to the Mississippi.

"How the hell are we gonna do that?" Claude wanted to know.

Les pointed to a stack of railroad ties neatly bundled beside the tree-lined bank and matter-of-factly answered, "We're gonna make a raft out of them and just glide down the river. It's all downstream."

They'd build the raft in knee-deep water, he explained, because it would be too heavy to lift once it was finished. Les was confident he could scrounge enough tools to do the job from his father's garage. Then he and Claude would be free of nagging mothers, household chores, and, better still, school.

After a couple of days of hard labor, they were ready to launch. Les figured that the natural current would float them down the Fox to the Illinois River, which eventually fed into the Mississippi. Little obstacles like the Thompson's Malted Milk plant less than a mile downstream never occurred to the boys. Never, that is, until great gobs of stinking goo poured from one of the factory's cavernous waste pipes and nearly engulfed them.

"We forgot all about that damn thing being there," Claude later said. "All of a sudden I hear Les hollering, 'Claude, Claude.' His pole was stuck in the mud and the raft was going out from under his feet. Well, he went into the drink, sewage and all. I was trying to pull him back onto the raft when the whole thing went under. We swam ashore, but we stank like a couple of pigs in a stockyard. We climbed onto a railroad trestle and stayed there bare-ass naked until our clothes dried. That was the end of our trip to the Mississippi. We didn't even get out of Waukesha."

Les wasn't the type to allow one minor engineering miscalculation to discourage his impulse to experiment. He eventually turned his attention to his mother's Kimball player piano, the centerpiece of the Polfuss household. At first he was content to just pump away at the foot pedals and enjoy the music. Then he came to the conclusion that the piano rolls could use a few improvements. He punched extra holes in the perforated rolls, adding a new introduction here, a new ending there. If he created a *really* sour chord, though, he'd tape up the holes and make new ones.

Evelyn's ears were assaulted by some of the most bizarre openings imaginable to "Barney Google," which, even untouched by mischievous hands, is a song of unsurpassing silliness. But her son refused to stop there. One day he grew tired of using the foot pedals to make music and decided it was time to try to combine his mother's piano and the motor of her old Hoover vacuum cleaner. She came home to find the inner parts of the Kimball upright spread across the living-room floor on a clean white sheet Les had clipped from the linen closet. A soldering iron sat nearby.

Evelyn burst into tears. "Don't worry, mother," Les said nervously, "I'll put it back together better than I found it."

The next day she asked Fritzie Carlsted, a friend who was a piano tuner, to come over and examine her prized Kimball. Everything was in perfect running order, said Fritzie, not a single piece missing or out of place.

Evelyn was not a woman to be trifled with, especially when it came to the orderliness of her home. But she knew she was fighting a losing battle with her precocious son, then nine or ten years old. To save the rest of her beloved piano rolls from being torn to shreds, she arranged to have him take piano lessons with Mrs. Williams, who taught in her home across from the beautiful limestone church near the center of town.

It was an unfortunate pairing. Mrs. Williams quickly grew annoyed by Les's unwillingness to practice her time-tested finger drills. He, in turn, made no secret of being bored to distraction by her conventional approach to teaching. After several sessions, Mrs. Williams gave up on her resistant student. She sent him home with a note that read: "Dear Mrs. Polfuss, Your boy Lester will never learn music, so save your money. Please don't send him for any more lessons."

That was the end of Les's formal music training. Evelyn claimed to have given her son additional lessons, but he insisted that he gradually taught himself to play by numbering the keys on the player piano. As the paper rolled along and picked out the song, he'd stop it and note which keys were depressed for each chord. Eventually he memorized enough chord patterns to begin playing on his own. He never did learn to read music, though.

Years later—when Les was at the height of his career—Evelyn brought Mrs. Williams to see him perform at Milwaukee's Riverside Theater. Backstage after the show, the piano teacher apologized profusely for having underestimated her former student's talent.

Radio became available to the general public on a limited scale by 1922. The earliest models were crystal sets, which could be heard only through earphones. Les built one of his own around 1927, using directions from a friend who had a mail-order crystal-set kit. He began by wrapping a cardboard toilet-paper roll with thin, pliable wire. When he was done, the makeshift radio emitted a crude, crackly sound. The stations drifted in and out of static and were barely audible, but Les still got a thrill out of hearing those disembodied voices. Like his mother, an avid radio fan, he enjoyed twisting the dial all evening long to see how many stations he could get.

The airwaves were clogged with radio evangelists like Billy Sunday and Aimee Semple McPherson. In between those fire-and-brimstone preachers, though, Les managed to tune in the folksy hillbilly sounds emanating from the Chicago, Nashville, and Memphis stations. One of his favorite musicians was Deford Bailey, *Grand Ole Opry*'s first black star, famed for his smoky, bluesy harmonica sound. Les tuned in the *Opry* broadcast every Saturday night so he could study the veteran entertainer's soulful style of blowing. When he was confident he had achieved a reasonable imitation, he began performing around town for tips. "All of a sudden," he remembered, "I was the king of Waukesha."

Les reveled in the sidewalk crowds. They let him know in no uncertain terms that they loved him, and he clearly enjoyed the sense of control he felt over them. If he told an amusing story, they laughed; if he blew a particularly clever chorus, they cheered. It was a wonderful feeling, a feeling he was determined to sustain for the rest of his life. Pretty soon, he claimed, he was coming home with thirty bucks a week while his older brother, Ralph, a laundry-truck driver, was making eighteen.

Les and Ralph were a study in contrasts. Both had inherited their father's sly charm—and lifelong aversion to unembroidered truth; neither could bear to let facts get in the way of an otherwise interesting story. But that's where the obvious similarities between the Polfuss boys ended. Ralph, like most people, flipped on a light switch without a thought; Les stubbornly insisted on knowing what made the bulb work. While Ralph toiled for more than twenty years at the same delivery job he took as a teenager, Les became a popular and well-traveled radio personality by the time he turned seventeen. Ralph was a hard-drinking, gambling man like his father, but Les took after his hotheaded mother, whose drive for perfection was supported by an impressive capacity for self-discipline and work. Lester Polfuss never wasted time or money.

Though he might have been more prudent than Ralph, Les often taxed his easygoing brother's patience. One winter he recruited his friend Claude Schultz to help him create his own private skating rink in the backyard of his West St. Paul Avenue home. Together they dug a shallow crater, about thirty feet wide and six inches deep, then flooded the area with a garden hose. It was a grand idea ... until the spring thaw came. Hundreds of gallons of muddy water drained into his mother's dirt-floor basement. Ralph, of course, had to help clean up the mess. Then there was the time Les "borrowed" a radio from Ralph's laundry truck to build a receiver.

What irritated Ralph more, though, was Evelyn's obvious preference for Les. She constantly fussed over her younger son. If his shirt collar was the slightest bit frayed, she'd pull it off and sew it back on so the worn part didn't show. When she realized he possessed extraordinary musical talent, she drove him to practice, practice, practice. The more he achieved, the more attentive she became, her praise growing in direct proportion to the upward spiral of his popularity as an entertainer. "I became a God to my mother," Les later said. "She'd say, 'Les is doing this; Les is doing that.' All Ralph heard all day long was how great I was. It got so he could hardly stand to hear my name."

Years later, Evelyn herself regretfully acknowledged that she had blatantly favored her younger son: "I gave all my attention to Les. I didn't do enough for poor Ralph, but I seen Les was making it, so I had to teach him music, piano."

Evelyn didn't teach her son so much as she freely indulged his fierce curiosity. "I left him alone," she said. "I let him experiment even though he was making a mess of my beautiful home."

Every so often she even let his friend Claude spend the night. One of the boys' favorite tricks was to tie the sheets from Les's bed together and lower themselves out the second-story window so they could walk the deserted streets of Waukesha till dawn. More often, though, they'd quietly hunker down in Les's darkened bedroom for the night, each wearing a set of earphones, coaxing as much hillbilly music as they could out of his ramshackle crystal set. Sometimes, if luck was with them, they'd catch a Jack Dempsey fight.

One evening Claude proudly presented Les with a handsome cathedral-style Majestic radio. It had intricate wood designs carved on the front, and a speaker—no need for earphones. Claude offered to leave the radio in Les's bedroom if Les promised to keep his hands off of it.

"I wanted it for us to listen to at night, not for him to tear apart," Claude recalled. "But it was up there about a week and that was the end of it. Les was so damn inquisitive about everything. He just wanted to know how everything worked. He had a terrible fascination. He used to ask me, 'How does a voice travel on a telephone?' All those crazy things. I'd say, 'What the hell do you care? It works, don't it? Why bother your head about it?' But he just had to know."

As radios and phonographs became more popular, Les's fascination with electronics grew. He augmented what he learned about electricity in shop class with frequent forays to the library, devouring books on radios, Victrolas, cars, anything mechanical. He hung around local radio stations, dogging the sound engineers with endless questions about microphones, transmitters, equalizers. He befriended the proprietor of Davis's radio supply shop, who used to give him battered electronic equipment that otherwise would have been sent to the dump. To Les, Davis's castoffs were pure gold. He eventually built a crude radio station in the basement of his mother's house, using a small vacuum-tube transmitter and a single-button carbon mike. He pretended he was broadcasting his records from coast to coast. But it was really just house to house.

With Les's growing interest in radio came a passion for the string players it featured. He got a banjo and taught himself to strum and sing along with all the popular hillbilly pickers. But he soon became even more enamored of pop- and jazz-oriented guitarists like Nick Lucas and Eddie Lang. Lang's distinctive rhythm playing and harmonic richness helped redefine the role of the guitar, which, like the banjo, had once been confined to the rhythm section. "I had to figure out what Eddie was doing," said Les. But first he had to get his hands on a guitar.

Chapter 3

HERE COMES
RED HOT RED

There are several conflicting versions of the story of Les Paul's first guitar. His mother always insisted she purchased it for him. But the way he once told it, "he bought it with the $5 paid him for picking the potato bugs off Si Perkins's patch up the road." Then there's another account by Claude Schultz, who thinks *he* brought Les his first guitar, if it could be called that. "It was really just a shell with a crack up the back," said Claude "no strings, no bridge, no nothing."

Whoever provided it, Claud J. Moye was indisputably the first to show Les how to use the instrument. Everyone knew this good-natured Illinois-born farm boy as Pie Plant Pete. His singular ability to sing funny, folksy songs and simultaneously accompany himself on harmonica and guitar made him a favorite among midwestern radio listeners. He held his double-reed mouth harp in place with a U-shaped shoulder brace fashioned from a piece of No. 9 wire. As far as Pie Plant Pete knew, his harmonica holder "was original and the only one of its kind in the world."

In 1927 he landed a job on Chicago's WLS, the Sears, Roebuck–owned radio station; the call letters stood for World's Largest Store.

He became a star performer on the famed *Saturday Night Barn Dance* and on a weekday-afternoon program called *The Dinner Bell*. For $50 a week, Pie Plant Pete told jokes and sang little ditties like "Oh Dem Golden Slippers" and "Eleven More Months and Ten More Days I'll Be Out of the Calaboose," the latter his most popular number. He eventually became master of ceremonies for the WLS Showboat, a touring group that played one-night stands in small towns throughout the Midwest. The cast, always costumed in hand-tailored silk sailor suits, featured the station's Top 10 hillbilly entertainers, including Whitey "the Duke of Paducah" Ford, whose "Let me on the wagon, boys, these shoes are killin' me!" was as famous in its day as Minnie Pearl's "Howdeee!"

Les rarely missed one of Pie Plant's radio shows. Neither did his mother. So it was easy for him to persuade her to drive him to any Showboat concert that came within a hundred miles of town. Evelyn's willingness to satisfy young Lester's fascination for the comedic hillbilly performer was apparently limitless. Once, for instance, when the Showboat came to a downtown Waukesha theater, Evelyn made sure she and Les had front-row seats. Pie Plant Pete noticed them the moment the curtain went up: mother and son were dressed in identical handmade sailor suits, just like the Showboat cast. After sitting through two matinee performances, Evelyn and Les raced to the stage door, where they ambushed Pete. "You are a hero to my boy!" Evelyn exclaimed breathlessly. "He just loves to hear you on WLS."

The torrent of flattery earned the pair an eagerly accepted invitation to lunch and a third show. Backstage, Les handled Pie Plant Pete's road-beaten guitar as if it were a sacred icon. Pete was so touched by this display of respect for his instrument that he decided to teach the boy a few of his favorite chords. He found a piece of paper and sketched a guitar neck with frets and strings. Then he drew circles to indicate where Les should place his fingers.

"He took that piece of paper home with him," Pete wrote in his unpublished memoir, "and within a very few days I received a letter from his mom saying she had purchased him a Sears, Roebuck guitar. Well sir, every time we would be within fifty to a hundred miles of Waukesha, here would come Mrs. Polfuss and her boy. And each time she would insist on my hearing how he had progressed on guitar. In only a month or two he had surpassed my guitar playing by a country mile."

Les nailed down the rest of Pie Plant's act pretty quick too. He liked it so much that he began mimicking it, right down to Pie Plant's choice of songs and homemade harmonica brace (which Les has always claimed to have invented). In fact, one Saturday afternoon several years later, around 1935, Pie Plant tuned in Chicago's WJJD and was astonished to hear his former protégé sounding "as much like me as could be."

Les still had a few more dues to pay, though, before he would carve out his own special niche in Chicago radio. He augmented the chords Pie Plant Pete taught him with the *E-Z Method for Guitar* instruction book. Of course, he made a few modifications along the way. Rather than play with his fingers, as the book recommended, Les wanted to play with a pick, so he broke the fat end tooth off a comb. He left his beloved new instrument propped on a chair at the foot of his bed every night so it would be the first thing he would see in the morning. At least once a week, he'd lovingly clean the guitar from top to bottom with warm water and Ivory soap.

Evelyn drove Les to be the best in everything, constantly reminding him that there was "always room at the top." And her unremitting haranguing served to fuel his ambition. He became an all-around athlete—strong and coordinated enough to be the captain of his junior high football team, as well as a magnificent swimmer. Nothing captivated him quite so much, though, as the guitar.

"He played that thing all day long," said Evelyn. "His friends would stand in the yard and holler, 'Come on, Les, let's go out to the quarry swimming.' Once in a while he'd go, but he usually just wanted to stay in the house and listen to the radio and diddle with his guitar. He scrounged all over town trying to learn as much as he could about the thing."

Once he figured out how to strum the guitar and blow the harmonica with equal facility, Les became a double threat to the local competition. He designed his harmonica brace so he could easily flip the harmonica over with his chin. This way he could play either the C or G side without taking his hands off the guitar. Then, too, he had the most potent weapon of all: the Polfuss gift for palaver. Nobody could outtalk George Polfuss's boy. He could floor a roomful of people with a few simple words. His mother helped him come up with a stage name that played off the color of his hair and freckled complexion: Red Hot Red.

By 1929, Red Hot Red was doing solo dates for PTA and Rotary Club meetings in the afternoon, and fast-talking his way into speakeasies at night. He performed for schoolmates at Wednesday afternoon assemblies and worked the crowds at local dance halls, stock pavilion shows, movie theaters, festivals—anyplace that called for live entertainment. But Thursday evenings were reserved for the concerts at the Cutler Park band shell (which now bears his name). Claude Schultz recalled Les's debut there. "He was probably thirteen at the time. He was up onstage all by himself, playing that crazy two-sided harmonica of his and the guitar. He sang 'You Can't Take the Rattles Out of a Ford.' It went over with a bang."

Les was too young to understand the howls of laughter when he warbled his way through old-time tunes like "Don't Ever Marry an Old Man" and "I'm a Stern Old Bachelor." People were dazzled not only by the breadth of the young guitarist's repertoire, but also by the ease with which he stood alone on stage and spun out one story or joke after another. "He was the fair-haired boy of our city," remembers bassist Warren Downie, Les's boyhood chum and onetime bandmate. "Everybody figured he'd go on to make a name for himself."

Les knew he was a gifted guitarist and entertainer, but he wanted to prove himself as a pianist as well. He was always after his friend Fred Rosenmerkel, a trained musician, to show him complicated chord combinations. Although he had the Kimball upright at home, Les often practiced at the South Street YMCA. He eventually worked up the courage to begin sitting in with a band of older musicians in nearby Genesee who played taxi dances, where girls danced with patrons for ten cents a dance. This was a particularly daunting challenge for Les: he had to learn dozens of new tunes in a hurry, because the ballroom proprietor didn't want the orchestra to dawdle too long on any song.

Evelyn was so enthralled by her son's obvious musical prowess and increasing popularity that she took him to a professional photographer, the same one she'd used when he was a baby. He dressed for the occasion in an outfit straight off the WLS Showboat: a white shirt, navy-blue tie, white pants, and a white sailor cap. Adopting a Pie Plant Pete–inspired pose, Lester proudly held his guitar in playing position, the harmonica resting in its brace just a few inches from his thin, smiling lips. This, his first publicity shot (which Les has erroneously claimed was taken on his "first pro job" at Milwaukee's Schroeder Hotel), was displayed in his 1930 junior high school yearbook, *The Megaphone*. There would be many more.

During the early 1920s—before the Federal Radio Commission existed—the government handed out broadcast permits almost as freely as driver's licenses. Stations popped up everywhere: department stores built in-house transmitting studios to attract customers, and hotels did the same to draw guests. Some aired from laundries, stockyards, poultry farms, and, in some cases, private homes. The smaller ones were generally run by a manager, an engineer, and— if the station had enough commercial sponsors to afford one—an announcer, who usually doubled as an entertainer.

These fledgling stations almost always had to rely on pools of amateurs to help fill hours of airtime, which was a boon to aspiring young musicians. Live programming often consisted of impromptu performances by local singers, sheet-music salesmen, and others eager to display their talents for free on this exciting new medium. There was no rehearsal time. Singers simply stepped up to the mike and prayed that whoever was on hand to accompany them on piano knew how to play in their key. If the station failed to recruit enough performers off the street, the "announcer" might be forced to run through his entire stock of songs two or three times. Given radio's dire need for a continuous flow of live entertainment, Red Hot Red had little trouble wheedling his way onto local stations like Marquette University's WHAD and Racine's WJRN.

Waukesha County had lost its mystique as a fashionable health resort by the late 1920s. The fancy hotels and spas were long gone, replaced by auto and aluminum factories, and before Prohibition, beer breweries. But the town itself still enjoyed a lively night life. The rapidly expanding ranks of blue-collar workers eagerly supported scores of new taverns and roadhouses, which usually offered good food and live music. It was customary around Waukesha to have a drink and a dance in one saloon and move on to the next.

Most of these drinking establishments kept operating right through Prohibition. They sold setups—a glass, ice, and a bottle of soda water—and customers brought their own booze. The mob-owned joints dispensed with the setup pretense entirely and sold bootleg hooch openly. If they got busted, they just figured that into the cost of doing business. The same rule applied to the slot machines, which were discreetly stashed in a back room if the proprietor was tipped off that investigators had targeted his place for a raid.

Cullen Casey, a lifelong Waukesha resident, remembered one of Les's earliest forays into one of these rough-and-tumble speakeasies: "I had just started playing drums, and Les decided to get a band together. It was 1929, the year I graduated from high school. Les was still in school. We rehearsed at his house on West St. Paul Avenue. We practiced in the living room, and his mother would go upstairs until we finished. She didn't seem to mind that we were making a racket for hours on end. In fact, she encouraged it. She was awfully proud of Les. She just worshiped him."

The fourteen-year-old bandleader called his group Red Hot Red and His Five Aces, although there were only four other players. The boys even had a reason to rehearse: a New Year's Eve engagement at the Firefly Inn. An older musician named Doc Carter originally had been hired for the job, which paid $4 a man, a paltry sum for the biggest night of the year. After another saloon offered to pay him a few more dollars, Doc dumped the gig in Les's lap.

In addition to Cullen, Les recruited Len Rich to play sax, Herbie Wilcox trumpet, and Norm Kranish piano. Half a dozen rehearsals later, the Aces were ready to make their mark at the Firefly. Trouble started as soon as they walked through the door, though. The bartender, who apparently had been lapping up booze all afternoon, exploded with rage when he discovered that Doc Carter had sent a bunch of gawky-looking kids to usher in the New Year.

"Right away," recalled Cullen, "he started in on our trumpet player, Herbie, who was the most timid guy in the band. He said, 'You keep that goddam mute in that goddam horn or I'll shove it down your goddam throat.' Poor Herbie. He pert near swallowed the mute on the spot."

The band had only about fourteen numbers in its entire repertoire, songs like "Confessin'," then a big hit for Guy Lombardo. But the boys thought they could get by, because the Firefly was just a typical roadhouse. The crowd changed every hour or so. When they ran out of material, Red Hot Red stepped center stage with his banjo and harmonica and began playing "Comin' Round the Mountain" and other hillbilly chestnuts that people liked to sing along with.

"Even as a kid he was terribly talented," said Casey. "He picked up music like he'd never done anything else. We got by fine that night. When we finished the job, it must have been twenty below zero. I had a 1928 Chrysler that never started when it dipped below thirty-two above. I still don't remember how we ever got home."

Chapter 4

ON THE ROAD
WITH SUNNY JOE

The locals looked forward to the end of winter, because it signaled the reopening of the Waukesha lake resorts and the amusement park. With the roads finally clear of snow and summer vacationers pouring in, the ballrooms and dance halls jumped every night, and that, of course, meant more work for young musicians like Les. One warm spring evening in 1931, Les met a twenty-five-year-old itinerant string player named Sunny Joe Wolverton. It was probably one of the most important nights of his life.

As Les recounts it, he used to tie a piece of thread around his big toe and throw the spool out the window with a note that said, "Don't pull unless it's an emergency." On this particular night, his friend Harold Vinger, a dance-hall connoisseur, gave the thread a yank and woke him out of a sound sleep. Harold spoke quickly and insistently: "Red, Red, get up! You gotta come down here! Now!" Les shinned down the rainspout by his bedroom window.

"Out in Genesee," Harold said, barely able to contain himself, "there's a guitar player, a fella named Sunny Joe Wolverton, who plays with Rube Tronson's band. You gotta see him. He's playing up and down the fret board like nothin' you ever saw."

"He's playing up past the third fret?" Les asked incredulously. "That's just impossible. There's nothin' up there! Those other frets are there just for decoration."

"Well, Sunny Joe sure knows how to use them," Harold answered. "I told him all about your playing and he wants you to come on out."

Les was sure that this was just some cockamamie tale, but his curiosity was sufficiently aroused to go and see the guy Harold was so excited about. He even brought his new National guitar just in case something interesting was happening.

Genesee, surrounded by rambling dairy farms, had more cows than people. It also had a huge country-style ballroom that attracted hundreds of people from all over the county. A few thirsty patrons choked down the dance hall's Prohibition beer, but most of them preferred to dash outside to the parking lot periodically to take a few slugs from the bootleg stash they kept hidden in their cars.

Rube Tronson's Cowboys, the featured performers, were well known to the WLS Saturday Night Barn Dance audience, and they played one-nighters throughout the Midwest during the rest of the week. All five musicians routinely crammed into Rube's sixteen-cylinder Cadillac, along with their instruments. A pair of longhorns protruded from each fender of the box-shaped car.

Rube's crew looked just the way a cowboy band should: They all wore ten-gallon hats, bandannas around their necks, and pants tucked into fancy cowboy boots. A tall, good-looking, Norwegian fiddle player with a powerful taste for drink, Rube presided over a group that included a banjo player, an accordionist, a drummer, and Sunny Joe, who often soloed on guitar, mandolin, violin, and banjo.

Too young to walk in the dance-hall door, Les waited till the coast was clear, then clambered through a lavatory window. Joe's picking exceeded anything Harold had described. Les hung by the lip of the stage, planting himself in front of Sunny Joe, just as he'd planted himself in front of the ditchdigger six or seven years earlier. His eyes locked on Joe's nimble fingers as they plucked out one fancy run after another. During intermission, Sunny Joe sized up the brash youngster. "You play guitar, I suppose?"

"Well, I thought I did," Les answered, "but I don't think I do now. How come you pick down there and I don't see you pick anymore and four notes come out?"

"That's what I learned when I studied violin," Joe explained. "That's left-hand pizzicato."

Before the evening was over, Joe invited Les to bring his guitar up onstage and sit in with the band. Les, in turn, asked Joe to play a few of his favorite tunes the following night on WLS. He promised Sunny Joe that he'd learn them by the time the Cowboys came back to town, and sure enough, he got them down pat.

Despite the fact that Joe was nine years older, the pair became fast friends. Les once brought Joe home, dragging the amused guitarist up to his bedroom for a private recital. He hit Joe with everything he had: the guitar, the double-sided harmonica, and three or four of his best Pie Plant Pete songs, including "I Had but Fifty Cents" and "The Cat Came Back." He even chugged out a few simple melodies on his jug.

Sometime in August 1932, Rube Tronson gave Les a call and asked if he wanted to hit the road with the Cowboys. Les thought the job paid only $8 a week, but he took it anyway, thinking he'd learn as much as he could from Sunny Joe. Evelyn, who already had visions of her son as a successful professional musician, agreed to let him go after he promised to come back for school in September. She made her boy star a slew of fancy cowboy shirts in several different colors, stitching them together on her old Singer, one of the few household gadgets her son had left untouched.

"People stopped Les on the street and asked him where he got his beautiful clothes," said Evelyn. "They wanted to know if I'd make some for them too."

Now properly outfitted with Western garb, guitar, and harmonica, Les boarded a bus to meet Rube in Escanaba, Michigan, where they were scheduled to play their first date together. He was delighted to discover that the job paid $8 a night instead of $8 a week, but disconsolate when he found out that Sunny Joe was no longer with the band. Although Les later claimed that he had been hired by Rube to replace his fired mentor, Joe in fact had quit the Cowboys to take a more lucrative radio job in St. Louis.

At seventeen, Les might have been the youngest of Rube's Cowboys, but he was certainly the most technically proficient. One of his first projects was to construct a PA system for Rube's Caddy so the Cowboys could announce their showtimes when they arrived in a new town. The innovation boosted the band's attendance rate considerably and proved early on that Lester Polfuss had an unerring instinct for self-promotion.

His first radio appearance with Rube's band was on a fifty-watt amateur station in Iron Mountain, Michigan. "The engineer kept telling the bass player to back up toward the door, to get him further away from the mike so he wouldn't overpower the rest of the band. The first thing you know, he was out in the alley. Then the engineer tells me to peek out the door and look to the left, toward the barber shop. The barber used to sweep the hair off the floor and put it in a pile in front of his shop. If he lit it on fire and the smoke went up, that meant we were coming in great."

After a few glorious weeks on the road with Rube Tronson's Cowboys, Les of course found his return to Waukesha High School to be a comedown. So the call from Sunny Joe Wolverton a few weeks later was sweet manna from heaven. By the fall of 1932, Les had had just about all he could take of school, where he had only reached tenth grade by the age of seventeen. Life at home apparently was equally unsatisfying. If Evelyn thought of herself as a devoted mother who did everything in her power to encourage her son's musical aspirations, at the time Les was more inclined to regard her as an overbearing meddler who tried to exert undue control over him and his older brother.

Then there was her radical political philosophy. "Waukesha was stiff Republican from the word go," said Les's friend Harold Vinger. "If you were a Democrat, that was like waving a goddam flag in front of a bull. So you can imagine that Evelyn was walking a lonely road in this town. I don't think Les liked what she stood for."

He was also eager to get more deeply involved in music. His only steady gig then was at a Pewaukee Lake dance hall run by Ted Jamieson, whose greatest claim to fame was that he had once been Gene Tunney's sparring partner. Les managed to teach himself enough piano to pound the ivories with Obie O'Brien's four-piece band every Saturday night. And although his playing passed muster for Jamieson's beer-chugging patrons, his friends knew he wanted more—a lot more.

"When it came to music, Les wouldn't stop till he got what he wanted," said Vinger. "He'd play someplace till he felt he wasn't learning anything; then he had the guts to move on. We all knew he had it in him to go places. You could feel it even then. He had an intensity about him that made him stand out."

By 1932 Sunny Joe Wolverton had a wealth of show business experience to pass along to his young protégé. Born Ralph Edwin Wolverton on July 8, 1906, he was the youngest of nine children raised in a musical family in Brazil, Indiana. His father was a crack fiddler who formed a string band with the Wolverton boys to play old-time favorites like "Sweet Bunch of Daisies" and "Over the Waves." When Joe turned seven, his father stuck a mandolin in his hands and told him to start strumming. Shortly thereafter, the boy won first prize in a talent contest in Carbon, Indiana.

Joe soon bought a banjo with money he earned helping his father repair chimneys and traded his bicycle for a guitar. His formal training began in junior high, with four years of violin lessons from the man who doubled as the high school band instructor and city park music director. As Joe later told Les, these lessons helped him relate intricate violin fingerings and chord positions to the guitar and banjo, which gave him an edge over other players. He could play scales all over the neck, and within a few years, perform a razor-sharp guitar solo of the frenetically paced "Flight of the Bumblebee," an astonishing technical feat for even the most accomplished string player.

Joe was rail-thin all his life, with skinny, clawlike fingers and a pointy chin. But he was powerfully attractive to women. In 1926 he married the first of six wives, Thora Keeler, a vivacious Illinois show girl who performed with the Red Path Chautauqua, a highbrow tent show that offered a mix of music and dance fare with educational lectures. The following year the couple became vaudeville regulars with a comedy act dubbed Keeler and Waldo, once splitting the bill with George Burns and Gracie Allen at the St. Louis Theater. Joe played piano and banjo and Thora, decked out in a little girl dress and pigtails, did child impersonations. "She'd come screaming out onstage, then settle down and sing a few songs," said Joe. Their lively blend of music and slapstick brought them to audiences all over the United States and Canada.

By 1929, though, the talkies had killed vaudeville, and along with it Joe and Thora's act. "Not long after that," says Joe, "she and I busted up. I got into a little altercation with her family around the dinner table. I got up and left the house and never came back."

Joe's versatility on a variety of stringed instruments helped him land a job on WLS in Chicago, playing strictly country-style banjo and guitar. He shared airtime on the station with Gene Autry, Red Foley, and Les's old friend and mentor Pie Plant Pete. Like most radio personalities in those days, Joe was given a stage name. His usually easygoing disposition earned him the title Sunny Joe Wolverton, which he used until 1934.

Sometime around 1930, Rube Tronson persuaded Sunny Joe to quit his WLS staff job, pack up his strings and join the Cowboys. The job paid $12 a night, plus three bucks extra for driving the Caddy whenever Rube got drunk, which was usually before the band finished its second set. But life on the road with Rube's band was hard work for little money, so the telegram that brought news of a job offer from KMOX radio director Hank Richards didn't come a moment too soon. Dated August 6, 1932, it was sent to Sunny Joe in care of the "Rube Tronson Orchestra," Conway Hotel in Appleton, Wisconsin: THINGS LOOK MARVELOUS HERE STOP WIRE ME IF YOU CAN ARRIVE IN TOWN THURSDAY STOP CAN ADVANCE FARE IF NECESSARY BUT WOULD RATHER NOT STOP CHANCE FOR YOU TO MAKE LOTS OF MONEY AND NAME FOR YOURSELF STOP NO WILD GOOSE CHASE. Now that was a deal Joe couldn't refuse.

KMOX, "The Voice of St. Louis," began in 1925 as a five-thousand-watt station based in the Hotel Mayfair. It was given the call letters K for its location west of the Mississippi, MO, for Missouri, and X for Christmas, the day of its first broadcast. The station had grown to a fifty-thousand-watt CBS affiliate covering forty-one states by the time Joe signed on. One of his first assignments was to back up the Girls of the Golden West, two saucy young brunettes who harmonized on good old cowpoke songs and wowed audiences with their flashy yodeling tricks.

Within a few weeks, Hank Richards asked Joe to pull together a bona fide hillbilly-style band for the early morning *Farm Folks Hour.* Free to hire whomever he pleased, Joe remembered young Lester Polfuss. The hillbilly format was perfect for Les's yahoo personality and bombastic entertaining style. His guitar strumming was still pretty clangy—especially since he insisted on using a guitar with a resonator to boost his volume—but Joe thought the boy's harmonica and jug playing would bring an added touch of frivolity to the act.

Joe offered Les about $45 a week to do the *Farm Folks Hour,* a handsome salary compared to what others were bringing home during the Depression. The average U.S. wage had fallen to $17 a week, down from $28 before the 1929 stock-market crash. Breadlines were forming in cities all over the country. And Rudy Vallee and Bing Crosby both had No. 1 hits in 1932 with the dolorous tune "Brother, Can You Spare a Dime?"

So Les dropped out of school on October 4, 1932, to hitch his wagon to Sunny Joe's star. Evelyn accompanied her son on the 350-plus-mile bus trip to St. Louis. "When we got there," Les later recalled, "Mother turned around and went right back home. She never left the bus station. She just wanted to be sure that I got there all right."

St. Louis, then the seventh-largest city in the United States, was a sprawling metropolis. Some fifteen railroad lines operated out of massive Union Station, which accommodated more foot traffic in a single afternoon than Waukesha saw in an entire week. Lying in the crescent-shaped bend of the wide brown Mississippi, the city was usually blanketed with a thick layer of smog from the vast quantity of coal burned in the close-packed belt of factories along the river. Breathing was sometimes a chore. But the *Farm Folks Hour* reached out to the verdant fields beyond the smokestacks. Monday through Friday mornings, it jump-started listeners with this perky salutation: "Yes, sir, it's five-thirty! The early bird gets the worm!" To attract sponsors, KMOX published an advertising flyer touting the show as "the ideal time to merchandise your baby chicks, breakfast food, overshoes, seeds, poultry feed, or, well, what have you.... "

Interspersed with the latest farm and weather reports were old-time numbers, minstrel shows, and comedy sketches. There were the good-natured hijinks of the Ozark Mountaineers, Sad Sam the Accordion Man, and hillbilly strummer Wyoming Jack Bryant, said in one radio trade magazine to be "as charming and as merry and as wholesome as the great West from which he comes." But Sunny Joe Wolverton and His Scalawags were reputed to be the radio audience's undisputed favorites. Joe played fiddle, guitar, banjo, and mandolin; Ken Wright, an organist Joe had met in a Green Bay, Wisconsin, theater, doubled on accordion, and Les filled out the sound with his guitar, jug, and harmonica.

Joe dubbed his younger partner "Rhubarb Red," which was a clever rip-off of Pie Plant Pete's stage handle, rhubarb being another description for pieplant. Les hennaed his hair every week to fit the name. His Waukesha friends were thrilled to hear one of their own on such a big station. "We all tuned in the week after he left town," his friend Cullen Casey later recalled. Ted Jamieson, Les's former dance-hall employer, pointed to the radio and said, "That's my boy!"

To stretch their KMOX earnings, Les, Joe, and Ken crowded into a single room in a boardinghouse on Lindell Avenue, near the heart of the city. Sometimes the boys engaged in a little post-midnight rowdiness. One night Joe decided he was going to wreak revenge on Les for all Les's rotten practical jokes, like the time he put glue on Joe's violin chin rest right before a performance. Les had a habit of snoring long and loud with his mouth wide open. On this particular evening, Joe mashed up a bottle full of quinine pills, poured them into Les's yawning maw, then quickly jumped into bed and feigned sleep. A moment later Les leaped out of bed in a total panic.

"Hey, Joe!" he yelled. "Wake up!"

"Whatsamatter, Les?" Joe innocently asked, stifling his snickers.

"My gallbladder's busted!"

That was probably the same night the trio were nearly evicted for smashing the landlady's window during a knock-the-stuffing-out-of-the-pillow fight. She told them they could stay after they promised to repair the window and act like grown-ups.

Outside the radio station, the Scalawags performed in nearby theaters, dance halls, county fairs—anyplace they could make an extra buck. Joe wore baggy dungarees scrawled with the names of all the stations where he had worked, Ken sported high-water pants and a half-squashed black top hat, and Les decked himself out in a pair of yellow high-button shoes, suspenders, and a straw hat.

One of the group's most memorable outside jobs was a goodwill mission. The station sent the Scalawags and Wyoming Jack to a Jacksonville, Illinois, mental institution to entertain a group of long-term patients. During his act, Wyoming Jack shot off a starter pistol as he sang one of his hokey cowboy tunes, inspiring a chorus of hysterical screams. "Half the people in the place went nuts," remembered Sunny Joe. "They started running around the room, diving for the floor." That was the end of the show.

Les was the sort of kid who might have fired a starter pistol under similar circumstances just to see what would happen, more out of a perverse sense of amusement than out of meanness. Recalling some of the antics that were to become lifelong traditions with Les, Sunny Joe cited the Saturday night in November 1932 that he and Delores Burt got married. At the program director's suggestion, the wedding was performed before KMOX's studio audience and heard by millions of weekend listeners. The over-the-air wedding was a radio first for St. Louis and probably for the rest of the country as well.

But Les added an unexpected twist to the proceedings. As the preacher led the couple through their vows, Sunny Joe looked up and saw Ken Wright rushing down the aisle. He was wearing a pair of farmer's overalls, carrying a double-barrel shotgun, and pushing Les in a giant pram. As soon as Les jumped out of the carriage and onto the stage, he pulled a baby bottle from his mouth, pointed at Sunny Joe, and cried, "That's my daddy!"

In a way, Sunny Joe was Les's surrogate father. He encouraged the teenager to continue to live with him and Delores and subsidized his membership in the St. Louis musicians' union. When Sunny could no longer stand the sound of Les's tinny-sounding guitar, he drove the boy 350-plus miles to Kalamazoo, Michigan, and bought him his first Gibson guitar—an L-50 budget arch-top that cost about $50. Then he began giving him lessons, eventually transforming the amateur guitarist into a professional to be reckoned with.

"I never wanted to spend time fooling around with a lot of dudes that wanted to learn guitar," Joe later commented, "but I thought I could teach Les something of importance. He was so willing. He'd set and watch me rehearsing and he'd say, 'Show me how you did that.' I'd say, 'Hey, we gotta get this radio program together. I'll show you after a while.' But he had to know right there and then. The first thing I did was make him throw away his capo and thumb pick. I taught him how to use his wrist. I also tried to teach Les how to read music, even though he never seemed to want to learn. But I did teach him chord spellings.

"Hell, he used to keep me awake at night. I'd go to bed and he'd go into the bathroom and practice his guitar for three hours. If he was having a tough time, he'd come and wake me up. He'd say, 'Show me how you did that again.' It was fun to watch him grow, to see how crazy he was to find out what makes music come out of the guitar. He was more than willing to spend the time to do it, which is something I rarely saw in other guitarists, then or now."

Les was so determined to learn as much as he could about playing the guitar from Sunny Joe that he temporarily lost interest in his electronics experiments. The closest he got to an electric during his years with Joe was the day in 1932 they visited a St. Louis music store that had a few on display. "They weren't made by any of the big companies that I can recall," says Joe. "We tried them and

laughed ourselves silly, 'cause they hadn't perfected them at all."
(Contrary to the repeated claims Les has made over the years, it was
at least 1934 before he began using an electric guitar.) In the meantime, he and Joe had all the work they could handle with their
Gibson acoustics.

Sunday was always the worst day of the week for Les. It was the
only day the band didn't work. Joe needed a little time alone with
his new bride, and Ken had his own friends outside the band. He
saw enough of "Red" the other six days of the week.

"I was around grown men all the time and I was just a kid," Les
later said. "The streets of St. Louis never seemed emptier than on
Sunday. I'd just stand on a corner and cry like hell because I was
so lonesome."

Those were the times when Sunny Joe's telephone trick came in
handy. Joe taught Les how to put a nickel in a pay phone and knock
it into the quarter slot, which saved him a fortune in long-distance
calls to Waukesha. In fact, seven or eight months after his arrival in
St. Louis, Les reluctantly called his mother to announce that he'd
be coming home to stay, at least for a little while. Though radio was
a particularly healthy industry during the Depression, KMOX wasn't
entirely immune to the sort of staff cutbacks other places were suffering. Sunny Joe's sidemen were among the first to go. For a while
he held on to his job at the station as a solo act, but it wasn't long
before he was fired too.

Within a few months, though, Joe found a new spot in Springfield,
Missouri, at KWTO, the call letters signifying "Keep Watching the
Ozarks." The station, which aired its first broadcast on Christmas
Day in 1933, was in the market for a lively hillbilly act. Once again,
Joe called upon his young sidekick from Waukesha. Just a duo now,
he and Les called themselves the Ozark Apple Knockers. Joe, re-
nowned as "the bad boy of the air," loved to drink and raise hell;
Les loved to tell corny jokes and laugh.

Shortly after they arrived in Springfield, Joe bought Les a handsome new Gibson L-5. It was just like the one Joe regularly used.
At the time, the L-5 was the instrument by which all other guitars
were judged, the model favored by all the leading professional play-

ers. At $275, it was by far Gibson's most expensive instrument, but Joe managed to get a discount because he was one of the company's endorsing artists. Now that he and Les were on equal footing with their guitars, Joe began teaching Les pop standards like "Sophisticated Lady," "Tea for Two," and "Lover," tunes that were much more demanding than the three-chord hillbilly songs that were the staple of their KMOX act.

Les's progress was stunning. His phonographic memory and agile fingers enabled him to begin imitating Joe's string attack in a remarkably short time. Even some of Joe's longtime fans began having trouble telling them apart. Indeed, Evelyn used to laugh when she'd tell people that her son was copying Joe's best runs when he wasn't looking.

Several months into the KWTO gig, Les, then eighteen, felt confident enough about his playing to turn his attention to an entirely new enterprise: girls. His fascination for music had all but eclipsed his interest in the opposite sex—that is, until he spied a pretty young piano player named Lou in a Springfield honky-tonk. Les used to run off with Joe's L-5 at every opportunity to sit in with Lou. That was the main reason Sunny Joe got Les one of his own.

Les's passion for his new companion could erupt at the most inopportune times. One day, after a good hard rain, Joe invited the couple to accompany him to a farm ten miles outside Springfield where he often pursued his favorite pastime, hunting for arrowheads and other Indian relics. Les and Lou remained huddled in the backseat of Joe's '29 Buick while he dug for the artifacts. Before long, though, they began steaming up the windows with some hot and heavy necking. The farmer's children watched from inside the house, giggling as they pointed at the car. Their horrified father, however, took the matter far more seriously. "Wait till I get my shotgun!" he hollered. Joe jumped into the driver's seat and beat a hasty retreat.

A couple of big talents like the Ozark Apple Knockers couldn't be confined for long to a little town like Springfield, Missouri. Sometime during the winter of 1934, they were befriended by Les Huntley, the creator of the Mescal Ike cartoon strip, which ran in several Midwestern newspapers. Huntley used his Chicago connections to get the Ozark Apple Knockers an audition at WBBM, CBS's powerful Chicago affiliate.

The station was headquartered in the prestigious Wrigley Building, the illuminated landmark at the foot of what was later known as Michigan Avenue's Magnificent Mile. It also did remote broadcasts of first-rate orchestras from the city's finest concert halls and hotels. All in all, WBBM had just the sort of big-city sparkle Les and Joe were looking for. After a successful audition, they returned to Springfield long enough to finish out their notice.

It was a threesome traveling to Chicago—Joe; his wife, Delores; and Les. They had lived together under the same roof for so long and were so excited about the new job that the trip should have been a relaxed affair. But it wasn't. They had less than twenty-four hours to drive some five hundred miles from Springfield to Chicago and report to the station for work.

Sheets of rain cut through a blanket of fog that reduced visibility to only a few yards. After driving all night, Joe was too exhausted and bleary-eyed to go any farther. He reluctantly turned the wheel of the Buick over to his young partner, who, unfortunately, was aching all over with a blazing fever. Outside Atlanta, Illinois, 150 miles from their destination, Les ran the Buick into the back of a semitrailer. The radiator collapsed on impact, and a jet of steaming water gushed onto the road. Joe was grateful that nobody had been injured, but beside himself after surveying the damage to his car. He was about to tear into Les when Delores reminded him that the boy was dreadfully sick.

"Look at the goddam car!" Joe wailed. "I'm sick!"

"I'm going home to my mother," Les cried.

"The hell you are," Joe shot back. "You're gonna be on the radio in Chicago with me tomorrow." He was.

Les later made light of the fact that his first love had given him a fierce dose of the clap.

The effects of the Depression weighed heavily on Chicago in the early 1930s. The municipal government was dead broke and the banks refused to extend it credit. In 1933, unruly mobs of schoolteachers stormed the banks for back pay after having been paid for more than ten months in scrip. Pinkerton guards, armed with the same kind of machine guns used by Al Capone's thugs, guarded Lake Shore Drive mansions. They protected the estates from riots by the hungry, which Chicago's wealthy constantly feared.

Within weeks of taking his first oath of office, Franklin D. Roosevelt began broadcasting his famous Fireside Chats in an attempt to calm economic fears and win support for the New Deal. Gangster violence was still creating havoc on the streets of the Windy City, though. One steamy July night in 1934, after Les finished playing a gig at a tavern on Sheridan Road, he and Sunny Joe heard that federal agents had just gunned down John Dillinger, who had terrorized the Midwest for more than a decade. The pair hightailed it over to the Biograph Theater in Joe's Buick in time to see a huge crowd of people surrounding the spot where Dillinger's bullet-riddled body had fallen. Some onlookers were digging bullets out of a nearby telephone pole; others used their handkerchiefs to mop up the gangster's blood. Les and Joe knew they had witnessed a small bit of history in the making.

Sunny Joe and Rhubarb Red continued to bill themselves as the Ozark Apple Knockers on WBBM, although Chicago's more sophisticated urban audience was now calling for fewer hillbilly tunes and more pop standards. That was no problem. The student was mastering his instrument with amazing speed. "Me and Les planned on being pretty important," remembered Joe, "so we went after the stuff nobody else could play, big-band tunes and the like. He did rhythm mostly, but I used to let him lead once in a while. He'd copy my style and say, 'Don't show anyone else, Joe.' "

Though Les later repeatedly boasted that he and his partner each earned the princely sum of $2,500 a week during this economically desperate period, Sunny Joe distinctly recalls that WBBM paid them closer to $75 apiece to play five or six afternoons a week for Sendol, which made patented medicine for colds. And that gig lasted for only a few months, until Sendol withdrew its sponsorship from the station. On March 3, 1934, the Apple Knockers received a tersely worded missive from Holland E. Engle, the assistant program manager. "Gentlemen," he wrote, "please consider this as two weeks notice of the cancellation of your contract."

Eight weeks later, Sunny Joe accepted a job at the Chicago World's Fair. He was contracted to put together a trio to play two three-hour shows a day for the Reliance Manufacturing Company exhibit. For $200 a week, the group was supposed to perform old-time country music, the kind that made people forget they couldn't afford to put clothes on their kids' backs or shoes on their feet. Once again Joe recruited Les; then he hired his friend Fry Peters, an Australian guitarist. Part of the deal required the newly formed trio to wear garments embroidered to advertise the Big Yank Shirt Company, a subsidiary of Reliance.

Despite the devastating impact of the Depression, the so-called Century of Progress fair, designed to celebrate Chicago's hundredth anniversary, was a raging success. Riots nearly broke out on the streets when the city tried to close the fair down at the end of 1933, so it was held over for another year, attracting 16 million more people. Among the exhibits were a partial reconstruction of a Chinese city, a Japanese teahouse, and a picturesque Mayan nunnery. By all accounts, though, Sally Rand was the main attraction. According to Chicago historian Emmett Dedmon, "Sally was an unemployed silent film actress who burst unexpectedly on the scene, astride a handsome white horse, in the role of Lady Godiva. When this outrageous bid for work failed, she gave up her horse, bought two ostrich feathers—on credit, she insisted—and persuaded the manager of the 'Streets of Paris' concession to hire her as a fan dancer."

The brazen twenty-nine-year-old actress reportedly earned up to $3,000 a week with her undulating interpretations of Debussy's "Clair de Lune." Fending off vigorous attempts to censor her act, writes Dedmon, "she all but pushed into obscurity the scientific theme that was intended to dominate the centennial." In fact, supple Sally was given much of the credit for making the Century of Progress a triumph.

She wasn't the only feisty performer at the fair, though. Les, now nineteen and more confident than ever, chafed at any attempt by Joe to curb his independence. Their partnership abruptly ended in August 1934, two years after it began.

As Les has repeatedly told the story, he and Sunny Joe broke up because Les wanted to begin playing jazz and to experiment with the electric guitar. Sunny Joe, he says, was a diehard country player who wanted to stick with acoustic instruments. Sunny Joe, however, remembers the episode quite differently. One day, he says, a girl Les was dating came to see him perform at the fair. During intermission, the couple planted themselves on a bench next to the Big Yank display and started kissing and hugging. The boss, all too aware that Les was wearing a shirt embossed with the company logo, told Joe to make them stop.

Les balked at the order. "Ain't it on our time?" he asked peevishly.

"Yeah, I know," Joe answered, "but the guy don't like it."

"Well, we're the two best guitar players here in Chicago, ain't we? To hell with him. We'll get another job."

"No!" Joe hollered, the heat rising in his face. "You can't haul off and do something like that when you're playing a contract. We got a commitment here and we're gonna finish it."

"It's my intermission," Les insisted. "I'm gonna do what I please!"

Joe gave him one last warning: "You neck around with that girl one more time and I'm gonna replace you!"

Les, of course, wrapped his arms around his companion and picked up where he'd left off. Joe fired him on the spot. He thought Les probably had imbibed one too many beers and "just wanted to smart off a little bit." But this time the boy had pushed him too far.

The truth is probably a combination of the two stories. Les more than likely would not have been such a wise guy if he'd thought there was a whole lot more to be gained by remaining with Sunny Joe. He was well past learning the fundamentals of guitar playing and eager to begin making a name for himself.

He had come light-years away from the days when he "considered it a privilege even to have a chance to carry Sunny Joe's instruments," as he once told Gibson sales manager Clarence Havenga. The engaging, inquisitive young boy was finally asserting himself as an adult. But he never entirely outgrew his childish resentment of Joe for abandoning him, just as his real father had a decade earlier.

Shortly after their estrangement, Les began complaining to other musicians around town that Sunny Joe was "stealing his licks." On the contrary, several acquaintances who knew both guitarists felt that Les wasn't giving Sunny Joe Wolverton the credit he deserved as a mentor. But this was just the beginning of a lifelong pattern. Over the years, Les routinely overlooked or downplayed the invaluable contributions fellow musicians made to his career: Pie Plant Pete, Sunny Joe, and others later on. That would come as no surprise to Joe: "Unless you knew him real well, you wouldn't know how egotistical he was," Joe later remarked. "Les always wanted to be tops, to go down in history as the greatest at what he did. Les and I got along better than most people, even though he could be uppish. But being around him that long, I overlooked a lot."

Joe Wolverton eventually left Chicago to work as a staff musician for Nashville's WSM. There he regularly backed an attractive young chanteuse named Fanny Rose Shore, who was better known later on as Dinah Shore. In 1937, he became a star endorsee for one of National's first electric Spanish guitars, and later recorded several albums with madcap maestro Spike Jones and His City Slickers.

Lester Polfuss remained in Chicago, where he continued to perform as Rhubarb Red on a variety of Chicago stations. In a few short years, though, he would shed his hillbilly persona, change his name to Les Paul, and embark on a whole new career path.

Chapter 5

JAMMING
ON THE SOUTH SIDE

Les's first independent steps into the music world were those of a fledgling. Sometime toward the end of 1934, after a brief stint at WLS, he began working at WGN, a radio station owned by the *Chicago Tribune*. His new act, sponsored by Rival dog food, offered the same freewheeling mixture of hillbilly tunes and corny one-liners as the Ozark Apple Knockers' show. He apparently didn't take the job too seriously, though.

One night, while filling in for a deejay who had failed to show for the late shift, Les told his listeners to stay tuned for fifteen minutes of breaking news. Instead of reading the incoming reports as they rolled off the wire, he propped a microphone next to the teletypewriter and took a leisurely stroll to the men's room. All the audience heard was the staccato click, click, click of the news printer. Naturally, the head of the radio station with the call letters that stood for "World's Greatest Newspaper" failed to see the humor in this juvenile prank. Les was fired that night.

By then he was tiring of his Rhubarb Red routine anyway. Eager to move on to something more challenging, he began toying with the idea of giving up the guitar and testing his skills as a jazz pianist.

He wanted to "be with the big guys, playing modern stuff," he said. Chicago was still a bubbling musical caldron, its streets teeming with honky-tonks and theaters where jazz players and bluesmen had been forging exotic new sounds since the 1920s. In addition to all the down-and-dirty clubs on the city's South Side, there were plenty of funky uptown hangouts like the Barrel of Fun, Liberty Inn, and Warm Friends.

Les eventually stumbled upon a gritty little strip joint called the Sundodgers Rendezvous (though he later claimed it was the 5100 Club on the North Side). As Les tells the story, the proprietor offered him a job playing piano in the bar and a bunk above the tavern if he promised to sweep the floor at closing time. The gig paid $5 a night—a fraction of what he had been earning as a hillbilly picker— but it gave him a chance to pull together a repertoire of jazz tunes and practice his new instrument in front of an uncritical crowd. He built his own sound system and sometimes used a phonograph as accompaniment onstage. "I didn't do very well, trying to impress a bunch of bar flies that I could play as good as the guy on the record," Les later confessed. "Bustin' the bubble for the bubble dancer was the high point of the night."

Relief finally came when a sympathetic acquaintance caught his half-baked act and sent him to Ralph Atlass, who then owned two of the city's biggest radio stations. WJJD featured old-time country music, while WIND, which was actually based in nearby Gary, Indiana, and featured more modern fare, catered to the South Side's sizable black population. Les was forced to resume his Rhubarb Red persona on WJJD five days a week. But his ambition to become a jazz pianist remained alive. Fortunately, he found some guidance from Harry Zimmerman, a staff organist at WJJD. One day Harry handed Les a pile of records. "Hey, I hate to do this to you," he said, "but I got some stuff here by Art Tatum that I think you ought to listen to."

"So," Les replied. "Who's he?"

Tatum was one of the most innovative jazz pianists of the century, an idol among musicians of every description. The nearly blind keyboardist effortlessly transformed popular standards of the day into dazzling displays of harmonic and rhythmic invention, sometimes playing so fast that he sounded as if he had four hands. After Les got an earful of the piano master's cascading notes and chords, he swore he'd never go near a piano again. However, he often dropped into the mob-owned club where Tatum played to bask in the pianist's miraculous, laser-quick improvisations. Newly inspired, Les resolved to make his guitar speak as articulately and passionately as Tatum's piano.

Once again, Harry Zimmerman offered some critical support. He brought Les a stack of recordings that featured a brilliant Belgian-born gypsy guitarist named Django Reinhardt. In 1928 a flash fire in Reinhardt's caravan had left two of his chording fingers badly deformed. Nevertheless he later became the first European guitarist to have a significant impact on American popular music. His recordings with violinist Stephane Grappelli were laced with soaring chromatic figures and chordal solos that fused exotic gypsy melodies and rhythms with jazz.

Les nearly wore the acetate off his new Reinhardt disks, reveling in Django's magnificent guitar tone and driving gypsy beat. He never imagined such exuberant expressiveness possible on a six-string instrument. The next day the young guitarist stopped Zimmerman in the WJJD studio and only half-jokingly threatened to quit the music business altogether. "Harry, what are you trying to do to me?" he asked in exasperation.

Les began making regular pilgrimages to Lyon and Healy's music store, a favorite hangout for Chicago musicians, constantly checking the bins for new Reinhardt releases. Before long, Django's sound would become Les's sound. And many of the tunes that Django performed with the Hot Club of France—"Avalon," "Tiger Rag," "Smoke Rings," "Nagasaki," and "Nuages"—would become lifelong staples in Les's act. Yet, according to one of his old Chicago jamming partners, the cheeky young guitarist typically refused to acknowledge Django's influence on his work.

By the mid-1930s, Lester William Polfuss had adopted his current stage name and teamed up with organist Harry Zimmerman to play jazz guitar on WIND, WJJD's sister station. "They just jammed for half an hour on the air," remembers Riley Jackson, who used to announce the pair. "They'd only play two songs during the entire show and it always seemed like one of them was called 'Who's Got the Ball?' "

Midwestern listeners had no idea that Rhubarb Red and Les Paul were the same person. Les wanted it to remain that way. Even though he was making a comfortable living from hillbilly music, he was keenly aware that other musicians regarded it with contempt. As far as he was concerned, hillbilly was out and modern music was in.

Indeed, in July 1935, under the famous headline "Hicks Nix Sticks Pix," *Variety* reported that even rural audiences were losing interest in movies with bucolic stories and rustic characters. America's entertainment tastes were growing more sophisticated. Noël Coward's suave musicals and dramas were in vogue. Cole Porter was beginning to dominate the Broadway stage, and Benny Goodman, bolstered by the hard-driving orchestral arrangements of a black pianist named Fletcher Henderson, introduced big-band jazz to America on his own network radio program, *Let's Dance.*

Chicago's South Side offered the sort of vibrant and expansive music scene that Les was determined to be part of. "That was easy," he told *Guitar Player* magazine, "because Chicago was a fireball. We lived jamming." All the music greats either worked or passed through the city—Teddy Wilson, Earl Hines, Roy Eldridge, Eddie South. And like New York's famed 52nd Street, the South Side had lots of jazz joints clustered together, which enabled musicians to stroll from one place to another and sit in several times in one night.

Lessons in improvising, phrasing, and showmanship were played out every night on the stages of Chicago's saloons and theaters, and Les eagerly took them all in. His ears soaked up the lusty, unscrubbed sounds of Louis Armstrong, Baby Dodds, Coleman Hawkins, Jimmy Noone. In fact, he once said it was Louis Armstrong who taught him how to turn a musical mistake into a triumph. One night he caught Louis's act at Chicago's Regal Theater: "Louie kept hitting a bad note, but he said, 'I'm going to stay on this stage until

I get it right.' And, by God, he did. When he finally hit that high C, the audience went crazy."

Although Les's musicianship would never match the inventiveness of, say, Art Tatum's, the speed and force with which he attacked his instrument did. His lightning-fast style, so full of grace notes and trills, distinguished him from almost all other Chicago guitarists. He was welcome to sit in on sessions all over town with far more established jazz artists. But when it came time to leave at four in the morning, he couldn't bring himself to tell his jamming partners where he was going. He'd quietly pack his gear and head for a couch in the lobby of WJJD, where he'd catch a few hours' sleep before his Rhubarb Red show. Then he'd pull out his acoustic guitar, slip the harmonica brace over his head, and begin the whole schizophrenic daily routine over again.

"I worked out a concept that every minute of my life was valuable," he later said. "If I got a chance to play with Art Tatum or Roy Eldridge, I made the time, even if it meant staying up all night." But it was Les Paul's rustic alter ego who made it to the recording studio first. On May 20, 1936, Rhubarb Red cut four sides for the Montgomery Ward label, including "Just Because" and "Deep Elm Blues," doubling as usual on guitar and harmonica. Shortly thereafter he hired a rhythm guitarist and an Iowa-born bassist named Bob Meyer to play a series of one-nighters at county fairs all over Wisconsin.

"At the time, I was working with my own jazz band at the Planet Mars on Wilson Avenue," recalled Meyer. "Les asked me to come down and audition at the radio station where he was working. All he wanted me to do was play this simple two-beat bass stuff and sing some simple harmonies. When we finally started making the rounds at the fairs, I was amazed by the reaction of the crowds. Rhubarb Red was very popular. Every time we finished playing, people would rush up to us and ask for our autographs. It made me realize how important that music was."

Around the same time, Les landed several Decca recording dates with Georgia White. The popular blues belter was usually accompanied by such established musicians as pianist/composer Richard

M. Jones, string bassist John Lindsay, and guitarist Ikey Robinson. Between May 1936 and January 1937, though, Les made nearly twenty sides with Georgia, including a number of bawdy ballads with names like "I'll Keep Sittin' on It If I Can't Sell It," "Dan the Backdoor Man," and "Daddy Let Me Lay It on You."

"Georgia couldn't do anything until she got completely stoned, so they'd put a jug on the piano and we'd go to work," Les recalled. The twenty-one-year-old guitarist's single-string solos on these disks had a distinctly diffident sound, suggesting that he was uncomfortable with Georgia's gut-bucket blues style. When he got lost, he'd pluck out one of Django's trademark runs, or throw in one of his old reliable hillbilly licks. But for the most part the country boy from lily-white Wisconsin held his own.

Showcasing his talent at the hottest places in town was easy for Les. The problem was finding a guitar that could be heard above the din of the clubs' brass players and hard-drinking patrons. The only plausible remedy, a decent-sounding amplified guitar, was not to be found in Chicago, or anywhere else for that matter. The Stromberg-Voisinet company (later renamed Kay) began advertising electrics as early as 1929. And in the early thirties, Rickenbacker's "Frying Pan," a circular hollow-body instrument with a disproportionately long neck, had attracted a great deal of attention to players like Alvino Rey and Ike Perkins, guitarist for boogie-woogie piano king Albert Ammons. But none of these instruments satisfied Les's discerning ear. Nor was he interested in the electrified Hawaiian steels that were gaining currency in the mid-thirties. With the help of a few more technically trained acquaintances, he began designing an amplified guitar of his own.

He built a series of pickups that were sufficiently powerful for use in public or on radio. Then he butchered dozens of secondhand guitars to properly position the electronic amplifying devices. He discovered that when he strummed his custom-built hollow-body, the wood beneath the pickup vibrated and inevitably absorbed some of the string resonance, muffling the sound of the guitar. So he

decided to create an instrument capable of producing a more powerful and evenly sustained string sound.

In the mid-1930s, he approached Carl and August Larson, two
Swedish-born luthiers who worked out of a three-story barn in Chicago, and paid them $15 to construct the first of his semi-solid-body
guitars. Inspired perhaps by National's electric Spanish model, which
had a solid top and no sound holes, he told the Larsons to build his
guitar with a half-inch-thick maple top and to eliminate the sound
holes. "They thought I was crazy," he told *Guitar Player.* "They told
me it wouldn't vibrate. I told them I didn't want it to vibrate because
I was going to put two pickups on it. As far as I know, I was the
first guy to put two pickups on a guitar."

Reaction to Les's custom-designed electric was immediate: "Everybody told me I sounded like a different guy." George Barnes, another early pioneer of the amplified guitar, was particularly
interested in the instrument. At fourteen, the Chicago-bred Barnes
was already playing electric guitar (built for him by his older
brother) and leading his own jazz combo in the Midwest. Instead of
becoming archrivals, though, he and Les held joint jam sessions
every Monday night at the Barrel of Fun, a North Side jazz club
where the cocky duo challenged other players to climb up on stage
and outgun them. Few succeeded. "There's no doubt about it," said
lifelong Chicago guitarist George Allen. "Those two were the top of
the heap."

Around this time Les also formed a quartet that duplicated the
repertoire and instrumentation of Django Reinhardt's Hot Club of
France. In addition to hiring a violinist and rhythm guitarist, he
once again called on bassist Bob Meyer, who would work with him
intermittently over the next several years. The Melody Kings began
performing at Chicago's Bismark Hotel, doing remote broadcasts for
NBC three nights a week. "Les and the violinist would stand right
next to the microphone and play all these fancy notes, doing their
best to sound just like Django and Stephane Grappelli," Meyer
recalled.

Meanwhile Les had someone back home recording the show off
the air on his primitive disk-cutting lathe. At the end of the evening,

the four musicians usually went back to Les's place to listen to the acetates. The quality of sound left a lot to be desired, but it gave the boys a fairly good idea of how they were coming across to their radio audience.

Like many of Les's unconventional recording methods, the lathe he used to record the Melody Kings evolved out of sheer necessity. Always a night owl, he sometimes had trouble finding partners who were willing to come over and jam till dawn. Since over-the-counter lathes were impossibly expensive for his meager budget, Les built one of his own with the help of a few friends and taught himself how to overdub, the process of layering a succession of musical parts on a single disk. Now he could accompany himself at any hour of the day or night.

It was this jury-rigged machine that would eventually become the basis of the "sound-on-sound" recording technique that would catapult Les Paul to international fame.

Chapter 6

THE BIG
WHITE LIE

Every Saturday night the Eighth Street Theater on South Wabash was hillbilly heaven, the weekend home of WLS's *National Barn Dance.* One of the stars in that firmament was the velvety-voiced singer-guitarist Tommy Tanner. Tommy was really Jimmy Atkins, Chet Atkins's older half brother.

Steeped from birth in the string-laden sounds emanating from kitchens and porches of the homes nestled deep in the hollows of East Tennessee, Jimmy was well known on WLS for his pleasing renditions of such old country chestnuts as "Bury Me Beneath the Willow" and "New River Train." But he was eager to break free from his hillbilly roots. As a teenager, he fell under the spell of pop singer-guitarist Nick Lucas, who was famous for his solo performance of "Tiptoe Through the Tulips" in the early sound movie hit "Gold Diggers of Broadway." In 1933, Jimmy became a vocalist and rhythm guitarist with George Morris's big band on Kansas City's WHB radio. Two years later, though, he moved to Chicago, accepting what he hoped would be a temporary job at WLS as Tommy Tanner, a sta-tion-owned sobriquet.

Like Les, Jimmy was more than happy to work under an assumed name. He had no desire to become any more closely identified with the hillbilly pickers than he already was. "Everybody looked down their noses at the hillbillies," he said. "But the odd thing about it was the country music boys were making the money! And the modern boys were eating hamburgers, when and if they could buy one." Nonetheless, by 1937, working with the "modern boys" was exactly where Jimmy wanted to be.

After finishing up his *Barn Dance* set one night, Jimmy walked backstage and saw a Gibson Super 400 resting in a corner. The gleaming new guitar was relatively new on the market. Much larger and more expensive than Gibson's premier L-5, it was a status symbol for those who could afford it.

When Jimmy asked about the handsome instrument, he was told it belonged to Rhubarb Red, whom Jimmy had long wanted to meet. He had been a fan of Rhubarb Red's jazz-playing alter ego, Les Paul, for some time. The two guitarists took to each other right away. Jimmy was flattered that Les had taken note of "all the big fat chords" he played on WLS as well. United by an ardent desire to escape the country-music scene, the pair agreed to form a trio. They invited Jimmy's friend Ernie Newton, who was also performing at the theater that night, to join them on bass.

Les, of course, was designated lead guitarist, and Jimmy played rhythm and sang with a voice that often drew comparisons to Bing Crosby's rich, silky baritone. The trio spent every spare moment practicing, sometimes at Jimmy's apartment, other times at Les's. In 1937 the two guitarists arranged to live in the same Winchester Street building on Chicago's North Side, which made rehearsing that much easier. By then Les had married Virginia Webb, a shy, genial girl who lived around the corner from a North Side tavern where he had worked a few years earlier. Though close to her family, who still lived in Chicago, she agreed to a justice-of-the-peace wedding ceremony, attended only by Jimmy Atkins and his wife, Wilma. But because she was not directly involved in the music world, Virginia would always remain on the periphery of her husband's life. In fact, few of Les's friends from this period knew he had a wife.

By 1938, Chicago was getting its last earful of up-from-the-delta jazz. Most musicians were making their way to the East or West Coast, and Les had no intention of being left behind. Around this time NBC launched a nationwide radio program called *Grand Central Station,* which opened each show with this compelling introduction: "As a bullet seeks its target, shining rails in every part of our great country are aimed at Grand Central Station, heart of the nation's greatest city . . . crossroads of a million private lives, gigantic stage on which are played a thousand dramas daily." The Empire State Building was still a novelty, Rockefeller Center brand-new, and the subway, which cost only a nickel to ride, still clean and efficient.

To Les, then twenty-two, New York City was a big, juicy apple waiting to be picked. It was the home of many national radio networks, gargantuan hotels begging for quality entertainment, Tin Pan Alley (then the main stem of the music world), and exotic jazz enclaves like Harlem and West 52nd Street, which were alive with nightclubs and after-hours joints that stayed open till dawn.

Les's friends told him he was mad even to consider giving up his staff position at WJJD. The country was still feeling the effects of the Depression. With unemployment stubbornly hovering near 20 percent, Roosevelt was frantically lobbying to pass dozens of social programs intended to alleviate the suffering of the dispossessed and forgotten. So the idea of dumping a steady job to go play jazz was thought to be sheer lunacy. Jazz was attractive only to a small audience of music lovers. Then too, the guitar was still not accepted as a solo instrument among jazz players. Because of the seemingly insurmountable volume problem—widespread use of electrics was still years away—most guitarists, no matter how talented, were resigned to being tucked away in the rhythm section, alongside the drummer and bassist. "Guitar was really put down," said Everett Barksdale, rhythm guitarist for such jazz greats as violinist Eddie South, bandleader Benny Carter, and Art Tatum. "If you were an orchestra leader, you threw a guitar job to a friend as a favor. At that time it just wasn't wanted."

Les brushed these concerns aside, but, as he later recalled, persuading Ernie and Jimmy to quit their lucrative country gigs for an uncertain future in jazz was another matter. Don't worry, he told them, they'd have no trouble finding a job. He and Paul Whiteman, the bandleader who starred in the 1930 film *King of Jazz,* were personal friends. In fact, Whiteman had never laid eyes on the brash young guitarist. The story was another of Les's dazzling con jobs— but it worked. Ernie and Jimmy's resistance was eventually undone by the magnetic force of Les's optimism.

Les promised his wife that he would come back to get her as soon as he was settled in the city. Virginia, as she would discover again and again, had married a man who would always respond to the call of his career first. This would be just the beginning of many long separations.

The first thing Les and Jimmy did was talk a WLS booking agent into putting the trio on a *Barn Dance* road show that was going to pass through upstate New York. The boys would have to play hillbilly music for several more weeks under their old stage names, but traveling with the tour would help defray some of the expenses of moving. Their mood, as they packed Les's Buick, was almost festive. A gang of musician friends helped them load their instruments and a few other prized possessions into the trunk and onto the roof.

Ernie set a chauffeur's cap on his head at a jaunty angle. "Well, we're ready to go," he announced with a flourish. So off they went, three fools with little to sustain them beyond their collective talent and Les's stubborn single-mindedness, an asset that would hurtle him over countless obstacles in years to come. They were, as Les later said, "young, happy, and stupid."

Once free of the WLS tour, the boys turned off the road whenever they spotted a tavern that might be willing to hire them for a one-night stand. They were pretty tapped out by the time the Buick coughed to a halt in front of New York's Chesterfield Hotel, a $12-

a-week dump on Broadway near Times Square where a lot of other musicians hung their hats until they could find steady work. Like everyone else, Les and his pals quickly discovered that New York was a dismal place to be without a job. They had to bathe and wash their clothes in a tub they shared with dozens of other hotel guests. "We'd sit in our room all day long and listen to Django Reinhardt records and try to copy every lick he ever made," Jimmy later said. "We did a lot of auditions, but no work. We were about ready to throw in the towel and go back to Chicago."

After a few weeks of lying around the Chesterfield, Jimmy began needling Les: "Don't you think it's about time we called your dear buddy Paul Whiteman?" Les was cornered. With Jimmy and Ernie in tow, he marched down to the pay phone in the lobby, dialed the bandleader's number, and proceeded to spin the same yarn for Whiteman's secretary as he had for his partners. When the woman came back on the line, she told Les that Whiteman didn't remember him. Les breathlessly began telling her that he had this great trio, but she interrupted, "Mr. Whiteman is very busy and doesn't have time to see you," and hung up.

"Well, what did she say?" Jimmy asked.

"She said to come right over," Les replied nonchalantly.

With the six-foot bass and two beat-up guitars slung over their shoulders, the trio traipsed a few blocks up Broadway to the bandleader's headquarters on the corner of West 53rd Street, the current site of the Ed Sullivan Theater. They didn't even have cases for their instruments. Stepping out of the elevator on the eleventh floor, they could see the secretary at her desk, and through another open door, Whiteman: rotund, mustachioed, and decked out in a pristine white suit. He sat behind a desk that looked as big as an airplane wing.

Les launched into another staccato introduction with the secretary: "I called a few minutes ago. I'm Les Paul and I've got my trio here, and I'm sure Mr. Whiteman is anxious to hear us."

Whiteman heard the commotion and shrieked, "Close that goddam door!" The dutiful secretary shooed them into the corridor and slammed yet another door.

"I thought you knew Whiteman real well," said Ernie.

"Well, from that distance," answered Les, "he more than likely didn't recognize me. And anyway, they're funny in New York."

Luckily for Les, just then Fred Waring happened to walk out of a nearby men's room. Waring was a megastar who had produced dozens of Top 10 hits with his orchestra and hosted a series of nationally broadcast radio shows. Few were the years between 1930 and 1950 that his "half a hundred Pennsylvanians" weren't heard on some network. In 1937, the versatile Waring, then in his mid-thirties, introduced a gadget he had developed that would help bankroll his musical efforts and forever make his name a household word: the famous Waring Blendor. The electric food and drink mixer sold more than 60,000 in its first year and a half on the market.

Waring's sprawling rehearsal studio, which occupied the entire tenth floor of 1697 Broadway, was one story below Whiteman's suite. As the famous bandleader stood waiting for an elevator with the three musicians, Les struck up a conversation:

"Hey, aren't you Fred Waring?" he asked with all the charm he could muster.

"Yeah, yeah, yeah," Waring wearily answered. "But if you're thinking what I think you're thinking, forget it. I've already got sixty-two Pennsylvanians, and I'm having a hard time feeding them."

"You've got nothing to lose," Les shot back. "The elevators are all down on the ground floor. Can we play till one gets here?

Before Waring could answer, the boys slid their instruments into playing position and tore through a cover of "After You've Gone," a hit that year for both Lionel Hampton and Django Reinhardt's Hot Club of France. The faster the elevator came up, the faster they played. Waring, apparently amused as much by their desperation as by their talent, told them to load their gear into the elevator and follow him to the main rehearsal hall. There they found the Pennsylvanians at work, including Waring's famous glee club. Waring told the band to stop so he could audition the trio right then and there. "If you like these guys as much as I do, we're gonna add them to the band."

Les picked and strummed on his modified Gibson electric, the one emblazoned with his hillbilly stage name. "But probably what impressed Fred Waring the most," he later said, "was the fact that my bass player, who was wearing a top hat, had a brush that he held in his right hand, like a drummer's brush, and he had a piece of sandpaper glued onto his bass. When Ernie plucked a string, he followed with a swoosh on the sandpaper. Jimmy, meanwhile, was an excellent singer, with a low voice like Crosby's. Very few people had heard the sound of an electric guitar in those days. Between the three of us, we had a unique sound."

Waring must have agreed. By the end of the afternoon, there were sixty-five Pennsylvanians. Les, the consummate con artist, had proved to his bandmates that he could deliver the goods: the trio had found a terrific job in New York, as promised. Waring gave each man a $30-a-week retainer until the local musicians' union allowed them to go on the air. Then their salaries would be automatically raised to $150, placing them among the highest-paid musicians in the country. All they had to do now was find a place to live and go back to the Midwest to retrieve Les's and Jimmy's wives.

Les had left Chicago unemployed. Now he returned a conquering hero. Not only had he found a comfortable niche where he'd get to show off his flashy guitar playing, he was going to be featured on a nationally broadcast show with *the* premier radio band. He stuck around long enough to bid a triumphant farewell to all the naysayers who had tagged him a fool for leaving his secure country music gig. Then he jumped in his Buick and headed for the Big Apple.

Chapter 7

LIVE—FROM THE BIG APPLE

Electra Court was a splendid place for young musicians to settle. The Jackson Heights, Queens, apartment house was cheap, conveniently located, and, best of all, *the* place to meet and mingle with New York's inner circle of players. It was home to musicians from the Benny Goodman, Tommy Dorsey, Artie Shaw, Bob Crosby, and Fred Waring orchestras, as well as many of the city's most sought-after studio players, including George Van Eps, Bob Haggert, and Bobby Hackett.

The six-story yellow-brick building was only a twenty-minute subway ride from the heart of midtown Manhattan, where most of the major radio stations and rehearsal halls were located. It was also one of the few places that provided three- and four-room furnished apartments, which made it attractive to musicians with families. The atmosphere was friendly and warm, instantly transforming an otherwise overwhelming city into a small town. The musicians could trade industry gossip, and the wives could keep each other company during the long, lonely nights their husbands were on the bandstand.

Les and Virginia moved into a cozy suite on the second floor, one flight below Jimmy and Wilma Atkins. The apartment had only one major drawback. It was far too small to accommodate the trio's much-needed practice sessions. Les eventually persuaded the building superintendent to let him and his partners convert what had once been a basement storage space into a rehearsal studio. The fifteen-foot-square room was already furnished with an old oriental carpet, an upright piano, a tattered couch, and a few tables and chairs. Before long, it also had a set of drums and microphones.

The subterranean warren soon became an after-hours club for the musicians in the building, as well as for players from Manhattan, who drifted in at all hours of the night. "There was something going on there constantly," said Johnny Blowers, a CBS staff drummer and well-known session player who lived next to Les in Electra Court. "It was a jam session made to order. The wives liked it, too. They could listen to the music by turning on the intercom system. If they liked it well enough, they'd come downstairs."

Nights of jamming helped Les and Jimmy shake loose after spending hours every day rehearsing and playing with the Waring orchestra. Waring had an inexhaustible appetite for work, and he expected the same level of commitment from his musicians. Before launching the first of several New York–based radio shows in 1933, the band leader typically staged two shows a night, seven days a week. Several private railroad cars were required to transport the musicians, singers, and dancers as well as a cadre of publicity people.

In addition to traveling hundreds of miles each day, the Pennsylvanians often performed a couple of live radio broadcasts to promote their upcoming concerts, one in the morning and another after the evening engagement. Their work schedule barely slackened after settling in the Big Apple. By the time Les joined them in the middle of 1938, Waring had signed a contract with NBC to conduct a live radio program every Saturday night from eight-thirty to nine. Sponsored by Grove's Bromo Quinine, the half-hour coast-to-coast broadcast cost the network more than $10,000 a week. If there were no out-of-town theater engagements, the bandleader expected his musicians and singers to show up at his midtown headquarters every Monday through Friday afternoon to rehearse. On weekends he often insisted that they perform at his Pennsylvania resort on the Delaware River.

The orchestra practiced in Waring's cavernous studio over Broadway, the glee club in a smaller room, and the featured acts, like the Les Paul Trio, in a yet smaller room. Waring outfitted each of these studios with microphones so he could sit in his office and listen to the Pennsylvanians rehearse their numbers, which he made them do over and over. Fred liked to say that he put his band through these exhausting drills because he was a perfectionist. Some of his sidemen, however, were convinced he did it because he was a poorly trained conductor who needed to hear the songs repeatedly to learn the arrangements.

Despite the way Waring's musicians felt about him, though, the reviewers commented favorably on his crowd-pleasing tunes and old-fashioned approach to entertainment. "Waring's comedy interludes come out soft and low," cooed an October 1938 *Variety*. "He features all sorts of melodious arrangements, with each item prettily wrapped and bow tied." NBC executives were so confident of Fred's ability to draw listeners that they expanded his airtime and put him up against the nation's most popular prime-time act, *Amos 'n' Andy,* after that comedy duo defected to CBS in the spring of 1939.

Waring's new program was sponsored by Chesterfield cigarettes, which also backed Glenn Miller's *Moonlight Serenade* on CBS. The Pennsylvanians were scheduled to perform two fifteen-minute broadcasts a day, Monday through Friday, with each show followed by an additional forty-five minutes of live entertainment for the studio audience. In order to fill the expanded format, Waring was forced to beef up his already considerable staff. By the time he was done, his organization included at least a dozen featured performers, sixteen chorus members, seven brass players, six reeds, five strings, three guitars, two string basses, two pianos, and two drums, as well as twelve arrangers, four copyists, and seven publicists.

Chesterfield Pleasure Time debuted on Monday, June 19, 1939. Broadcast live from the Vanderbilt Theater on 48th Street in Times Square, the program was eventually heard on more than a hundred stations from Schenectady to San Francisco. It was run very much on the lines of a regular theatrical production; the orchestra played before a studio audience, complete with elaborate stage lighting effects and backdrops. Broadcasts began precisely at 7:00 and 11:00 P.M., the later one to accommodate West Coast listeners.

In addition to making several pitches for Chesterfield cigarettes, Waring's announcer, Paul Douglas, routinely rattled off dozens of major league baseball scores. The Pennsylvanians played a cheery chord for the winners and a sad one for the losers and squeezed in as much music as possible in the little time remaining. "This meant we had to move like clockwork," said Virgil "Stinky" Davis, Waring's lead saxophonist and arranger for twenty-two years. "With all the commercial announcements we had to make, that gave us about twelve minutes of actual playing time. It could not be thirteen minutes. Every song was shaved to its barest necessity."

"Fred occasionally called me into his office to tell me he wanted an arrangement done for the next day. I'd work all night and bring it in the next morning. Sometimes the band would end up rehearsing the first part of the score while I was finishing the rest of the arrangement. I'd end up going on the air and playing something I'd never heard."

Because the show was done live before a studio audience, Waring insisted that his troupe be as well attired as guests at a swank Long Island cocktail party. The musicians were expected to march out onstage every night decked in crisp cream-colored evening jackets, starched white tux shirts, and black trousers and satin cummerbunds. God help the man who forgot to grace his lapel with a bright red carnation.

Into this highly disciplined band of New York City slickers came Les Paul from the farmlands of Wisconsin, Jimmy Atkins from the southern mountains of Tennessee, and Ernie Newton from laid-back California. They complemented each other perfectly. Jimmy was an unassuming guy with a manner as pleasing and relaxed as his voice. Ernie's bass playing was barely adequate, but he had a natural gift for stand-up comedy. And Les came across as "the real jive cat of the band," commented *Down Beat* writer Leonard Feather. His

*W*earing banana curls and one of his mother's handmade outfits, Les, circa 1917, with brother Ralph
Courtesy of Waukesha County Museum Collections

*L*es's boyhood home at 320 West St. Paul Avenue was torched in 1988 as part of Waukesha's firefighter's training program.
Mary Alice Shaughnessy

*L*es *(front row, fourth from right)* in 1921 with his first-grade class. Later on he preferred playing hooky to school.
Courtesy of Waukesha County Museum Collections

𝒫ie Plant Pete *(above)*, star of Chicago's famous *WLS Barn Dance*, taught Lester how to play his first guitar chords. Shortly thereafter Lester began mimicking Pete's act, adopting his hillbilly repertoire and guitar/harmonica combo. Taken in the same photo studio as his baby picture, Les's first publicity shot *(right)* found its way into his 1930 junior high school yearbook, *The Megaphone*.

Courtesy of Nashville Country Music Foundation and Waukesha County Museum Collections

*K*nown to locals in the late 1920s and early 1930s as Red Hot Red, pint-size bandleader Lester Polfuss dazzled a holiday parade crowd with his guitar/harmonica act. Two decades later Warren Downie *(third from left)* played string bass with Les Paul and Mary Ford at Chicago's Blue Note jazz club.

Courtesy of Waukesha County Museum Collections

*R*ube Tronson's Cow Boys featured Rube as fiddler and Sunny Joe Wolverton *(far left)*, the versatile string player who became Les's mentor and gave him his first big break in radio. Les briefly took Joe's place with Rube's band in the summer of 1932.

Courtesy of Joe Wolverton

In October 1932 Sunny Joe Wolverton invited Les to join The Scalawags on KMOX's *Farm Folks Hour* in St. Louis. Joe dubbed his seventeen-year-old jug-playing protégé Rhubarb Red, a take-off on Pie Plant Pete's moniker. Ken Wright was the accordianist.

Courtesy of Joe Wolverton

In 1934, Sunny Joe and Rhubarb Red renamed themselves the Ozark Apple Knockers and moved to WBBM, CBS's wide-ranging Chicago affiliate. That year the Gibson catalog advertised both guitarists as endorsees.

Courtesy of Joe Wolverton

Sunny Joe Wolverton, now eighty-six, lives with his wife, Betty, in their Cottonwood, Arizona, home, which is packed with show business artifacts dating back to vaudeville.

Mary Alice Shaughnessy

Gypsy guitar master Django Reinhardt strongly influenced Les's playing style.

Courtesy of Richard Lieberson

_F_eatured on Fred Waring's nationally broadcast radio show from 1938 to 1941, Les Paul *(third row, far right)* plucked stunning single-string solos on electric guitar that helped break the instrument out of the rhythm section.

_L_es occasionally strummed an acoustic Gibson on Waring's weeknight show with his trio, which included bassist Ernie Newton and vocalist/rhythm guitarist Jimmy Atkins, Chet's older brother.

$\mathcal{D}$uring the 1940s Les generally favored hot-rodded Epiphones, whether recording in his Hollywood garage studio or performing at Club Rounders on Sunset Boulevard.
Courtesy of Bob Summers

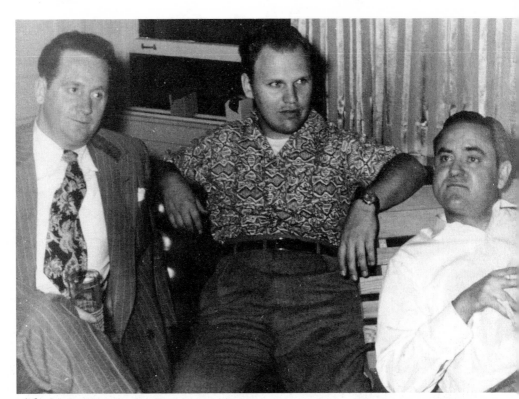

$\mathcal{R}$eputed to be the hottest guitarists in Chicago during the 1930s, Les Paul and George Barnes *(center)* often staged cutting contests at the Barrel of Fun, a popular North Side saloon. Here they are in George's apartment with bassist Bill Moore *(right)* in the late 1940s.
Courtesy of Evelyn Barnes

"*You* could throw a grenade in here and straighten it up," Les once said of his cluttered Mahwah, New Jersey, home *(left)*, where he stores his famous eight-track recorder, which he designed in the early 1950s. In 1988 he set up a display of earlier recording equipment *(center)*, including the modified Ampex he used to make "How High the Moon." Scores of guitars now occupy the master bedroom he once shared with Mary Ford *(bottom)*.

Mary Alice Shaughnessy

Mary Alice Shaughnessy

Mary Alice Shaughnessy

single-string solos provided all the jazz for the entire Waring orchestra, but he'd slip in some country licks just for kicks.

Jamming for years on Chicago's South Side with masterful improvisors like Nat Cole and Earl Hines helped Les create his own increasingly unique and supple sound. "He knew how to take a tune and make it his own special arrangement," recalled Stinky Davis. "He'd leave the melody and go off on a tangent, but thematically it always made sense. He never got lost; he always knew where he was going. He had an incredible ear and it governed everything he played."

Regardless of the excitement he generated among his new colleagues, though, Les still had to adhere to Waring's strict afternoon rehearsal schedule. One day he was horrified to find he had overslept. Hurtling over the Queensboro Bridge en route to Manhattan in his Buick at seventy-five miles an hour, he was stopped by one of New York's finest.

"Where are you going in such a hurry?" the cop asked Les.

"My wife and kid. They're hungry," he replied. "I left them in my apartment in Jackson Heights. If I make this audition, I'll get an advance and be able to buy my family some food. If I'm late, I'm gonna blow the whole thing."

The cop must have filled his quota for speeding tickets that day. He let one of New York's newest con artists off. "Get movin,' pal," he said. "But don't ever make me stop you again." Over the years, Les became nearly as famous for his demonic driving as for his music. A speeding ticket was of little consequence compared to Waring's wrath if anyone was late for a Pennsylvanian rehearsal.

Waring was often in a foul mood, even if everybody showed up on time. He once swept into the studio and began a practice session by sarcastically asking his orchestra, "Why don't you all just try to *imitate* musicians?" On another occasion, he turned to the glee club and said, "You know, I have two thousand people waiting to take your place."

Les was one of the few band members who consistently escaped Waring's bad-tempered attacks. Waring seemed to have taken a special liking to Les, who was exactly fifteen years his junior. The two had a lot more in common than their June 9 birthdays. Neither could sight-read, but both became legends in the music and electronics businesses.

They also shared a perverse sense of humor. Egged on by the unrestrained imagination of his publicity chief, Jim Moran, Waring sponsored some of the most outrageous self-promotion campaigns in history. One of them was inspired by a series of insipid novelty numbers that had been written specifically for the Pennsylvanians' radio show. "One of the songs," recalled Moran, "was called 'Shoot the Sherbert to Me Herbert.' This song was popular for a week or two, then the boys in the band came up with a new song called 'Shoot the Meatballs to Me Dominick.' If this trend kept up, we would soon be playing 'Shoot the Goose to Me Moose,' or 'Shoot the Fruit to Me Brute.' I decided to put a stop to this custom."

Moran got his hands on a Manhattan phone book, jotted down the last name and address of every Herbert and Dominick he could find, and instructed a few of Waring's minions to send them invitations on specially engraved stationery: "In honor of the songs 'Shoot the Sherbert to Me Herbert' and 'Shoot the Meatballs to Me Dominick,' Herberts and Dominicks are invited to come to a sherbert and meatball shooting contest to be held in the main ballroom of the Strand Hotel. Orchestra leader Fred Waring will be the victim for the sherbert and meatball shooters with his head in a cut-out bull's-eye with a bow-and-arrow target. We will have various shooting devices such as slingshots, crossbows, catapults, and so forth and plenty of sherbert and meatballs. Each contestant will be given five shots. There will be a $50 prize for each Herbert and Dominick winner. Please come and fire away."

Moran, once headlined "The High Priest of Hoopla" in the *New York Times,* made sure his pals from every media outlet in metropolitan New York were on hand to report the food-flinging contest. "It got great coverage," he later boasted. Moran's madcap maneuvers were part of the glue that melded his friendship with Les in years to come. He would eventually play a vital role in an infamous publicity campaign for Les Paul as well.

On November 12, 1938, after satisfying the union-imposed waiting period for out-of-town musicians to go on the air, Les was straining at the bit to mount the stage and show Waring what he and his partners could do. Failing to come up with a catchy name, the trio simply called itself String Swing. "I'll never forget it," Les later said. "We were at the Strand Theater. Fred asks, 'How would you like to be introduced?' I said, 'Just put your hand out like this and say, 'Ladies and gentlemen, here's the Pennsylvanians' latest addition,' and we'll go get 'em!"

Fred raised his eyebrows and smirked at the bold young guitarist, but delivered the hackneyed intro as requested. A cascade of brightly played amplified notes danced above the chung-a-chung rhythm of Jimmy's Gibson acoustic and Ernie's upright bass. Les made every note count, effortlessly blending the sounds of hillbilly hoedowns with the hot rhythms of the Chicago jam sessions.

Unfortunately, the trio's debut was a resounding flop. Perhaps the live audience, attuned to the full, round sound of Waring's oversized orchestra and glee club, found the subtleties of a simple, self-contained trio anticlimactic. Maybe they had trouble tapping their feet to Les's machine-gun-rapid electric guitar runs. Whatever the reason, Les was crushed by the indifferent response to his trio's premier performance. Around midnight, after the Pennsylvanians wrapped up their second show of the evening and returned to the Broadway rehearsal hall, Les meekly approached Waring's tenth-floor office.

"Come on in, Les," commanded Waring from behind the closed door.

"How'd you know it was me?" Les asked in amazement.

"I knew it was you. You wanna know what you did wrong, huh?"

"Yes, sir, I do."

"Well, I'll tell you what to do. Next show, you boys sit up there in the orchestra with all the rest of the fellas. When I call you to come on, you stumble through the music stands. And *make sure* you knock a few over as you work your way up front. I guarantee you'll stop the show."

Les did as he was told the following night and found that Waring, who prided himself on taking "the common man's approach" to show business, was absolutely on target. Les now understood that it wasn't enough to be a skilled musician. If he intended to break free of the herd, he'd have to work even harder on his showmanship. Hence he not only came up with bright new arrangements for each performance, he also crafted dynamically varied solos that *demanded* the audience's attention. He'd segue into a whisper-soft melody from a stinging, improvised run.

Still one of only a dozen or so electric guitarists in the entire city of New York, "Les was startling for the times," said Pennsylvanian Glen Moore. "Nobody else played like him then and nobody tried." The fact that he used the only amplified instrument in a strictly acoustic orchestra made him stand out even more. After a heated discussion with Jimmy and Ernie, he persuaded them to let him rename the group the Les Paul Trio.

Within a few weeks of their debut, Les and his triomates became one of Waring's most popular acts. They were among the Pennsylvanians' featured performers at FDR's White House. Back home in Wisconsin, Evelyn Polfuss reacted to the news of her son's latest career coup with unabashed enthusiasm, even placing a little piece in the hometown paper. "Waukesha Boy on Waring Broadcast," trumpeted the headline of the November 19, 1938, *Waukesha Freeman*. Still bitter toward her ex-husband, she chose to name herself in the article as Les's sole parent, even though George Polfuss was still a prominent Waukesha citizen.

Meanwhile, down in Tennessee, Jimmy Atkins's family tuned in the local NBC affiliate every weekday night and eagerly awaited the Pennsylvanians' opening theme song. Chet Atkins, then an aspiring guitarist, "was as proud as a kid brother could be. Sitting there by the radio and listening to Jim was like being on a throne." Intrigued by Les's complicated single-string solos and lilting instrumental fills, Chet begged his brother to write to tell him "how Les Paul managed to play so damn much guitar."

Les's prominent role on Waring's nationally broadcast radio show had a profound impact on many young guitarists, most of whom had never heard the sound of an electric guitar—or thought of the guitar as a solo instrument. In this sense, he helped redefine the instrument's place in performance. Charlie Byrd, Tony Mottola, and Johnny Smith are just a few of the guitar greats who cited Les's early work with Waring as an abiding influence on their careers. "At the time," recalled Smith, "I was traveling with a hillbilly band, but every night, when the Chesterfield show came on the air, I'd have my ear glued to the radio to hear Les. I felt about him the way he felt about Django. As far as I'm concerned, he did more to popularize the electric guitar than any other player."

Every Tuesday night, the Pennsylvanians wrapped up *Chesterfield Pleasure Time* with "Round Robins," improvisational sessions in which the strongest musicians in the band were allowed to solo for a few bars. If all went according to Waring's carefully drawn plan, the solos were followed by a two-minute song from the Les Paul Trio. Then the glee club was supposed to launch into a multiharmonied arrangement of "Sleep," Waring's sign-off theme.

All too often, though, Les was so rapturously transported by the sound of his own picking that he'd run over the trio's allotted time slot and throw the normally unflappable Waring into a fit of white-knuckled panic. The bandleader would wave his arms, make frantic signals, point at his stop watch—all to no avail. Les would keep on strumming, his eyes closed, his expression blissful, oblivious to everything around him. Forced to shave precious moments from his choir's exquisitely crafted finale, Waring would angrily warn the young guitarist to refrain from expropriating his colleagues' airtime. But the warning was often disregarded.

Soon after moving to New York, Les resumed the dual life-style he had begun in Chicago. He showed up every day to do his bit on radio with the Waring orchestra, but around midnight he'd bolt up to Harlem or over to 52nd Street to jam with friends like Art Tatum, Ben Webster, Stuff Smith, and Roy Eldridge. Though he remained solidly rooted in the swing school of playing, Les knew Harlem's musical mavericks—Dizzy Gillespie, Kenny Clarke, Thelonious Monk—were on to something special. He was well on his way to developing his own distinct style, but Reinhardt-like improvisations were still strongly evident in his playing. In fact, Leonard Ware, one of Les's favorite New York guitarists, once spent an entire set on the bandstand with Les, assuming he had finally gotten to play with the great gypsy guitarist.

Fred Waring couldn't fathom what Les hoped to learn from these musical anarchists. Young black jazzmen were just beginning to formulate the complex rhythmic style that eventually came to be known as bebop. As the style continued to flower into a full-fledged jazz revolution, the established school of musicians—both black and white—saw it as a threat and condescendingly referred to it as "Chinese music."

Before the late 1930s, bands were racially segregated. Benny Goodman made a radical statement on June 16, 1938, when he invited Count Basie, Lionel Hampton, Lester Young, and members of Duke Ellington's band to join him onstage for a performance at Carnegie Hall. This historic event was the first time the venerated concert hall had ever offered a nonclassical program. When the house manager asked Goodman how long an intermission he planned to take, the bespectacled bandleader innocently replied, "I don't know. How long does Toscanini take?"

Les Paul was never politically progressive. In fact, throughout his life, he appeared to have no interest in politics at all, except as politics applied to the entertainment world. But when it came to music, he, like Goodman, was color-blind. One night he persuaded Waring to accompany him to the Cotton Club to hear the way Cab Calloway's orchestra handled some of the same material the Pennsylvanians routinely performed. After listening to Calloway's arrangement of "FDR Jones," Waring swore he was going to tear the tune out of his band book. "They got something we don't," he confessed.

Les jammed wherever other musicians could be found. He'd sit in for a set or two with pianist Edgar Hayes at a gin mill up on Harlem's 140th Street—nursing a single bottle of beer all night long—then he'd wander over to an after-hours club in the back room of a nearby funeral parlor. "Les would come uptown and cut everybody's head," said Melvin Moore, one of Count Basie's vocalists.

Then Charlie Christian came along. Charlie was only twenty-three years old when he moved from Oklahoma City to New York in September 1939 to join Benny Goodman's band. But he scared the hell out of every guitar player in town, including Les Paul. The two musicians often traded solos on the bandstand at Minton's Playhouse in Harlem. Les, the musical speed demon, was amazed at how many exquisite musical ideas Charlie could convey with so few notes: "Charlie's phrasing showed excellent taste. He knew when to lay out and leave a hole. He straightened my head out fast."

While Les stayed out every night until six or seven the next morning, Virginia remained at home. She cleaned the apartment late at night so her nocturnal husband could sleep during the day. Although she found several new friends among Electra Court's other orchestra widows, Virginia longed for the company of her mother and sisters back in Chicago. But the dutiful wife never complained.

Once in a while Les and Jimmy Atkins took their wives up to Harlem for an evening of entertainment. One night the two women were shocked to find themselves in a *gay* black jazz club. If Les and Jimmy noticed, though, they apparently didn't care. "They just liked listening to those guys," said Wilma Atkins. "They'd go anywhere to hear a great band."

Fred Waring vigorously suppressed those who sought stardom in his firmament. This was an endless source of frustration for many of the musicians in his orchestra, especially Les Paul. Sometime during 1939, Les came up with a unique outlet for his thwarted talents by creating an illegal radio station in his Electra Court basement rehearsal studio. Now he could flaunt his guitar artistry and abundant wit with abandon, simultaneously playing deejay, comedian, and bandleader on his own pirate radio broadcasts. Every Thursday morning, between one-thirty and eight-thirty, Les's voice could be heard for blocks across his densely populated Queens neighborhood. "Good evening, ladies and gentle-men, the Booger Brothers are on the air. We're the pink-and-yellow network at the top of your dial."

Jimmy Atkins told *Guitar Player* magazine that it was he who unwittingly set the "Booger Brothers Broadcasting Company" in mo-tion. One day he went out and bought himself a rather unusual Philco radio/record player. Equipped with a built-in oscillator, it was capable of broadcasting the sound emanating from the turntable to any nearby radio. After giving the Philco set a test run in his Electra Court apartment, Jimmy walked over to the intercom and buzzed Les. "Turn on your radio," he instructed. "You've got to hear this tune."

Les dutifully spun the dial on his receiver until he landed on the right frequency. "Yeah, yeah, I can get it," he said, wondering why his friend thought it was such a big deal.

"Well, that's my record player!" Jimmy proudly announced.

"What do you mean, your record player?" Les asked.

"Come up here," Jimmy insisted. "You've got to see this."

Les threw on a pair of dungarees and a sweatshirt and flew up the stairs to Jimmy's flat, his suspenders dangling by his thighs. Bursting through Jimmy's door, he headed straight for the Philco. "Hey, that's quite a load!" he remarked. "Where's the record player?"

Jimmy brought him into an adjacent room and pointed to what looked like an ordinary turntable. "Where are the wires?" Les inquired.

"No wires," Jimmy replied.

"Now, come on," Les said, certain that his pal was putting him on.

"There are no wires anyplace, Les. This is for real."

"Let me see it," Les insisted, as he made a beeline for the record player.

"Now, wait a minute," Jimmy implored. "I know you. You see something, the first thing you do is tear it up to see how it works."

"I won't touch a thing," Les promised. "I'll just lift the back off. Just let me look at it."

Jimmy finally gave in and anxiously watched as his friend went to work with a screwdriver. A few minutes later, Les turned to Jimmy. "Mmmm, put this back and come with me."

The two men jumped into Les's Buick and headed for a nearby radio supply shop. "I want the biggest damn oscillator you got," Les told the proprietor.

"What do you want with it?"

"I'm going to build my own record player."

"Well, where do you want to locate it?"

"I want one that will get me across the building someplace."

"I don't know if we can get that far or not. The government will only let you build a one-tube transmitter."

Somehow Les managed to talk the owner into constructing one with two tubes. As soon as it was ready, Les set up the transmitter in his apartment and connected it to his amplifier and record player with long lengths of wire. Then he flipped through his record collection and slapped one of his favorite tunes onto the turntable, the Benny Goodman Trio's version of "After You've Gone." Much to his delight, the song could be heard static-free on radios scattered throughout Electra Court. He could even hear it on the radio in his car, which was parked in front of the building on 81st Street.

He thought his custom-made transmitter could do better than that, though. He asked Ernie Newton to climb into the Buick, keep the dial tuned to "After You've Gone," and head for Manhattan. Then he went back up to his apartment and played the record over and over. About half an hour later, Ernie walked through the door and delivered some promising news: He could hear the song clearly, without static, until he reached the middle of the 59th Street Bridge, nearly four miles away from Electra Court!

After Les figured out how to transmit the sound of voices and instruments, he moved his new toy into the basement studio and began broadcasting all-night jam sessions. The station's no rules, no sponsors, play-whatever-you-please policy attracted many notable entertainers, including singer Jo Stafford, Lionel Hampton, and the Merry Macs, a vocal quartet that reached national prominence on Fred Allen's radio program.

The musicians concocted fanciful names for each other. Les sometimes performed as Even Steven the Piano Demon. To add a little variety to the show, he interspersed snippets of FDR's Fireside Chats with the music, casually referring to the President as Fearless Frank, the Ferocious Philosopher. "At four in the morning, that building was just like an anthill—alive," Jimmy Atkins later said. "No one could possibly live there but musicians, it was such a beehive of late-night people. All day long everybody was asleep."

The Booger Brothers Broadcasting Company eventually found a couple of unofficial sponsors: a restaurant owned by Joe Raibo, an old banjo player, and a deli run by Gus Katukas. Both eateries were right around the corner from Electra Court, near 81st Street and Roosevelt Avenue. Whenever Les mentioned them on the air, the owners showed their appreciation by sending over generous quantities of food and drink for everybody at the jam.

There was always a bathtub full of ice-cold bottled beer and a lot of laughs to relieve the tension that was growing in the wake of the Nazis' relentless drive through Europe. The Germans had already annexed Austria and invaded Poland and Czechoslovakia, and it was becoming increasingly apparent that America could well be drawn into the European conflict. Les's famous sense of humor was a welcome palliative. One night he was sitting at his makeshift control board when he looked up and spotted a woman through the window in an adjacent wing of the apartment building. He surmised from the way she was dancing around the kitchen as she cooked that she was probably listening to the Booger Brothers' broadcast. But he had to know for sure. After the woman sat down to dig into her meal, she heard a strange command from her radio: "Will the lady eating the pork chop please put the pork chop down?" She looked slightly stunned but didn't move. "You heard me," Les shouted. "Put the pork chop down!" This time the woman quickly complied. "Thank you very much," he said, inspiring gales of laughter from the other musicians in the room.

No amount of merrymaking, though, could entirely repress the wartime anxieties of Les and his jamming partners. They knew they would eventually be called upon to trade in their instruments for guns if the country mobilized to enter the war. To keep track of the Germans' progress through Europe, they stuck pins in a giant map of the world hanging on the studio wall.

Completed in 1939, North Beach Airport (later renamed La Guardia) was only about a mile and a half from Electra Court. One night, in the midst of a particularly raucous jam session, Les and Jimmy were startled by the arrival of two uniformed pilots. "We enjoyed your music very much," said one of the pilots, "but you were blocking out our signal on the southwest vector. It's a good thing that it was good contact flying, or we could never have found the airport."

The following morning a couple of FCC representatives dropped by Electra Court to conduct a more thorough investigation. Les eventually convinced them that he was neither a spy nor a wild-eyed radical bent on sabotaging U.S. air traffic. But the dour-looking officials issued a stern warning anyway. One of their agents would be patrolling the Jackson Heights neighborhood over the next few days in an antenna-equipped car. If he picked up the illegal signal on his car radio, Les would face stiff criminal charges. Sadly for all, that was the end of the Booger Brothers Broadcasting Company.

Soon after arriving in New York, Les began making records, some leading his own trio, others as a sideman. This did not sit well with his boss. Although Fred Waring had achieved considerable fame with dozens of chart-topping disks throughout the 1920s and early 1930s, his attitude toward recording had undergone a radical change. "Our professional life is longer without records," he told a *Down Beat* reporter. "We haven't recorded since 1932, and never will until I can get a guarantee that the records won't be played promiscuously on radio and coin machines in competition with our own live music."

The bandleader also discouraged his men from taking outside gigs. "Fred and I didn't agree on a lot of things, mostly because he had a policy to never let anybody become famous," Les later said. "He was just the opposite of Tommy and Jimmy Dorsey and Glenn Miller. They all had singers who became famous while they were still with their bands. Fred sort of sat on his people."

Waring, however, failed to stifle the ambitions of his star guitarist. On October 3, 1939—less than a year after his debut on the Waring broadcast—Les and his triomates cut four songs for Columbia's Vocalion label: "Goodbye, My Lover, Goodbye," "Out of Nowhere," "Where Is Love," and "Swanee River" (The latter pair were released as a single on OKeh after Vocalion temporarily folded in April 1940.)

The first two sides were released on a 78 single six months later. Les's picking and strumming on "Out of Nowhere" framed Jimmy's sonorous vocal like a platinum setting around a fine-cut diamond, intricate but never intrusive. On his own solo, though, the guitarist cut loose with a myriad of exquisitely executed ideas, including a cleverly placed quote from "Rhapsody in Blue." "Goodbye, My Lover, Goodbye," however, was unable to transcend Jimmy's funereal vocal arrangement. The disk netted favorable reviews anyway: "The highly talented, long-neglected guitar soloist with Fred Waring's band is highly impressive here with his breakneck, single-string guitar solos," reported *Down Beat*. "Paul, while playing in the Reinhardt tradition, still manages to insert original ideas. And he plays with great lift." The same issue of *Down Beat* also included Les's single in its "Best Solos on Wax" column, alongside Django Reinhardt's "Georgia on My Mind" and Louis Armstrong's "Wolverine Blues." High praise, indeed, for a hillbilly from Waukesha.

During this period, Les continued to search for new ways to enhance the volume and sustain of his guitar. In 1941 he persuaded the proprietors of the Epiphone guitar company to allow him to use their West 14th Street factory to test out some of his theories concerning the solid-body guitar. Working there on Sundays, when the shop was normally closed, Les eventually built a twenty-pound monstrosity he called "the Log."

Now one of the most popular attractions in Nashville's Country Music Foundation Museum, the Log derived its name from the four-by-four-inch length of pine that Les used for the body of the instrument, which, when completed, resembled a railroad tie with strings. He added a Vibrola tailpiece, a Gibson neck with a Larson Brothers fingerboard, and two pickups he fashioned from the inner coils of an electric clock. Then, to make it look more like a guitar, he clamped on a pair of side wings from a used acoustic Epiphone.

Although Jimmy Atkins thought the rough-hewn instrument produced a fine tone, Les was never quite satisfied with its sound, preferring, for the most part, to stick with his modified Gibson, or later, one of his hot-rodded Epiphones. But if he was in a particularly mischievous mood, he'd take the wings off the Log and tote the stick-straight guitar into clubs just to shock the patrons.

It was an unusually hot, humid afternoon in May 1941, too hot to venture outdoors. Les, Ernie Newton, and a few other musicians decided to jam in the Electra Court basement studio, the coolest spot in the building. There was no escaping the heat, though. It seeped through the cement walls of the basement and made Les's hands moist with sweat.

Holding the neck of his electric guitar with one hand, he absentmindedly attempted to move a live microphone with the other. He froze to the mike stand as 220 volts of electricity tore through his body. His friends froze too. Les kept screaming, "Shut it off! Shut it off!" But it took a few seconds for anyone to grasp what was happening.

Finally, Ernie put down his bass and picked up a broomstick and knocked the mike stand out of Les's hands. According to the guitarist, his friends packed him in a bath of ice water until an ambulance transported him to a nearby hospital, where he remained for several weeks. "The muscles and ligaments in my chest were all ripped loose," he later said. "After they healed, my hands were numb and I felt like I was wearing a hat."

The doctors told Les that patients suffering similar traumas to the nervous system sometimes developed neurasthenia, a chronic condition characterized by localized pain, irritability, anxiety, and fatigue. His concerns, however, were much more immediate: Would he ever be able to play again?

Faced with an uncertain recuperation period, Les decided to quit the Pennsylvanians. He had been yearning to stretch himself beyond the narrow musical confines of Fred Waring's orchestra anyway. "We rehearsed everything till it was so perfect that it didn't have a stitch of soul to it," he later complained. And his ongoing conflict over recording with Waring also had come to a full boil when the orchestra leader threatened to fire him if he insisted on making more disks. Les had already begun putting feelers out for a new job earlier that year, even though Virginia had just given birth to their firstborn son, Les junior (Nicknamed Rusty, the boy was born in June 1941 in New York City, not in Chicago as his father has publicly stated in the past.) The accident simply encouraged the guitarist to quit the Pennsylvanians sooner.

When Jimmy refused to move on with him, Les disbanded the trio and eventually accepted a job as a music director for two radio stations in Chicago. He returned with his wife and infant son to the midwestern city where he had first made a name for himself. But his heart and mind were elsewhere.

Chapter 8

A TEMPORARY
SETBACK

Les had fantasized for years about performing with Bing Crosby, who was enjoying epic popularity as a singer and actor. That dream seemed entirely possible before the Electra Court mishap. Thanks to Fred Waring's daily broadcasts, Les's electrified guitar solos had become familiar to millions of listeners from coast to coast. Landing a spot on Crosby's Hollywood-based radio show was, to Les's way of thinking, the next logical step.

Like Les, Crosby had gotten his first break with a radio orchestra. He was the lead vocalist for a jazzy and innovative trio called the Rhythm Boys, stars in Paul Whiteman's band in the latter part of the 1920s and early 1930s. After his engaging performance in *The Big Broadcast,* Crosby won lead roles in a parade of outstanding musicals that helped make him the most sought-after figure in show business. By 1941, his resonant baritone and breezy stage persona had earned him more than twenty-five movie roles and nearly two hundred top-selling records, a number unmatched by anyone else in recording history.

Now Les grew obsessed with rubbing elbows with this powerhouse of talent and success. And when Les set his mind on a goal, it was usually only a matter of time before it was achieved. He even told Fred Waring that he was moving to California to go to work for Crosby.

"Where did you meet him?" Waring inquired.

"I never met him, just like I never met you," the guitarist replied. "But I'm going to play with him."

As Les tells it, he planned to head for L.A. as soon as he recovered from the accident. However, Ralph Atlass, his former boss at WJJD, spun him into an entirely different direction. Atlass asked him to come back to the Chicago radio station to serve as musical director for both WJJD and WIND. Les reluctantly accepted the offer, but it was probably a prudent decision. He was in no condition to begin another grinding round of auditions in a new town.

The new job promised to be far less taxing than his role with the Waring band. His main responsibilities involved hiring other musicians and overseeing the daily programming schedule. During off hours, he concentrated on learning to read music (which he claims never to have mastered). But he felt he had taken a step backward. Here he was, working at the same place where he had been a hillbilly performer three years earlier. Worse than that, he could barely play his instrument.

Troubled by persistent numbness in his hands, he sought treatment at the Mayo Clinic in Rochester, Minnesota. He was told there was nothing to do but wait until the damaged nerves in his body healed themselves. "He was terribly discouraged," said guitarist Doc Parker, who used to jam with Les around Chicago. "He was the sort of guy who could be sound asleep in bed, and if some lick came to mind, he'd have to get out of bed to try it. He'd pick twenty-four hours a day if he could. If you took the guitar away from him he'd die."

Fortunately, within a matter of weeks, Les's natural resilience prevailed and he gradually began playing again. He left his job at WJJD, briefly resurrected his country twin, Rhubarb Red, on WLS, then accepted a full-time job as a staff musician at WBBM, the CBS affiliate where he and Sunny Joe Wolverton had performed nearly a decade earlier as the Ozark Apple Knockers. There he worked as

Les Paul with the WBBM studio orchestra, using the opportunity to practice his newfound arranging skills. The gig fell short of the Hollywood high life Les had envisioned for himself. But at least he was performing full-time under his own name with an orchestra that included many excellent jazzmen. His spirits rose even higher when he landed a regular spot on a new musical show conducted by Ben Bernie, the well-loved radio personality known as the Old Maestro.

By the spring of 1942, WBBM was so pleased with Les's "hot licks" that it began advertising him as "one of America's electric guitar virtuosos." That April he discussed his approach to playing in an interview with *Music and Rhythm* magazine, his comments reflecting the self-assured voice of a maturing artist:

"Phrasing is one of the toughest things about guitar playing. Getting the right phrasing is like a man talking. Some men can speak forcibly and express exactly what they wish to express. Others dribble on, talking words and more words, but somehow they never put across their ideas. Well, that's the way it is with phrasing on guitar. It takes not only constant, persistent study, lots of experience, and lots of listening, but it also takes that extra spark of something which enables a man to intuitively know what is good taste—what expresses his idea most forcibly in terms of musical phrasing. Tone is created by the musician himself; it's his individual character expressed in music. On a guitar you 'buy' the tone. Whenever it is struck, it gives out a certain definite tone. But the phrasing added to that is what makes the difference and brings out the individuality. Mass production makes all guitars sound pretty much alike. To get distinctiveness you must experiment, try different phrasing, different gadgets, amplifiers, speakers, tubes, strings, etc. But above all, it's the style, the phrasing, which sets you apart."

WBBM was one of the most profitable radio stations in the country. Owned by Ralph Atlass's older brother, H. Leslie Atlass, it was considered "the Cadillac of the business" by advertisers. The elder Atlass governed his station with one overriding philosophy: "Hire the best you can hire and pay them more than they are worth." Gene Autry, Dale Evans, Judy Canova, the Andrews Sisters, and Fran

Allison (later the star of TV's whimsical puppet show *Kukla, Fran &
Ollie*) were among the big-name performers whose careers were
given a substantial boost on Les Atlass's station.

During the day, WBBM listeners eagerly followed some of radio's
first soap operas—*Aunt Jenny's Real Life Stories, Our Gal Sunday,
Road of Life*—and conscientious homemakers jotted down Betty
Crocker's "kitchen-tested recipes." After dinner, millions of men,
women, and children gathered in the parlor around their Philcos to
take in one of the all-time favorite comedy shows, *Amos 'n' Andy,*
which was broadcast live from the Wrigley Building five nights a
week.

WBBM reflected the country's wartime concerns throughout the
early 1940s, when both the Merry Macs and Kay Kyser's band scored
big hits with patriotic morale boosters like "Praise the Lord and Pass
the Ammunition." Every weekday afternoon, *Victory Matinee* invited
service men and women of varying rank to describe their roles in
maintaining U.S. defenses. On Saturday mornings, *Fashions in Ra-
tions* taught Americans how to maximize their government allot-
ments of meat, shoes, and sugar. (Basic U.S. food prices were 61
percent above prewar prices.) In fact, the war was much closer to
home than natives of the Windy City ever imagined: In June 1942 a
small group of scientists, including thirty-four-year-old Dr. Edward
Teller, secretly gathered behind the ivy-covered walls of the University of Chicago to lay the groundwork for the world's first atomic
bomb.

One casualty of the war era was recorded music. From 1942 to
1944 it was banned on radio largely because of the muscle-bound
maneuvers of James Caesar Petrillo, the colorful and combative president of the American Federation of Musicians. Petrillo was elected
head of the national union in 1940, a time of rapid change in the
music industry. Talking pictures had thrown thousands of musicians
out of work, and Petrillo predicted early on that phonograph records
and electrical disk transcriptions would create a tidal wave of canned
music that would eventually sweep live performances off the radio.
But the strong-minded union boss didn't see why his boys should
be compelled to have a hand in their own doom. "Electric refrig-

erators put the iceman out of work," he argued, "but the iceman didn't have to make them!"

In July 1942 he ordered musicians across the country to refrain from recording until record companies agreed to pay the AFM's Music Performance Trust Fund a royalty on every disk sold. It took the personal intervention of President Roosevelt and the War Production Board to bring the strike to an end twenty-seven months later. By then, though, all the major record companies had caved in to Petrillo's demands, agreeing to pay royalties of up to two and a half cents per disk. Broadcasters were so incensed by Petrillo's autocratic style that they eventually persuaded Congress to pass the Lea Act, better known as the Anti-Petrillo Law, which prohibited the union boss from encouraging his musicians to carry out acts that could be regarded as coercive.

Les, of course, benefited from Petrillo's vigorous campaign to keep live music on the air. As a member of WBBM's studio orchestra (which was conducted by Petrillo's younger brother, Caesar), he not only backed every big-name entertainer who came to the station, he was also on hand to do sustaining programs, network shows designed to fill airtime that was not paid for by a commercial sponsor.

He often accompanied vocalist Fran Allison, who also starred in several of the station's weekly comedy sketches. A fan of Les's from the Waring show, Allison was thrilled when he joined the WBBM staff: "I used to love to have Les play fills while I was singing," she recalled in 1989. "It was like having a thirty-piece band behind you. He was constantly thinking about how he could make a song better. I knew he wouldn't stay at the station long. He had the kind of talent that just had to move on."

Before he did, though, he took a lesson or two from Ben Bernie, who affectionately referred to the boys in his dance band as "all the lads." Bernie's show, sponsored by Wrigley gum, was broadcast live every weekday afternoon from five forty-five to six from WBBM's first-floor studio. The Old Maestro greeted radio listeners with his trademark introduction—"Yow-sah, yow-sah, yow-sah"—and peppered his program with humorous remarks. He often performed as a vocalist, tossing off songs in a sly, half-talking manner. The steady hand with which Bernie managed his musicians and audience quickly earned Les's admiration and respect.

On the surface, the two men seemed to have little in common. Bernie, born Benjamin Anzelevitz, was a cigar-chomping New York City–bred Jew who had begun his career on the vaudeville circuit three decades earlier as a monologuist-violinist. But he and Les were both self-made men with a flair for waggish showmanship. At the height of their fame both would rank among the nation's highest-paid entertainers.

Bernie acted as a mentor to many of the struggling young talents who crossed his path. He helped launch the careers of jazz trombonist Lou McGarity and Dinah Shore, whom he fought to keep on his show after the sponsor insisted she didn't sing loud enough. Now he found an eager protégé in Les Paul. "Ben taught me what could be done *without* a musical instrument," Les later said. "I learned from him that you have to be in the right place at the right time with the goods. But he said it isn't any good if you haven't got the goods to deliver."

Although Les was probably the only musician in Bernie's band who couldn't read music, the orchestra leader gave him ample solo time. One of Les's most valuable assets was his ability to grasp new material after a single listening. Blessed with perfect pitch and a phonographic memory, he rarely missed an opportunity to show them off.

Bucky Pizzarelli, a guitarist who later toured with Benny Goodman and formed a highly respected jazz duo with George Barnes, used to mark his radio dial with a pencil so he could easily find the early-evening program that featured the astonishing electrified sounds of Les Paul: "In those days, everybody was looking for the Gibson Super 400 or the Epiphone Emperor, because they could be heard without a microphone. But Les was way ahead of them all because he had his own electric guitar. I was taking lessons at the time, and I just couldn't understand this monstrous guitar playing. It scared me. I'd think, 'How does he do that?' Nobody in the world played a melody like Les. He sang with his instrument. It made me realize that there was more to the guitar than strumming as part of an orchestra, which is all anybody did at the time."

Jimmy Atkins's younger brother Chet, then a guitarist with a group called the Dixie Swingsters on KNOX in Tennessee, was also following Les's career closely. A staff musician, he had no trouble slipping into the station's transcription library at night or on weekends to borrow disks that featured his two favorite pickers, Les Paul and George Barnes. "I copied a lot of Les's choruses," Chet later said. "But I discovered that when I played one of Les's licks around other musicians, they'd say, 'Hey, that's Les Paul.' I found out right away that you had to get your own licks, which I did in a hurry."

In his spare time, Les continued to refine the Log, the crudely crafted solid-body guitar he had built in New York the previous year. He even brought the outlandish-looking instrument to M. H. Berlin, president of the Chicago Musical Instruments, which owned Gibson, to try to persuade him to manufacture a line of solid-body guitars. But Berlin laughed him out the door, insisting the Log was "nothing but a broomstick with a pickup on it."

In the meantime, Les was busy developing a dramatically different sound for his amplifier. For this he sought the hands-on help of John Kutilek, who was then building amplifiers for Gibson. Night after night, Les trekked over to Kutilek's basement workshop on the northwest side of Chicago and, as was his habit, refused to leave until he got the sound he was after.

"With a little distortion and overload, we were able to produce an echo effect," Kutilek later recalled. "At this time Les was also toying with multiple recording. He was determined to do it and spent most nights working on it. He was a very single-minded boy."

By the beginning of 1943, Les was once again feeling frustrated by Chicago's shrinking music scene, which grew even smaller with Ben Bernie's departure in February. Weakened by years of rugged road life and hard drinking, the bandleader developed a near-fatal case of pleurisy and retired to the West Coast. But he encouraged Les to follow, promising to groom the young guitarist to take over his orchestra. That was all Les needed to hear. He was also eager to begin his campaign to work with Crosby. He decided to pull up stakes, form a new trio, and move out to L.A. right away. He even persuaded a friend, pianist Joe Rann, to move out there with him.

He would have had his bags packed the next morning if it hadn't been for the contract that committed him to remain in Caesar Petrillo's band for several more months. "When I gave Caesar my resignation, he just tore it up," Les later claimed. "He told me I wasn't going anywhere. When his brother Jimmy found out that Ben was trying to get me out on the Coast, he had him fined a thousand dollars for trying to solicit a man from his brother's orchestra."

Around this time, Fred Waring's longtime business manager came to the Windy City. According to Les, Johnny O'Connor just happened to have a few street-hardened pals of his own: the Irish mob. One night O'Connor invited Les to a bash in one of the big private suites in the luxurious Sherman House Hotel. Thrilled by the prospect of seeing his old New York friend, Les grabbed his guitar and headed straight for the hotel on the corner of Clark and Randolph streets in the Loop.

After Johnny greeted him at the door of the suite, Les quickly realized that O'Connor's Chicago friends were members of "Terrible Tom" Tuohy's gang, one of the most powerful bootlegging clans in the greater Chicago area. "The whole damn family was there," said Les. "It was a pretty strange get-together. There were bodyguards everywhere with guns strapped on. And every one of them was roaring drunk!"

Johnny was fairly well shellacked himself when he told Les why he had invited him up to the suite: Waring wanted his star guitarist back and was willing to pay $1,000 a week to get him. Les ruefully explained that he couldn't go anywhere because "Caesar Petrillo has got me locked in." Johnny assured him that everything would be taken care of. Before the evening was over, the smooth-talking Irishman reached Jimmy Petrillo by phone.

"Look, I want Les Paul," he said. "Tell your brother that as of Friday, he is no longer with CBS."

That was that. Les was free to leave.

A few days later Fred Waring called Les from New York, frantically looking for his business manager. Les had left O'Connor at the train station. He didn't know where he was. "Well, what the hell am I paying you?" Waring asked

"Johnny said a thousand bucks a week."

"I don't pay anyone a thousand a week," Fred hollered.

"As a matter of fact," replied Les, "I don't think that's enough."

Johnny, who apparently had gone on a bender, soon called and sheepishly admitted that his magnanimous offer had been fueled by a full head of scotch. The deal was off. "You wanted to go to California anyway, right?" asked O'Connor.

"Right!" Les exclaimed.

Driving over the ribbon of highway that led to a new dream, the young guitarist savored an uncomplicated moment of triumph. He was twenty-seven years old, just entering his prime, with all sorts of wonderful possibilities stretching before him.

Chapter 9

REACHING FOR
THE BRASS RING

Hollywood in the early 1940s was still in the midst of its golden age. Americans believed it was a charmed place. Scores of stage-struck young men and women arrived there daily, making their homes in cheap hotels and rooming houses where they talked shop, read the trades, and patiently waited to be discovered.

Les, of course, was far more aggressive about spreading his name around. Wheeling into town in 1943, he headed straight for Hollywood Boulevard and Vine Street, Tinseltown's miniature version of Times Square. Within a few blocks of this famous intersection were a myriad of opulent theaters, luxurious hotels, and widely publicized watering holes where the consumption of food and drink was incidental to seeing and being seen by the right people.

Among the hotels was the elegant Hollywood Roosevelt, a four-hundred-room Spanish Colonial structure co-owned by such movieland notables as Douglas Fairbanks, Mary Pickford, Louis B. Mayer, and Marcus Loew. Advertised as "the social occasion of the year," its 1927 opening had attracted the likes of Greta Garbo, Gloria Swanson, Will Rogers, Charlie Chaplin, and Wallace Beery. From that night on, the trendy hotel across from Grauman's Chinese Theatre was dubbed "the home of the stars."

With electric guitar in hand, Les wandered into the Roosevelt Cinegrill, an intimate cabaret club that attracted Hollywood's fast set. It was in this room that fifteen years earlier Ben Bernie became one of the first orchestra leaders to do a live broadcast outside a radio studio, creating a new style of on-air informality with his wry remarks to the radio audience and dancers.

That night, as luck would have it, a local radio station was doing a remote broadcast of the Cinegrill house band. Les knew that the leader would invite him to sit in if he stuck around long enough. Although the American Federation of Musicians vehemently opposed this time-honored tradition—"Why should customers pay for a seven-piece band and get twelve pieces?" AFM president Jimmy Petrillo brayed—Les plugged in one of his modified Epiphones and let his fingers fly. Unfortunately, a representative from the ever-vigilant Local 47 collared him after the first set. "How come you guys have to jam all the time?" the union man demanded. "Why don't you practice at home?"

"For the same reason you don't dance with your wife in the kitchen," Les teased. "You gotta have the response of an audience to amount to something, to know what you're doing right and what you're doing wrong."

The brassy guitarist was a two-time winner that night. He got off without a fine—and he put Hollywood on notice that Les Paul, former star soloist of the Fred Waring and Ben Bernie orchestras, had arrived.

Hollywood now rivaled New York and Chicago as a radio center. More and more nationally broadcast shows originated in its network studios. The booming film capital was also becoming an important music publishing hub. A profusion of record companies, independent recording studios, and transcription services churned out an avalanche of disks with the latest new dance numbers and musical revues for commercial and domestic consumption.

Naturally Les was eager to stake a claim in this vast field of possibilities. He settled with his family in West Hollywood, just a few
blocks north of Santa Monica Boulevard. By then, Ben Bernie was
too ill to be of any help to his protégé, battling the pulmonary disease that would claim his life only a few months later in October
1943. So Les scrambled to pull together a new trio. He already had
Joe Rann, the bespectacled, baby-faced pianist who had followed him
from Chicago. But he still needed a bass player. Somehow he managed to track down Bob Meyer, the bassist he had used six years
earlier in his Hot Club of France–inspired quartet at Chicago's Bismark Hotel.

Meyer had moved to California in 1941 and was now happily leading his own jazz quartet, the Rhythmaires. "One night," Meyer later
recalled, "we were working at a club called the Seven Seas and in
walk Les and Joe Rann. Now Les being Les, I knew he would want
to sit in. But I was amazed when he handed me several of his own
arrangements for the other musicians to play. Les himself did everything by ear. I doubt if he even knew the name of some of the chords
he was playing. His thing was speed."

Meyer immediately abandoned the Rhythmaires and joined the
new Les Paul Trio. The three musicians practiced daily at Meyer's
home in North Hollywood, converting a spare bedroom into a makeshift rehearsal studio. They deadened the walls with blankets and
sheets and rolled in an old upright piano for Joe. Harry Zimmerman,
the organist who had done so much to teach Les about jazz in Chicago, occasionally came by to offer advice and encouragement.

The rehearsals were a time of experimentation. One of the first
things Les did was persuade Bob Meyer to retune his symphony-
style string bass: "He had me change the tuning his way, which was
a good idea because it brought up the tone of the instrument. It
made it sound more brilliant."

The trio briefly considered adding a singer. One afternoon a
plump, curly-locked young man dropped by to show off his pipes. A
new Hollywood arrival, Frankie Laine had a jazzy vocal style, but he
lacked the glossy veneer traditionally associated with band singers
of the day. "We could see that this guy was never going to make it,"

Meyer said of the former talent agent from Cleveland. However, within four years of his failed audition with the Les Paul Trio, the leather-lunged Laine, later known for his robust rendering of the theme song for TV's *Rawhide,* became one of the country's best-selling recording artists.

As soon as they tightened up their repertoire of jazz and pop standards, Les and his pals began making transcription disks for C. P. MacGregor, an independent recording studio which, among other things, produced packaged radio programs for national distribution. Shortly thereafter they landed jobs as staff musicians at NBC in Hollywood, home of Bing Crosby's weekly *Kraft Music Hall* show.

As Les has often recounted the story, he and his triomates oiled their way into the network—sneaking past NBC's security guards during lunch-hour rush. They slipped into a vacant rehearsal studio, then hastily launched into an impromptu jam session. Lured into the room by the sound of the trio's hot licks, a friendly program director helped them get hired right then and there.

Bob Meyer, however, couldn't recall any such chicanery. He was certain that the trio got the job at NBC on the strength of Les Paul's already considerable reputation. After all, Les had been a star player on the same network with Fred Waring's orchestra just two years earlier. "I'm sure we would not have been in that building unless we were invited," Meyer insisted. "Maybe we used an empty studio to rehearse in until they figured out what they wanted to do with us. But the story sounds a lot more interesting the way Les told it."

In any case, added Meyer, NBC paid the trio union scale to do several sustainers, programs designed to fill unsponsored airtime that could be heard on stations all over the country. In the meantime, the group guested on everything from *The Elgin Watch Show* and RCA's *What's New* to Hedda Hopper's gossipfest. They managed to work everywhere, it seemed, but Bing Crosby's *Kraft Music Hall.*

By late 1943, the new Les Paul Trio had garnered enough attention to win a cameo in a film that was eventually titled *Sensations of '45,* starring Eleanor Powell, Dennis O'Keefe, W. C. Fields, and Sophie Tucker. Repeating the vaudeville-type format of movies like *Follow the Boys* and *Song of the Open Road, Sensations* was nothing more than a string of half-baked sketches loosely tied together by a flimsy story line about a failing publicity agency. A diverse collection of talent—the Woody Herman and Cab Calloway bands, the Flying Copelands, and the Pallenberg Bears—lent a touch of luster to this otherwise vacuous movie. But it was still a resounding box-office flop.

Sensations sole importance was that it was W. C. Fields's last film before his unquenchable thirst for alcohol drove him from the silver screen forever. The bulb-nosed comedian hated the picture even more than the critics did. "They panned the hell out of it, but they were pretty kind to me," Fields wrote his sister Adel two weeks after the June 1944 release of *Sensations.* "The producers take some little starlet and surround her with names and in their effort to make the little girl a star they ruin the picture, as the little girls haven't the experience to carry the load. . . ."

The "little starlet" to whom Fields referred was, of course, Eleanor Powell, although she was already a star in her own right. In fact, one of the few scenes Les could later recall from the entire movie was the young, leggy Powell tap-dancing on top of a giant, flashing pinball machine. *Sensations* was forgotten almost as quickly as it hit the theater, but it represented one more step toward the stardom that Les had sought so desperately since leaving his native Waukesha a decade earlier.

He certainly had come closer to achieving fame than any of his hometown friends, one of whom visited him in late 1943. Cullen Casey, then a sailor en route to Pearl Harbor, hadn't seen "Red" since they played together in 1932 at Jamieson's honky-tonk on Pewaukee Lake. Curious to see how his boyhood pal was faring in the dream capital of the Western world, Casey gave Les a call and they agreed to meet at a Hollywood restaurant. Casey brought along a shipmate, a good old boy from the backwoods of Mississippi. The two sailors listened in silence for more than an hour while Les lectured them on "what it took to be a genius."

"I don't know anything about football. I don't know anything about basketball. I spend twenty-four hours a day playing my guitar," he exclaimed between bites of pizza. "You have to give up everything if you want to be a good guitar player, play around the clock. You can't be monkeying around with anything else. You have to give your whole life up to it."

Casey's young friend was astonished by Les's rambling monologue. "When we got outside the restaurant," Casey later said, "this fella turned to me and said, 'You know something? That guy is nuts!'"

Les's characteristic self-absorption was already creating a chasm between him and those who did not share his obsessions. It was a chasm that would widen with each passing year.

By the end of 1943, the supply of unmarried, draft-age men was exhausted, forcing Selective Service to widen its net for new inductees. Twenty-eight-year-old Lester William Polsfuss, as he was still known in legal documents, was soon plucked out of the remaining pool of prospects and placed in the Army. Fortunately he had friends in high places. One of them was Meredith Willson, the multitalented music director of NBC, where the two probably met.

Willson began his career as a flute and piccolo soloist with John Philip Sousa's concert band in the early 1920s. He later earned rave reviews for the music he wrote for *The Music Man* and *The Unsinkable Molly Brown,* both smash hits on Broadway. In the interim, the composer gained widespread recognition for his scores for such early-1940s movie favorites as *The Great Dictator* and *The Little Foxes.*

Shortly after the onset of the war, Uncle Sam commissioned Willson to serve as music director for a special entertainment division that would eventually be called the Armed Forces Radio Service. Major Willson had one overriding charter: to buoy the morale of American GIs here and abroad with engaging music and variety shows. He accomplished that task with the help of more than five hundred enlisted men and women. Based in a modest suite of offices on Santa Monica Boulevard near Gower Street in West Hollywood, the khaki-clad recruits worked at a furious pace to create seventy-six hours of prerecorded entertainment a week for hundreds of GI radio stations all over the world. They produced shows like *Command Performance, At Ease,* and *Mail Call,* which boasted such mainstream glitterati as Bob Hope, Dorothy Lamour, and Frank Sinatra, as well as *Jubilee,* which showcased America's premier jazz talent—everyone from Duke Ellington to Dizzy Gillespie—and simultaneously counterbalanced the largely white fare found on the rest of the AFRS.

Among Willson's personal duties was the recruitment of top-notch musicians for the AFRS's ubiquitous nineteen-piece orchestra. Because the band was often called upon to break into smaller units to provide support for a wide variety of acts, Willson prized versatile players. He gladly used his influence as a high-ranking officer to get Private Polsfuss into his unit. Aware that Les was an electronics whiz as well as an ace guitarist, Willson cautioned him, "Play as dumb as you can or you'll end up in the Signal Corps." The reluctant conscript followed Willson's instructions to the letter.

After surviving six weeks of vigorous basic training, Les returned to the palm-lined streets of Hollywood and to the comfort of his own home. He had the good fortune to live only a few blocks above the GI radio service's Santa Monica Boulevard headquarters. "All I had to do to get to work every day was climb into my car and release the brake," he later boasted. "I didn't even have to turn on the engine."

The AFRS was not only one of the best-possible wartime assignments but also one of the greatest breaks in Les's career. He got to strut his stuff with the highest echelon of Hollywood entertainers, and he also became familiar to millions of soldiers all over the world, men and women who would thereafter associate his name and upbeat music with the good life back home and better times ahead. He soon formed a new trio—and new alliances, sharing the AFRS recording studio with such Hollywood heavyweights as Jack Benny, Rudy Vallee, Groucho Marx, and Kate Smith. Later he became a regular on the hard-swinging Jubilee shows, where with his longtime idol, Art Tatum, he made some of the finest music of his career. And he worked once more with one of his *Sensations* costars, W. C. Fields. Scarred and puffy from years of drinking, Fields was now frequently in and out of hospitals. He often performed with Edgar Bergen on the AFRS, as well as on civilian radio. The veteran entertainers frequently staged on-air feuds between W. C. and Bergen's wisecracking dummy, Charlie McCarthy. ("How'd you like to take a piggyback ride on a buzz saw, my little friend?" Fields would sneer at Charlie.) In reality, Fields and Bergen were best of friends. Les, however, recalled at least one AFRS recording session in which Fields worked himself into a state of righteous indignation over some wry comment Bergen made via Charlie. After the duo finished recording their bit in the studio, W. C. slipped into Bergen's dressing room and sawed the head off his freckle-faced wooden companion.

Les's Army days were not all glitter and glamour, though. He had to help edit hundreds of hours of prerecorded entertainment down to scores of tightly constructed thirty-minute variety shows for Armed Forces network distribution. With tape-recording technology still four years away in this country, it was exceedingly tedious work. To put together one half-hour transcription required a master disk recording lathe, two playback machines, three technicians with split-second timing, and several painstaking hours. If someone missed a cue or prematurely dropped the recording needle, the process had to begin again from scratch. But it was excellent training for Les, who was now aggressively pursuing the study of audio engineering. He used to pray that his partners would make mistakes so he could use the discarded disks to practice on his own homemade lathe.

Although the Armed Forces Radio Service gave Les ready access to a network of powerful stars, Army life apparently cramped his style. He began bucking for a medical discharge within months of his recruitment. Nobody associated with him at the time could recall the nature of his ailment. "I used a staff car on several occasions to drive him to an ear, nose, and throat specialist who took care of all our boys," said former AFRS press liaison Sue Chadwick.

Whatever his complaint, though, it was good enough to get him out of khaki by early 1944. Nevertheless, he continued to make a broad assortment of transcriptions for the AFRS's music library—many at C. P. MacGregor, one of the finest independent recording studios in the country. Sometimes he recorded with his own newly formed group, now comprising rhythm guitarist Cal Gooden, bassist Clint Nordquist, and pianist Tommy Todd. Other times he strummed up a storm with the AFRS All-Star Quintet, which included alto saxman Willie Smith and drummer "Big Sid" Catlett. And every now and then he trotted out his country cousin Rhubarb Red. The rube act appeared to be as much for the amusement of the musicians and technicians in the studio as for the boys overseas. "He'd roll on the floor laughing when he sang that stuff," said C. P. MacGregor recording engineer Carson Taylor. "He was just a crazy nut, in it for fun."

Juxtaposing hillbilly horseplay with serious musicianship greatly enhanced Les's reputation as an all-round entertainer. "If you told him you wanted him to build a melody or harmony in a certain style, whether it was jazz, pop, or country, he could do it right there on the spot," added Taylor, who later engineered disks for Nat King Cole and Frank Sinatra. "He got to take solo turns with every AFRS band he played with."

The MacGregor studios represented much more to Les than simply a place to make a few bucks. Whenever he wasn't recording there, he was in the control room, plying the engineers with questions. "His thirst for knowledge was insatiable," said Taylor. "He was desperately trying to understand what we were doing. And he kept at it and at it until he did. That set him apart from all the other recording artists we worked with."

Les soon ingratiated himself with a couple of other MacGregor engineers—head sound man Art Felthausen and Art Partridge, both highly respected within the recording industry. Felthausen and Partridge were members of the Sapphire Club, a fraternity of audio engineers that took its name from the sapphire stylus used to cut grooves in disk recordings. The Los Angeles contingent met at least once a week to talk shop and experiment with new types of equipment. From these men—and several other equally adroit engineers—Les Paul received the equivalent of a Ph.D. in audio engineering. He relied upon their technical expertise during his remaining years in Hollywood—and beyond.

At the end of June 1944, shortly after the release of *Sensations,* Les got a call from Nat Cole. The two musicians had jammed together on several occasions in Chicago's South Side saloons during the 1930s. Now Nat wanted to know if Les was ready to trade some licks in a much classier venue: the Los Angeles Philharmonic Auditorium. The superb Nat Cole Trio had been booked to perform there on July 2, 1944, with such jazz greats as Joe Sullivan, Barney Bigard, Buddy Rich, and Benny Carter. But Nat's regular guitarist, Oscar Moore, couldn't make it. Les, of course, jumped at the chance to fill the last-minute vacancy.

Advertised as Jazz at the Philharmonic, the Sunday-afternoon show was planned and sponsored by a brash, twenty-five-year-old impresario named Norman Granz. No musician himself, Granz had organized spirited off-hours jam sessions in 1943 at Herb Rose's 331 Club in Hollywood. Unlike most jams, which were spontaneous, unpaid affairs, Granz offered local musicians and star sidemen union-scale wages to come to the 331 Club and do what they would have done for free after hours anyway. Pretty soon he was attracting such name soloists as Nat Cole and Lester Young.

Through the jams, Granz not only spread the gospel of swing and bebop but also promoted his social agenda: racial unity. He abhorred the segregationist policies at most Hollywood nightclubs and the racism that divided the musicians' unions into separate black and white branches. His jams featured racially mixed bands, and he always insisted on an open-door and open-seating policy.

The Jazz at the Philharmonic concert would also combat prejudice. The previous year, twenty-one Mexican youths had been jailed in San Quentin during the Los Angeles "zoot suit riots." "We needed a benefit to raise money," Granz later said, "so this seemed like a chance to try out one of my ideas, which was to put on a concert at the Philharmonic."

Throughout the concert, Les's humor and spontaneity were evident. He hit the ground running on such tunes as "Lester Leaps In" and "Bugle Call Rag" and grew more musically surefooted as the night wore on. Seeing he could evoke waves of laughter from the crowd by strategically plucking an off-key note here or humorous quote there, Les milked his solo on "Body and Soul" for all the laughs he could get, earning a dubious review in *Down Beat:* "The kids squirmed with glee as guitarist Les Paul produced novelty sound effects on his electric guitar, registering presumably 'hot' facial expressions for the galleries."

Years later, the guitarist boastfully recalled one of his sizzling musical exchanges with Nat Cole:

> I listened to everyone onstage that day and decided that Nat was the guy I was going to do battle with. I knew from being a piano player myself what he couldn't do. I also knew I couldn't play some of the things he could play, so I made sure he was following me, though he didn't know it. . . . I threw out one of my easiest runs and Nat picked up the bait. I threw out a tougher one, and Nat climbed on my back again. He didn't know I was walking him into the center of the ring. He didn't even know he had his gloves on. Well, I had a few runs I knew would kill him. I waited until I got everyone in the audience on the edge of their seat, then I let Nat have it with both barrels, and the whole place went crazy.

In fact, there was no winner or loser in that sparkling musical chase. Nat's exquisite piano runs echoed Les's note for note. Then the rest of the band jumped in, bringing that segment of the concert to a close and the entire audience to its feet.

By the end of the matinee, it was abundantly clear that Granz had played his hunch right. It was time to take jazzmen out of sleazy saloons where they had to compete with ringing cash registers and drunken patrons and put them in a concert setting. The young promoter staged another jam at the Philharmonic three weeks later—this time as a strictly commercial venture—and eventually produced dozens more across the United States and Europe, all under the Jazz at the Philharmonic banner. Ella Fitzgerald, Billie Holiday, Dizzy Gillespie, Charlie Parker, Roy Eldridge, and Oscar Peterson were among his regular stable of artists.

Granz used the success of the concert series to continue his fight against Jim Crow. Though he lost money in Southern cities where promoters and auditorium operators refused to relax traditional rules on segregation, other bandleaders followed his lead. Nat King Cole, Artie Shaw, Tommy Dorsey, Count Basie, Charlie Barnet, and dozens more promised to put integrationist clauses in their contracts. By then, the Mexican youths who had inspired the initial Jazz at the Philharmonic concert were freed.

The release of the JATP concerts on records was entirely unplanned. A recording engineer from the Armed Forces Radio Service just happened to show up at the debut concert with a portable disk cutter. Granz, completely enthralled by the results, took a demo to Mannie Sachs, the reigning guru of RCA. But Sachs could hear only clinkers and crowd noises. Columbia and Decca were similarly unimpressed. The idea of issuing a live concert was simply too radical for the recording establishment. Moe Asch, who owned a tiny disk company in midtown Manhattan, thought otherwise. He helped Granz make the JATP recordings the country's first live concert records. (Benny Goodman's 1939 Carnegie Hall concert album wasn't issued until years after the JATP sides were in circulation.) The first four volumes sold more than 200,000 copies within the first few months of their release, an impressive number for jazz. And the complete fourth set, which featured Les on a couple of cuts, even made it into jukeboxes.

Les, who performed in two more JATP jams, later bragged that he "helped make Norman Granz a millionaire." There was more than a grain of truth in this claim. The JATP concerts initiated a selling reciprocity between box-office and record sales no one had predicted. The albums encouraged listeners to go to the concerts, and the live performances sent them running to the record stores. Together they made Norman Granz the world's first jazz mogul.

But Les profited as well. In years to come, the JATP recordings represented the only enduring evidence of his jazz artistry. For his life would soon undergo another radical metamorphosis, his restless muse rushing headlong toward more financially rewarding ventures.

Chapter 10

TOPPING THE CHARTS
WITH DER BINGLE

Returning to NBC after his brief stint in the Army, Les picked up where he had left off. He played several sustainers a week and eventually made regular guest appearances on everything from Rudy Vallee's Thursday-night variety show to George Burns and Gracie Allen's giddy free-for-all. Sometimes he led his own trio, other times he accompanied singers like Kay Starr or Dinah Shore. But he always performed as if there was nothing else in the world he would rather be doing. Cullen Casey, who witnessed Les at work at the NBC studio in July 1944, said: "He was incredibly relaxed. I couldn't believe he was on the air. It looked like he was just fooling around."

He still hadn't grabbed the brass ring, though. Passing Crosby in the corridors of NBC week after week, he was unable to attract as much as a nod of recognition from his idol. As Les tells it, he resolved to study every detail of the star's day-to-day existence—where he slept, where he ate, where he worked and when. He noticed that Crosby liked to rehearse for his Thursday-evening show in a tiny studio in the basement of the NBC building. The dingy, poorly lit room was barely big enough to hold an upright piano, but Crosby evidently enjoyed the privacy it offered.

Les legitimately needed to book a rehearsal space for his trio as well. He just made sure it was the same one that Crosby was in the habit of using, especially on Thursday late afternoons. The scheduling secretary encouraged Les to practice in one of the larger, more modern rooms. But the guitarist explained that he liked the one in the basement precisely *because* it was small. "It has a nice, intimate sound," he said. Les's triomates had no knowledge of the impending ambush. He simply warned them not to get rattled if a surprise visitor dropped in.

They were playing the daylights out of "Back Home in Indiana" when Bing entered the room at his regularly scheduled hour. "Oh, excuse me, fellas," said the startled singer as he began backing out the door.

"Hey, aren't you Bing Crosby?" Les coyly inquired.

"Yeah. What do you boys call yourselves?"

"We're the Les Paul Trio."

Crosby, who more than likely had heard Les on Armed Forces Radio, stuck around long enough to listen to a few more tunes. Perhaps Les's lively single-string solos reminded Crosby of his long-time friend and guitar accompanist Eddie Lang, who had died at the height of his career a decade earlier. "Where have you boys been hiding?" he asked.

"Right in this room," answered Les.

"Well, do you have a steady job with anyone?"

"Right now we're negotiating a deal with Rudy Vallee."

"Well, how'd you like to come on my show?"

Crosby didn't have to wait long for Les's reply. "Then we'll see you there next Thursday," he said as he disappeared down the corridor.

Thereafter Les became a frequent guest on Crosby's radio show and their friendship blossomed. With Crosby's sponsorship, the guitarist cut the first of several disks with his trio for Decca. His group—now comprising Cal Gooden, Clint Nordquist, and pianist Milt Raskin—recorded four sides in Hollywood on December 14, 1944: "Dark Eyes," "Blue Skies," "Begin the Beguine," and "Dream Dust." These tastefully arranged standards revealed Les's growing instrumental command. Gone were most of the obvious Django Reinhardt embellishments. At age twenty-nine, he was finally shaping his own sound.

Two weeks later, his trio appeared on Crosby's *Kraft Music Hall* to push one of the group's freshly minted tunes. The NBC show, broadcast live every Thursday evening before a packed studio audience, was heard by millions of listeners nationwide. Its lightweight blend of relaxed conversation and music gave the public respite from the bitter realities of a world at war—or at least tried to put the best possible face on them. "What with all the holiday buying and the new rationing rules," said announcer Ken Carpenter, "we suppose that point budget of yours is strained, so we want to mention in passing that the four grand varieties of delicious Kraft cheese spreads take just two points apiece."

The sixty-minute show proceeded on a strict schedule, but Crosby hosted as if he were chatting with friends in his living room. He opened with the theme song he had used since 1931, a languorous, string-laden version of "Where the Blue of the Night (Meets the Gold of the Day)," Les's feathery guitar fills providing an elegant backdrop for Crosby's husky, virile voice. Then he brought his new protégé center stage with a flourish.

"It's a pleasure to welcome the world's largest trio, a four-boy combo headed by composer/arranger/electric-guitar playing ex-GI, Mr. Les Paul," Crosby told the radio audience. "Seriously, folks, they are a really great foursome, Les and his group. They've sent so many jouncy and interesting arrangements overseas on shows like *Command Performance* and *Mail Call* that they are prime-time favorites of the boys overseas. And when you hear Les's tremendous treatment of 'Dark Eyes,' you'll see why."

Les opened the adapted Russian folk song with three melodramatic glissandos. His solo, a dizzying cascade of single-string notes, was enhanced by understated piano support from Milt Raskin, who followed with a hard-swinging chorus of his own. The two musicians then brought the up-tempo instrumental to a playful conclusion with a lightning-quick musical interchange.

"Sensational, Les!" Crosby exclaimed for the whole nation to hear. A wildly enthusiastic round of applause washed over the NBC stage. Less than two years after his arrival in Hollywood, the boy from Waukesha was on his way.

Seven months later, on July 12, 1945, Les made his disk debut on Decca with Crosby, the first of several collaborative efforts for the label. They cut two romantic ballads, "It's Been a Long, Long Time" and "Whose Dream Are You?" Although Les was paid a flat fee of $400 for the session—with no prospect of collecting royalties in the future—he firmly believed it was an important breakthrough in his career. He was right. Within weeks of the disk's October 13 release, "It's Been a Long, Long Time" shot to *Billboard*'s No. 1 spot, and it remained on the charts until the following March.

The disk was a critical success as well. "The Crosby/Les Paul Trio combination," trumpeted *Down Beat,* "is an excellent one and an attractive change of backgrounds for Bing. He's tried most everything during all these years with Decca, and Les provides better accompaniment than most. Both sides are well done, both just what you might expect from the names involved."

Crosby was equally impressed by Les's growing command of the technical aspects of recording. The day they made "It's Been a Long, Long Time," he encouraged the guitarist to open his own studio, even offering to put some money into the venture. Les, however, shunned the idea. Though he enjoyed recording himself and friends in his own home, he didn't want to get bogged down in the complications of running a business.

Later that day Les told his friend Lloyd Rich about Crosby's proposal, more or less laughing it off. But Rich, a fellow audiophile, eventually persuaded him to reconsider. If Les didn't want to get involved in running a commercial operation, Rich argued, how about building a personal studio in the garage behind the house. As Rich noted, it would be a perfect place to put some of his unconventional recording theories into practice. Besides, it was time Les moved his ever-expanding collection of recording equipment out of the house. In August of 1944 he and Virginia had had a second child, a boy they named Gene, and their home could no longer accommodate the small army of musicians and engineers who customarily dropped by at all hours of the day and night.

By then, the Paul family had settled into a small stucco bungalow on North Curson Avenue, a stone's throw from Sunset Boulevard. Before it was demolished to make way for a used-car dealership, the single-story house looked like every other home on the block. It was dwarfed by two towering columns of palms that lined the steeply sloping street leading deep into the Hollywood Hills. To the right of the grassy front yard, a narrow driveway led to a sixteen-by-thirty-foot garage with a ten-foot ceiling. The low-slung building was a perfect location for a studio: close enough to duck into the house for an occasional phone call or snack, but far enough away to escape the clamoring demands of a harried wife and two young children.

Before the summer ended, Les tore the garage apart. Lawn mowers, rakes, and other household tools were quickly replaced by microphones, music stands, a baby grand, and other assorted instruments. Unconcerned with building permits or fire hazards, Les boarded up the garage door and partitioned off a four-foot-wide control room with double glass, forcing visitors to climb through the small side window until he cut a proper entrance several months later. The control room was just barely big enough for a disk-recording lathe, mixing console, turntable, and monitor. His cobbled-together audio equipment was sorely inadequate, but he couldn't possibly afford the over-the-counter models.

So, Les claimed, he and Lloyd Rich built a Rube Goldberg–style recording lathe, using a solid-steel Cadillac flywheel rummaged from a nearby junkyard as a turntable. The sheer weight of the flywheel, Les reasoned, would cut down on the speed variations, which were common to even professionally designed lathes. To reduce vibrations, he used dental belts to drive the turntable, then mounted the lathe on a bed of steel and concrete. A contraption fashioned from an old vacuum cleaner, a bell jar, and some rubber tubing sucked debris out of the disk grooves as they were being cut.

Though Les possessed the keen intuition of an inventor, he required the help of more formally trained friends to refine his raw ideas. In time Vern Carson, Art Felthausen, and Art Partridge helped him assemble much more sophisticated recording equipment, including a four-channel microphone mixer. C. V. Olsen, RCA's leading sound engineer, built him a set of custom-made record heads that went "way out beyond the standard frequency response," and Jim Lansing, the founding father of JDL audio equipment, handed over a prototype of one of the country's first coaxial speakers, which Les incorporated into his monitoring system.

The makeshift studio was uncomfortably crowded: People had to step over instruments, recording gear, and sometimes each other to get from one end of the tiny room to the other. But it cost only a few hundred dollars and it gave Les the freedom to experiment anytime, day or night, totally unfettered by commercial studio rules and schedules.

It also served as a guitar workshop. Although commercially produced hollow-body electrics were widely available by the mid-1940s, Les continued to build his own peculiar hybrids, mixing and matching parts from various models. The one he seemed to favor most, though, was a customized, f-hole Epiphone, to which he added two "super hot" hand-wound pickups. Mounted on a $\frac{3}{8}''$ steel plate that was bolted to the body, the pickups were completely immune to vibrations from the bridge or neck, giving his instrument the long-sustaining sound of a solid-body guitar.

Over the next five years, tinkering in this backyard garage, Les would pioneer new guitar sounds and recording techniques that would help change popular music forever.

Chapter 11

SWINGING WITH THE HOLLYWOOD SWELLS

Although it was originally intended to be a private hobby shop, Les's garage studio rapidly evolved into a thriving cottage industry. By the summer of 1946, he was producing master platters for record companies, as well as disk transcriptions and spot announcements for radio stations. Dashing back and forth between the control room and studio, he served as recording engineer, bandleader, and arranger, and he played guitar or piano in between.

His piano playing, however, was less than adequate. An acquaintance suggested he recruit a young San Diego pianist named Paul Smith, who sounded as if he had twenty fingers. Les relished the idea of finding someone with whom he could trade lightning-fast fours, the kind he used to rip through with Art Tatum. But he had no desire to drive 130 miles down the coast to audition the twenty-four-year-old pianist. So he listened to him over the phone.

"Les wanted me to play 'Tea for Two,'" remembered Smith, who later became Ella Fitzgerald's music director. "I got about eight bars into it and he said, 'That sounds pretty good to me,' and told me to come up to L.A. to give it a shot. All I knew about him was that he had a jazz trio and that he supposedly played a lot like Django Rein-

hardt. But when I actually got to listen to him, I thought he played better."

Les regarded Smith with equal respect, something he didn't necessarily extend to all of his musicians. If one of his sidemen played an ill-conceived solo, he typically offered a two-word critique: "It stinks." His perfectionism apparently paid off, though. As word of his unique approach to record producing spread, well-known personalities like Andy Williams, Judy Canova, Tex Williams, and Perry Como began flocking to the studio to cut demos—or simply to see what all the talk was about. André Previn, then a hot young jazz pianist, "was completely intrigued by Les's guitar and recording techniques," said Doc Parker, who lived at Les's house for several months in the mid-1940s. "He was there all the time."

The most interesting recording subject to visit the Curson Avenue studio, though, was W. C. Fields. The comedian was in and out of hospitals by the fall of 1946 with what was charitably described to the press as pneumonia. But just a few weeks before he died on Christmas Day, he came to the garage studio with Hollywood writer Bill Morrow, one of Les's AFRS colleagues. At Morrow's request, Les agreed to produce what is now reputed to be W. C. Fields's only disk recording.

In a scene reminiscent of one of his comedies, W.C. showed up for the session with an entourage from his sprawling Spanish-style mansion in the Hollywood Hills. First his chauffeur waltzed into the garage with a couple of jugs of gin, which he carefully placed on a prop table in the center of the room. Then his valet carried in a linen-covered cocktail tray loaded with glasses and a bucket of ice. A few moments later, the sixty-six-year-old comedian himself hobbled in on a cane, followed by his ever-present nurse. He appeared to be in a great deal of pain. Stepping forward to greet him, pianist Paul Smith extended a hand and exclaimed, "It's a pleasure to meet you, Mr. Fields, but I'm sorry to see that you're limping. What happened?"

Fields, who always insisted he had trouble telling where Hollywood ended and his booze-induced apparitions began, replied: "Well, my boy, one night I was in my bedroom minding my own business when I saw a giant chartreuse octopus on the wall. It was right next to the bright blue ostrich with the Mixmaster for a tail. I mounted the dresser to smite the little devil, but I lost my footing. I've been walking with a cane ever since."

Despite his obvious discomfort—and near-blindness, which forced him to rely on poster-size cue cards—W.C. hunkered down like a pro to work on the first side, "Temperance Lecture," a tongue-in-cheek repudiation of booze. The session opened with an exuberant burst of Smith's honky-tonk piano playing. "Ahhh," growled W.C., "give me a little pi-an-issimo, professor, please. I would like to speak a few words on temperance."

Smith's playing became soft and spare.

"That's fine, my boy, keep it down there." Taking a sip from his iced gin, Fields turned back to the microphone and thundered:

"LADIES AND GENTLEMEN, *DOWN WITH RUM!* Ever since the beginning of time, there has been a drink problem. Quite a problem. Even a *greater* problem now that it's so scarce. . . . Through the years, enlightment came, and with it the control of spiritus fer-ment-ti, and controlling spiritus fer-ment-ti is tougher than tying a hair ribbon on a bolt of lightning. . . . In my younger days I was prone to take a nip. I chortle now at the fault of weakness in my otherwise strong character. How well I remember my first encounter with the devil's brew. I happened to stumble across a case of bourbon, and I went right on stumbling for several days thereafter. . . . Friends, my heart bleeds when I think that right at this moment throughout our fair land, there are thousands of misguided souls who are hitting the bottle. Yes, they are consuming rivers of highballs, lakes of cocktails, and oceans of distilled damnation. . . . Back in my rummy days I would tremble and shake for hours upon arising. It was the only exercise I ever got. . . . A man who overindulges becomes conceited. He thinks the whole world revolves around him . . . and it usually does."

Later on in the session, Les wove hillbilly guitar licks around W.C.'s bizarre tale of nurse Dorothea Fizzledockel ("pretty, blond, and starched") and the Happy Buzzard Gas Station and Tap Room. Although Fields improvised on the script as he went along, he still managed to wrap up both sides in just a couple of takes. The brilliance of his mind was apparent on the finished disk, which was eventually released on a bootleg label.

Years later Les complained that he never received the paltry $40 he charged for the date. But at the time he was running too hard and fast to concern himself with such inconsequential matters. He was a busy man about town. In addition to doing more than a dozen sustaining shows on NBC—half as Rhubarb Red—he continued to be a regular on George Burns and Gracie Allen's Thursday-night variety show and on Crosby's *Kraft Music Hall.* He also made scores of soundies for MGM and innumerable guest appearances on everything from Groucho Marx's Saturday-evening clambake to RCA Victor's *Sunday Matinee.*

Meanwhile, he turned out a steady stream of prerecorded radio shows and records with his trio, including a four-disk set of Hawaiian songs. Most were for Decca or its transcription service, World. But sometimes he played sideman for jazzmen on other labels, using an assumed name to avoid contractual problems with Decca. Regrettably, the subterfuge deprived him of claiming public credit for some of his best work. "Exceptional guitarist!" *Down Beat* raved of the "comparative unknown" Paul Leslie on bassist Red Callender's Sunset single "Get Happy"/"These Foolish Things," which hit the record bins in late 1945.

These sides—and others he did around the same time with saxman Willie Smith—pulsed with an excitement and drive that was lacking in his own releases. Their sales, however, paled beside those of the disks he cut with more pop-oriented artists. In July 1946, one year after cutting "It's Been a Long, Long Time" with Bing Crosby, Les teamed up with the country's most famous female harmony trio—Patti, Maxene, and Laverne Andrews—to make another multimillion-selling ballad.

At first the Minneapolis-born singing sisters were reluctant to work with Les. Some of Maxene's Hollywood friends, she said, had warned that he "was too much of a prima donna to be content working behind girl singers." Maxene and her sisters happily discovered otherwise, though. Far from causing trouble, Les helped create a relaxed atmosphere in the studio. "He loved to joke around," Maxene remembered, "but it never cost us any production time." In fact, Les's single-string solos helped earn the disk enthusiastic reviews. Released in September 1946, "Rumors Are Flying" quickly climbed to the top of pop charts in *Billboard*, which also touted Les's "stellar electric guitar picking" in its new platters column.

A few weeks later, Les landed his first Hollywood nightclub gig, an open-ended run at the Club Rounders, a glitzy Sunset Boulevard cocktail lounge across from the NBC studios. He brought in Paul Smith on piano and rehired rhythm guitarist Cal Gooden and his old friend bassist Bob Meyer, who was fresh from a two-year stint with Uncle Sam.

The Hollywood nightclub scene was jumping in the fall of 1946. The Mills Brothers were drawing crowds at Zanzibar, while Ray Bauduc's band had them swinging in the aisles at Susie Q's. And in a funny twist of fate, Frankie Laine, the singer Les had rejected for his trio two years earlier, was playing to full houses every night at Billy Berg's, by far the hippest nightspot in town. But that didn't bother Les. He was reveling in his own newfound fame just a few doors away.

The Club Rounders mounted a larger-than-life portrait of him beneath a marquee emblazoned with his name in fancy three-foot-high letters. The stick-straight image looming over Sunset Boulevard, however, was an uncharacteristically starchy-looking Les Paul, dressed in a crisp white shirt, pastel sport coat, and dark tie and stiffly cradling his modified Epiphone in his arms, with his fingers splayed in an unnatural position over the tailpiece.

Onstage, though, Les was downright rowdy. People who came to the club expecting to hear a live version of the demure background music he had played on the Decca releases with Bing Crosby and the Andrews Sisters were shocked. During the course of a single set he careened from exquisitely crafted jazz-tinged solos on such standards as "Begin the Beguine" and "I Found a New Baby" to goofy hillbilly tunes culled from his Rhubarb Red radio show. But he pulled it all off with such surefooted style that the sophisticated Rounders crowd happily accepted either extreme. Les was the master of flash and flair.

His numbers ended, as often as not, reported *Metronome,* "with heavy stomps on the floor, grunts and groans, sometimes on the instruments, sometimes out of the mouths of the Paul Trio. The music, when it gets serious, as it does a little more than half the time, is very good. It springs from dazzling technical displays by Les, who can make the guitar sound like anything from a balalaika and a mandolin to a guitar. . . . It is further propelled by Cal Gooden and Bob Meyer, who make lots of rhythmic sense, keeping the ensemble together, which is hard to do when Les is all too likely to get up from his stand, pirouette around it, and yell to the audience, "God, we're hot tonight!"

Even Les's sidemen were startled by his relentless showboating. "What he lacked in ideas he made up for in style," remembers Bob Meyer. "It was hard for Les to hold back and play just one single line of melody without putting in a couple of sixteen-note runs, which were part of his signature," added Paul Smith. "He wasn't the typical jazz musician who performed with a straight face and thought he was playing great classical music. He always played to the crowd, deliberately dropping in a wrong note or two once in a while just to make people laugh. He never forgot that you're up there trying to please an audience, not just to amuse yourself and the guys with you, and he communicated that philosophy to all of us."

The lesson evidently brought rich dividends. By the end of the first week at the Club Rounders, waiters had to drag extra tables out of the storeroom to accommodate the growing number of patrons. The Sunset Boulevard club was a popular watering hole for musicians. Meredith Wilson, Les's former commanding officer, dropped by regularly. So did Benny Goodman, Artie Shaw, and guitarists Howard Roberts and Barney Kessel. Whenever Barney walked into the darkened nightclub, Les usually broke into a hillbilly number to tease Barney about his Oklahoma roots. When Les looked out into the house and saw more guitarists than regular customers at the bar, he'd half-jokingly drape a little black handkerchief over his fretting hand. He didn't want those guys stealing his runs as he'd stolen Sunny Joe Wolverton's.

Lou Levy, the Andrews Sisters' manager (and then Maxene Andrews's husband), was an intuitive judge of talent. He grew up peddling fruits and vegetables from his father's horse-drawn cart on New York City's Lower East Side. By the time he was twenty-five, though, his street-honed business skills and finely tuned ears were earning him a tidy sum in the music publishing business. Shortly thereafter he fished the Andrews Sisters off the stage of the Big Apple's Edison Hotel, encouraged them to record a cranked-up version of an old Yiddish folk song, "Bei Mir Bist Du Schoen," and launched their show-biz career with a bang.

Levy believed Les was a singular talent, too, and he could tell by the way the guitarist drove himself in his garage studio and onstage that he was hungry for stardom. Les had, after all, helped make "Rumors Are Flying" a chart-topping single. To give the disk an even bigger boost, Levy decided to use Les and his trio as an opening act on the Andrews Sisters' next road tour. "Watching his fingers work was like watching a locomotive go," he said. "People hadn't seen anything like that before. He was one of a kind, perfect for the girls."

The Andrews Sisters never felt confident enough to open their show with musicians. In the past, they had hired comics, acrobats, dancers, animal acts. This was due in part to the shabby treatment female vocalists—or "canaries," as they were called—typically suffered at the hands of orchestra musicians. The boys in Artie Shaw's band were particularly cruel to the Andrews Sisters, who always outsold them at the box office. "If Artie's guys didn't like a certain passage we were singing, they'd play it out of tune, or miss it entirely," Maxene Andrews later complained. "They hated us because we were the stars and they had to be background music for us."

Les's attitude toward the Andrews Sisters was far more respectful. He admired nothing more than commercial success, and these brash young sisters happily enjoyed an abundance of fame. Just a few years earlier, they had been struggling to make $45 a week on radio. Now the effervescent "Rum and Coca-Cola" girls were earning more than a million a year on stage, screen, and records. Les welcomed the opportunity to study them in full flight.

The Andrews entourage left Hollywood for Cincinnati's Albee Theater in November 1946, the first stop on a circuit that would take them to Philadelphia, Providence, New York, and finally Boston. The tour required boot-camp stamina. When the Andrews Sisters weren't traveling by train for hundreds of miles at a stretch, they toiled for applause six or seven times a day, beginning well before noon and ending after midnight. In between, there were live radio appearances and newspaper interviews. "We were young, blessed with boundless energy, and incredibly naive," Maxene commented. "It was a murderous schedule, but it was standard in the industry. We all did it."

Les's daily routine was equally taxing. He and his trio served as both the Andrews Sisters' opening act and as their rhythm section. For this music director Vic Schoen was eternally grateful. It was entirely too expensive to carry a full-size orchestra across the country. So Vic had to hire local talent, which diminished in direct proportion to the distance the tour traveled from major metropolitan areas. It was Vic's job to teach these musicians forty or fifty minutes' worth of material, an exhausting process he repeated three or four times a month. At least Les's trio provided a good strong foundation for the changing roster of bands, which was half the battle.

The Andrews Sisters' performance benefited as well. "It was a cinch to go out and sing after Les's act," Maxene later recalled. "We could just walk out and lay on top of what he'd already started. And it was wonderful having him perform with us. He'd tune in to the passages we were singing and lightly play the melody, sometimes in harmony. He made it much easier for us to enjoy what we were doing because he really propelled us along. We'd sing these fancy licks and he'd keep up with us note for note in exactly the same rhythm. He was totally attuned to what we were doing, almost contributing a fourth voice. But he never once took the attention away from what we were doing. He did everything he could to make us sound better."

Sometimes he reached into his grab bag of pranks to liven up a performance. One evening he wrote the name of Paul Weston, a well-known orchestra leader, on a big piece of white cardboard, which he secretly hung on Vic Schoen's back moments before Vic stepped onstage to strike up the band. Vic couldn't understand why the audience erupted into a riot of giggles when he turned to lead the orchestra through one of his beautifully arranged ballads. Once he figured it out, though, he vowed to repay Les in kind.

A few nights later, he fastened a long nylon rope to the bottom rung of the three-legged stool Les planned to use during performance. Right in the middle of one of Les's favorite solos, Vic and a couple of confederates slowly began dragging the stool into the wings. But Les had the last laugh. He went right on strumming, as though nothing out of the ordinary were happening. The audience roared.

Then, too, there were occasions when Les unintentionally made people laugh. Vic mercilessly teased him about his headless aluminum guitar. "It was like something from Mars, very wide across, with tuning pegs that protruded from the top of the wings. Les was always trying to build some damn electronic contraption. Some of it worked, some of it didn't," said Vic. "But you could always count on him to come up with something no one else had thought of."

The "headless monster," as Les called the black, lightweight aluminum guitar, certainly had a few drawbacks. Overall, it had a pretty good sound. (He claims to have used the homemade instrument to record a few of his hit tunes, including "Caravan," one of his early solo instrumentals for Capitol.) But it was a disaster onstage. "When the hot spot lights hit it, it started doing all kinds of crazy things," Les later said. "At first I didn't know what was happening. I thought, 'Holy God, what's wrong with my ear?' So I tune it again and get it right. Then the guy pulls the spotlight off the Andrews Sisters and onto me, and I started sinking into another key again. I said, 'There goes my invention.'" (Not entirely. Forty years later, Ned Steinberger marketed headless guitars and basses that sold briskly on the market, though his were made of wood instead of aluminum.)

By all accounts, the casualness of Les's attire matched his performing style. He usually trotted out onstage wearing an open-neck shirt and a pair of baggy pants that made his five-foot-nine,

180-pound, potbellied frame look even paunchier. One night the audience burst into laughter at the sight of his mismatched socks—one white, one blue—which became clearly visible when he sat on his stool and crossed his knees in the middle of a song. A few days before the group was scheduled to begin their month-long engagement at New York's renowned Paramount Theater, Lou Levy laid down the law. "Your clothes are driving me crazy!" he exclaimed.

"Look," Les replied. "I'm only here to present my music, not a fashion show."

"You'd go out in your underwear if I let you," snapped Levy.

"So?"

"Well, people like to see the presenter look good too, you know."

Les not only went along with Levy's demand that he spruce up but also attempted to shed a few pounds.

It was a crowded roster of artists that debuted December 18, 1946, at the Paramount, the Times Square theater where thousands of screaming bobby-soxers had helped launch Frank Sinatra's solo career three years earlier. Backed by Tony Pastor's hot big band, the Andrews Sisters shared the stage with a puppet act, a dance team, and, of course, Les and his trio. Rosemary and Betty Clooney were hired to sing with Pastor's band, but Lou Levy sent the pretty blond teenagers home on opening night. "He didn't think they needed two sister acts," Rosemary later recalled with a laugh.

A few days after it opened, the show was warmly praised in the trades. "It packs speed, gets laughs in the right spots and is strong enough to sustain itself for the full hour it runs," wrote one *Billboard* critic, who also added that Les "plucked a terrific guitar."

But for Les, the high point of the Paramount date occurred backstage. He was shaving in his dressing room, preparing for the fifth or sixth performance of the day, when a stagehand hollered from downstairs, "Mr. Paul, you have a visitor."

"Who's that?" Les asked.

"Django Reinhardt is here to see you."

"Yeah, sure. Send him up with a case of beer and Jesus Christ and I'll give 'em both an autographed picture," Les wisecracked as he continued to lather his chin.

A few moments later, the tall, swarthy gypsy guitarist walked through the door. Reinhardt, who just happened to be performing in New York with Duke Ellington's orchestra, was eager to meet the flashy American guitarist he had heard borrowed so heavily from his style. Les, of course, was honored that Django had sought him out. But he was saddened by the sight of his hero's shriveled and scarred fretting hand, the aftermath of a fiery accident that occurred early in the guitarist's life, leaving two of his fingers badly deformed. Django spoke little English ("America, oui les beeg ranches, le guitar, le moon—ici pour le Gypsy, c'est formidable!"). And Les didn't understand a syllable of French. They had to communicate through music.

"I gave him my guitar to fool around with while I finished shaving," Les later said. "Well, I have never come so close to cutting my throat. The guy sat there in the dressing room ad libbing. The tone was so great when he was playing my guitar. He made it sound like a different instrument. And the ideas! I wouldn't even attempt to think of anybody who could play as much guitar as Django."

Les picked up another guitar and they started playing "Night and Day," accompanied by Cal Gooden and Bob Meyer. Les and Django dissolved in laughter as they exchanged musical sleights of hand. This was probably one of the lighter moments during Django's American visit. Stung by the relatively cool reception he received outside New York—and the harsh realities of the city itself—the homesick guitarist returned to Paris.

By the end of December, Les had arrived at a crossroads in his career. He had played jazz on dozens of well-received records and transcriptions. But the only disks he had made that sold in the millions were those with pop singers, Bing Crosby and the Andrews Sisters. For weeks he had watched from the stage as the Andrews Sisters' ecstatic fans danced in the aisles to the up-tempo beat of novelty numbers like "Rum and Coca-Cola" and "Boogie Woogie Bugle Boy." But when he and his trio performed their jazz-tinged tunes, "only certain audiences got our message."

Les surmised that people would always prefer songs with melody, songs they could hum and tap their feet to. Besides, the swing style he had played so well for the past decade was becoming passé. Bebop was now shaking up the jazz world, and Les found little to enjoy in the intellectualism of this "nervous music."

The letter from his mother was the last straw. "I heard you on Bob Hope's show last week," she wrote. "You were great." Les called her right away. "How could you have heard me on the radio?" he asked in exasperation. "I've been performing with the Andrews Sisters."

"Well," she replied, "can't you copyright your style? They're all sounding like you now. If your own mother can't tell if it's you or not, then you just don't mean a thing."

Les was devastated. The person who had followed his career more closely than anyone else couldn't distinguish him from another guitarist (later said to be George Barnes). Of course it was impossible to copyright his style. But Les resolved right then and there to come up with an entirely new approach to music.

After wrapping up a four-day run at Boston's RKO theater, he went into Decca's midtown Manhattan recording studio on January 23, 1947, to cut a couple more sides, the last under his own name for the label. The session offered the first real indication that Les was serious about turning out more accessible music. Moving away from the jazz standards that had long been the mainstay of his repertoire, he tried to capitalize on America's renewed interest in country music, recording such hillbilly-flavored tunes as "Steel Guitar Rag" and "Guitar Boogie."

He returned to the West Coast a couple of weeks later. It was time to regenerate.

Chapter 12

THE NEW SOUND

After his return, Les rarely left the West Hollywood garage studio, and when he did, he seemed preoccupied. One Friday night his friend Lloyd Rich persuaded him to try to relax for a couple of hours at a tavern on Santa Monica Boulevard. Settling at a table near the bar, the pair washed down bowls of salty popcorn with beer as they watched a few rounds of boxing on television. Les wasn't paying much attention, though. Lloyd challenged him to an arm-wrestling match and effortlessly won. "Hey, you're not concentrating," Lloyd complained. "Where's your head tonight?"

"I'm still thinking about that echo problem," Les listlessly replied.

"Well, what is it you're looking for?" Lloyd inquired.

"I want an echo effect on my records, but I don't want the kind of long time delay you get from an echo chamber."

Lloyd sat quietly for a moment. "You mean like if you put a playback pickup behind the record head?" he asked.

"That's it!" Les cried as he flew out of the tavern with Lloyd in tow. They headed straight for the Curson Avenue garage studio and began tearing apart Les's disk recorder. The pair worked through the night until they hit upon the rich, reflected sound Les was after.

138

At the time, record companies relied on specially built reverberant rooms or simple tile bathrooms to fatten the sound of their disks. But Les, informed perhaps by Art Felthausen's earlier experiments with echo, figured out how to do it electronically. After several days of tinkering with his disk lathe, he determined that a one-tenth-of-a-second time delay was a pleasing delay for an echo—not too long, not too short.

Les took a break from the garage studio for several weeks in April and May of 1947 to work with the Andrews Sisters in San Francisco and Chicago. Then he drove to New York, where he played a Jazz at the Philharmonic concert at Carnegie Hall, his last performance for promoter Norman Granz. But his personal recording experiments remained his highest priority—and best-kept secret. For a while he discouraged friends and professional colleagues from visiting the backyard studio for fear they would steal his ideas.

Les was determined to increase the range of musical colors on his disks, to paint pictures in sound. He placed microphones within inches of—or in some cases inside—the instruments he was recording, and cut tunes over and over with different microphone arrangements. Feeding his amplified guitar directly into the mixing system, he simulated the sound of various instruments by altering the recording speed, sometimes synthesizing entirely new ones. He created odd percussive effects by drumming on the top of the guitar with his hands. And he enhanced the sound of other performers by miking them separately, which gave him greater control in the mixing process.

Like many of the recording methods he employed during this intense period of experimentation, Les's penchant for "close miking" was born of necessity. The sound of buses and trucks rumbling over Sunset Boulevard kept turning up on his disks. At first he stationed friends on the garage roof, instructing them to watch for offending vehicles and signal when the coast was clear. When that cautionary measure proved to be inadequate, he began encouraging his instrumentalists and singers to stand within inches of the mike, which also helped drown out unwanted amplifier noise. He trained vocalists to sing across, not directly into, the microphone and to use the letter *b* in words that began with *p* to avoid popping sounds.

His crowning achievement, though, was his ingenious method of overdubbing. Using his modified disk lathe, Les routinely began overdubbing several generations of sound on a single disk, this at a time when the major record companies were still struggling to get a good clean sound out of two or three. Les first observed this process on the movie lots of Hollywood, where overdubbing was used to great effect in the early 1930s in such MGM musical films as *The Cuban Love Song.* Metropolitan opera baritone Lawrence Tibbett sang the title song in his customary range, while a superimposed double image of him harmonized in the tenor range.

A decade later, in 1941, saxophonist/clarinetist Sidney Bechet made recording history by overdubbing himself in RCA's New York studio on tenor and soprano saxophones, clarinet, drums, piano, and string bass on jazz versions of "The Sheik of Araby" and "Blues of Bechet." Bechet's intricate lead lines, however, became increasingly muffled with each new generation of music.

By squeezing the recording frequency down and painstakingly filtering out unwanted sound, Les began producing overdubbed recordings that were relatively free of surface noise and distortion. He was certainly the first musician to master such a complicated technical achievement in his own home studio. Generally speaking, performing artists and audio engineers are two distinct species. Musicians often lack the vocabulary to successfully convey their needs to technicians and vice versa. But Les, fluent in both languages, managed to meld the two disciplines.

Others in the industry, like audio engineer Bill Putnam, another early pioneer of overdubbed disks, were flabbergasted by what Les was doing in that little garage of his. "Les lived and thrived on the gratification of achieving things that were beyond the current state of the art," said Putnam. "Nobody was producing the quality of multigenerational disks he was producing in the mid-forties. And the number of overdubs he was getting—impossible! Considering the fact that he had no formal education as an engineer, his knowledge was absolutely amazing."

Another reason Les's overdubbed disks were so clean was the unconventional order in which he recorded the instruments. If, for instance, he had an arrangement for drums, bass, rhythm guitar, and lead guitar, he began the session by laying down the drum part and rhythm guitar, leaving the lead and bass parts till last. "The drums and other rhythm instruments are *supposed* to be in the background," Les later explained. "But the bass player, he's the one who helps set your tempo, so you better have him right up front. And that lead guitar better shine. He better be brand new."

Les discarded some five hundred disks before producing one he thought worthy of release. ("My life is littered with failed experiments," he once said.) By the fall of 1947, however, he came up with a radically different reading of "Lover," an old Rodgers and Hart chestnut. Les's version was a feverishly fast multilayered arrangement for eight guitars (a combination of the Log and the modified Epiphone), all played by him. Some parts were pushed far beyond the normal recording speed, creating a surging techno-pop sound. The fact that he didn't read music made "Lover" that much more amazing. He had to work from an architectural blueprint in his head, imagining how eight different guitar parts would sound together before ever laying down a single note. He repeated the process for the multirhythmic, Latin-tinged "Brazil," which he eventually put on the B side of the disk.

Before approaching any record companies, though, he wanted to see how his friends in the industry would react to his technical tour de force. One evening at a party at publicist Jim Moran's Hollywood home, Les slipped a copy of the record onto Moran's turntable. Then he melted back into the crowd and waited for a reaction. When every jaw in the house dropped, he knew it was time to shop the disk around.

His timing was perfect. Jimmy Petrillo, the headstrong boss of the American Federation of Musicians, was threatening to call another recording strike, this time over a provision in the Taft-Hartley law "that overturned his plan for reuse payments to the union for films or records replayed on television." And when Jimmy Petrillo talked, musicians usually listened. This gave Les a strong bargaining chip. He was in a position to throw scores of home-recorded masters into his prospective recording deal, a strong negotiating point in the face of the looming disk ban. Decca and Victor, however, still turned him away, a decision they surely must have regretted later.

Les had much better luck at Capitol, a younger, more daring company on the corner of Sunset and Vine. Jim Conkling, the savvy but mild-mannered head of the label's A&R department, had been hearing about Les Paul for years from Hollywood's musical in-crowd, which included Conkling's brothers-in-law, ace guitarist Alvino Rey and pianist Buddy Cole, who once played in Les's trio. "Alvino said, 'I don't know how that guy is doing what he's doing, but you ought to get ahold of him fast,'" Conkling remembers.

So when Les unexpectedly turned up late one Friday afternoon at Conkling's office, then over a music store owned by Capitol cofounder Glen Wallichs, he received a warm reception. Unfortunately, Conkling was rushing to catch a flight to New York.

"Les, you'll have to come back another time," Conkling explained. "I've got to run."

"Just let me play this one side while you're packing," Les pleaded. "It will only take a minute."

Before Conkling could respond, Les slapped "Lover" on a nearby turntable. The record executive was stunned by the instrumental's richly woven tapestry of single-string guitar lines of contrasting tempos. "My God, Les, that's a guaranteed hit," he exclaimed.

As Les told the story years later, Conkling promised him a contract right then and there: "He said he would give me five percent of the royalties and that the contract would be in my hands by Monday morning."

When Conkling returned from the East Coast, he played the otherworldly-sounding disk for several Capitol engineers. "They asked, 'How many guitarists did he have in the room at the time?' And I told them that he was the only one. They couldn't believe it. They used to say, 'You can't overdub, you can't overdub.' But when they heard "Lover," they all went scrambling. Les's engineering was as radical as his playing. He was feeding in the bass end and top end of the scale all at the same time, which was a feat I never understood.

The industry learned a lot from what he did, although he made people figure it all out for themselves."

The overdubbed guitar lines on "Lover" and "Brazil" were a stunning contrast to the pedestrian fare dominating the record charts in the late 1940s: simple-minded ditties like "Too Fat Polka (I Don't Want Her, You Can Have Her—She's Too Fat For Me)" and the theme song from the Woody Woodpecker cartoon series. The executives at Capitol realized from the start that they had discovered a canny new artist with a dramatically new sound. In fact, that's how they promoted Les's overdubbed instrumental—they called it "the New Sound."

"Les Paul has created quite a commotion with his amazing and secret guitar technique," exclaimed one Capitol press release. "On these sides, as well as on subsequent releases, as many as eight guitars are heard playing simultaneously, and Les is playing them all! How he does it has even Capitol's veteran engineers baffled, and Les isn't letting the secret out."

The critics were equally enthusiastic. "As a combined performance and technical achievement," wrote *Down Beat,* " 'Lover,' will have few parallels this year."

At last, Les was on his way to making a name in his own right, not as an appendage to some already established show business personality. Although he was not responsible for introducing overdubbing to commercial recording, he was certainly the first to make it a major selling point of his disks. This studio technique, which took him roughly two years to perfect, would ultimately force the industry to reexamine its approach to recording—and make Les Paul a fabulously wealthy man.

Chapter 13

RHUBARB RED MEETS THE SUNSHINE GIRL

While Les's career soared, his life at home with Virginia was sinking. The marriage could no longer endure the stresses and strains of his show-business career, and he could no longer resist the persistent charms of Iris Colleen Summers, a young, beautiful country singer who looked as though she belonged in the movies.

Their affair began innocently enough. They had met two years earlier, in the summer of 1945, through Eddie Dean, then one of the hottest singing cowboy stars in Hollywood. One afternoon, in the midst of building his garage studio, Les asked Eddie to come over and help test some of his freshly assembled recording equipment (which Eddie later judged to be equal to anything he had encountered in Los Angeles's professional studios). After the session was over, the guitarist began telling Eddie that he wanted to add a female vocalist to his Rhubarb Red radio show, one of several sustaining programs he did for NBC. "When he described the sort of girl he was looking for," Eddie later said, "I immediately thought of Colleen Summers. Everyone knew Colleen and the Sunshine Girls."

Colleen had been a fixture on the West Coast country-music scene since the early 1940s, when she began singing and playing guitar every weekday afternoon on KXLA's *Dinner Bell Roundup Time*. By the time she turned twenty, she was a respected guitarist and featured performer—both as a solo act and with her own aptly named trio, the Sunshine Girls—on *The Hollywood Barn Dance* and on Jimmy Wakely's immensely popular hillbilly radio show.

She was also a vociferous Les Paul fan. "She idolized him on the Waring show," remembers her oldest sister, Esther Williams, a Los Angeles professional organist. "We used to get into heated debates over who was the best guitar player in the country and she would *always* argue for Les." She cried when she heard Hedda Hopper tell her radio audience in 1943 that Les had been drafted.

So, two years later, when the guitarist telephoned her one afternoon to invite her to a private audition in his garage studio, Colleen was delighted. Hopping into her beat-up 1940 Plymouth, she headed straight for 1514 North Curson Avenue. As Les later recalled the episode, she spotted him mowing the lawn in front of his house, but didn't recognize him because he was so shabbily dressed. He was wearing a threadbare plaid shirt and a pair of faded fatigues tucked into unlaced Army boots that flopped dogeared around his ankles. Peering out from beneath a wild mass of red curls, Les watched silently as Colleen approached.

"Excuse me," she said, thinking she was addressing the gardener. "I'm looking for Les Paul."

"Walk to the end of the driveway there and into the garage," he answered, pointing to the right of the house. "He'll be there in a minute."

A couple of Les's friends were on hand to help the petite blonde climb through the garage window, which was then the only way into the studio. Moments later, the guitarist himself stepped through the narrow opening. He looked at Colleen and smiled.

"You're Les Paul?" she asked, barely able to mask her disappointment. She had been expecting a tall, handsome, sophisticated figure, not this intense, disheveled little man. The guitarist had to pick out a few of his filigree runs to convince her that he was indeed the genuine article.

Les, on the other hand, was thoroughly enchanted by Colleen, who had just turned twenty-one. She was perfectly proportioned, with a beautiful, round, open face. Thick blond locks cascaded around her shoulders. Though she was shy and blushed easily, her sound was rich and full-bodied, with the sort of relaxed sincerity Les admired in Crosby's performance. She had an unparalleled ability to harmonize, and strummed her guitar like a runaway locomotive.

There was just one problem: Colleen Summers was already too well known in the country field. The only solution, Les decided, was to give her a new tag: "I wanted something that sounded familiar. The name Mary was meant for her and Ford just came to me. It sounded rich."

"Mary" was born on July 7, 1924, in Pasadena, California, the third of seven musically gifted children in a strict Protestant family. Her father, Marshall Summers, was a Nazarene minister who later became a painting contractor. He was a steady, hardworking man, successful enough to eventually buy a sizable piece of land in nearby San Gabriel to build several rental properties. Tall and well proportioned, Marshall was a stern man of few words. But his children always felt they could go to him when they were in trouble, which, as they grew older, was quite often.

Mary's mother, Jenny May White, hailed from the heartland of Missouri, where she married Marshall. A headstrong young woman, Jenny May changed her name to Dorothy because she thought "Jenny sounded too mulish." It was Dorothy who persuaded Marshall to move to California in 1919, shortly after their first child, Fletcher, was born. In fact, Dorothy made most of the major decisions in the family, including how to discipline the handsome, rambunctious Summers brood.

Dorothy bore several uncanny similarities to Les's mother, Evelyn. Both were advocates of health food long before it became fashionable, and both enjoyed arguing politics, though Dorothy's were decidedly conservative Republican instead of radically leftist. "Mom could get pretty intense, depending on how intense the other person got," remembers Bob Summers, the baby of the family. "She never backed down."

Dorothy played guitar, piano, and organ with equal skill and, like Evelyn, was eager to pass her gift for music along to her children. Holidays around the Summers home were filled with song. "Music was drummed into us from the time we were babies," said Mary's sister Esther. "Mom was responsible for all of us picking up instruments. She was our best and worst critic. If we didn't play something right, she kept after us until we did. She never went into the entertainment field, but I think she secretly lived it through us."

Shortly after the United States entered World War II, Marshall and Dorothy devised an ideal way to combine their three presiding passions—God, family, and music. They began airing their own religious radio program on Pasadena's KPAS. Marshall preached, Dorothy played organ, Esther picked lap-steel guitar, brother Bruce plucked a big bass fiddle, Mary strummed acoustic guitar, and everybody sang, including the three youngest children, Carol, Eva, and Bob. "I stood on a chair in front of the microphone and sang 'Jesus Wants Me for a Sunbeam'," remembered Bob.

Much to Marshall and Dorothy's dismay, though, the children loved their first taste of show business. The Nazarene faith not only forbade the use of liquor (Marshall cranked out temperance tracts on his garage printing press) and tobacco (most of his children became heavy smokers), the church eschewed almost all forms of popular entertainment, including movies. "The devil is in the theater!" Dorothy constantly reminded her youngsters. Her warnings apparently fell on deaf ears. Six out of seven of her children eventually earned their living on the stage.

Mary was a bright, creative girl. She was positively compelled to play music from the age of seven, when her mother taught her to strum a few simple chords. After that there was no stopping her. "She used to sneak Fletcher's guitar out of the closet every time he left the house, no matter how high up on the shelf he put it," said Esther. In junior high school, she and a feisty neighborhood girl named Milly Watson began performing in churches all over Pasadena, and later they made a few religious recordings with Milly's older brother, Marvin, for which Mary wrote some reasonably competent songs. In 1939 the two teenagers claimed first prize in a Pasadena talent contest judged by several Hollywood notables, including a very young Judy Garland. Unfortunately, the girls became so enthralled with their budding music careers that they completely lost interest in school. They began skipping classes at every opportunity, ducking into cinema houses that offered live entertainment between movies.

Appalled when they discovered her spotty attendance record, Mary's parents shipped her off to live with her older brother Fletcher in El Centro, California, a sleepy little town fifteen miles north of the Mexico border. She enrolled as a freshman in El Centro's Union High and soon began studying guitar with Stan Atkins, a professional violinist who doubled as the school's music instructor. Atkins was so impressed by Mary that he arranged to have her perform at several local Kiwanis Club affairs—often accompanying her on fiddle—and encouraged her to compete in the Imperial County Fair amateur show, which she handily won. But Mary was terribly homesick. After a restless year in El Centro, she persuaded her parents to let her quit school, return to Pasadena, and get a job at a local movie theater. In the interim she renewed her friendship with Milly and Marvin Watson, performing with them at church socials and other public functions.

Mary and Marvin, however, had more in mind than music. By the time she was sixteen, Mary had more suitors than the American flag had stars. They came in droves, attracted by her beauty, her talent, and, above all, her obvious vulnerability. "She was very insecure, like all she needed was someone to provide some steadfastness in her life," said Dave Palmquist, who fell hopelessly in love with her in the early 1940s. "She was appreciative of anyone who would step up to the plate and take charge. In return, she made you feel like you were the most important person in the world."

Palmquist, a dangerously good-looking young bachelor, managed the downtown movie theater where Mary worked. He knew several other local swains were aggressively courting the pretty cashier—especially Marvin Watson—but that only fanned the flames. "Marvin's had his chance," Palmquist declared, quickly sweeping Mary off her feet. One night after work, in a burst of reckless passion, the young couple drove 250 miles to Yuma, Arizona, and got married. Before returning to the movie theater the next day, Palmquist dropped his blushing bride off at her San Gabriel home. Mary gingerly walked through the front door in nervous anticipation of her parents' reaction to the news. But her misery was compounded when she found Marvin standing in the living room with a stricken look on his face and a lush bouquet of flowers in hand. "Do you *really* love him?" he quietly asked.

"No!" she exclaimed, bursting into tears. Marvin immediately rushed the distraught young woman off to his parents' home, where she remained until they arranged to have the hastily exchanged wedding vows annulled. Dave Palmquist was heartbroken. "He lay on our couch and cried for a whole week," remembered Bob Summers.

Mary married Marvin sometime around 1941, shortly after the annulment was official. "Mom and Dad were very upset," Esther later said, "but she'd known Marvin for so long, they hoped it might work out."

Of course it didn't. Even at seventeen, the new Mrs. Marvin Watson was bursting with unexplored creative potential. Yet her new husband immediately tried to stifle her performing career. Mary did want to have a stable home and family like the one in which she had been raised, but Marvin's attempts to reel her offstage were premature. She was far too young to retire. Her second marriage lasted less than a year.

The airwaves were crowded with hillbilly radio shows in the 1940s, the heyday of the singing cowboy and cowgirl in Los Angeles. This wacky era was mostly the result of Hollywood's desire to combine two of its most popular forms, the Western and the musical. And Mary walked right into the center of it. Her older sister Esther was dating one of the staff musicians on Stuart Hamblen's well-known country music show, and Mary often tagged along to the studio.

One night Hamblen invited the younger Summers sister to do a number for his radio audience. "She sang a song called 'Chime Bells,' " Esther recalled. "She played her guitar and yodeled, which she was really good at." Hamblen apparently thought so too. He encouraged Mary to come back to the show with her guitar again and again, though he never offered to hire her.

She did, however, become acquainted with an up-and-coming young cowboy picker there named Cliffie Stone. Cliffie called Mary soon after landing his own radio show in 1942 on KXLA. Broadcast daily from 11:30 A.M. to 12:30 P.M., Cliffie's *Dinner Bell Roundup* was as full of corn as an Iowa field at harvest time. Every day at twelve on the dot, he shook a big brass cowbell and hollered "High noon!" and his entire cast routinely hollered back "Hi, Cliffie!" He rang the bell after each song too, to cover for the fact that he didn't have a live studio audience.

The warm, homespun style of the show found a natural audience in Los Angeles, a city filled with people who missed their old lives on the farm. Mary auditioned for *Dinner Bell* with a ballad, "I Care No More."

"She was a delicate talent with an amazing ear," Cliffie later said. "She sang quietly, succinctly, and always in tune. But the most remarkable thing about her was her guitar playing. She was a terrific rhythm player, which was very hard to find. She had such a natural feel for the instrument. I eventually started giving her lessons on upright bass. She was already playing bass notes on the guitar, so it was merely a matter of teaching her proper fingering and how to use a bow. She picked it up immediately.

"It was very unusual to find the combination of talents Mary had. I made her a large part of the show, even though she was afraid to open her mouth. When it came time for her to go on the air, I'd say, 'What are you going to do today?' And she'd just name the song and begin to sing without further comment."

When they weren't in the studio, Cliffie and Mary performed all over Los Angeles County—at nightclubs, dances, private parties, American Legion picnics. One summer they even did grand openings for the Crawford's supermarket chain. With a single microphone and speaker between them, they set up a makeshift stage on the back of Cliffie's pickup truck and serenaded prospective customers under the blazing Saturday-afternoon sun.

Saturday nights were reserved for KNX's *Hollywood Barn Dance,* where the versatile Stone served as band contractor, staff musician, and standup comic. Here Mary found her widest audience yet, for the network broadcast ranked in importance with Nashville's *Grand Ole Opry* and Chicago's *Saturday Night Barn Dance.* Most of these Western-style radio shows had the same format: the entire cast remained seated onstage in a large semicircle throughout the program, which usually included singing cowboys and cowgirls, male and female vocal trios, comedians, horse and rope tricks, and lots of aw-shucks patter from the master of ceremonies.

Mary's favorite act was the Riders of the Purple Sage, a popular stage and recording trio who patterned themselves after the Sons of the Pioneers. She fell in love with the group's handsome, smooth-talking leader, Foy Willing. But the relationship never got off the ground, because Foy was married. For the time being Mary was content to dress up in her little cowgirl outfit and white tasseled boots and sing such Western classics as "One Has My Name, the Other Has My Heart."

Then along came Les Paul. Though Les claims they fell in love the day they met, Mary's family and friends insist she resisted his initial romantic overtures. Still infatuated with Foy, Mary apparently didn't want to complicate her life with another married man. She ducked Les's phone calls, instructing her sisters to tell him she had gone out even when she hadn't. In time, though, she surrendered, overcome by Les's persistence, playfulness, and power.

In Les she found a perfect mate. He was a strong-willed individual who was determined to make it to the top of the business, and she was a raw bundle of talent in need of shaping. He was looking to lead, she to follow. Besides, he was full of new and daring ideas, constantly tinkering with one thing or another in his garage studio. Mary had never met anyone so completely consumed by music. It was inspiring.

From the start she found Les's devil-may-care attitude irresistible.

His pranks sent her into spasms of sidesplitting laughter. One day while she and her sister Carol were in the midst of a song on his hillbilly radio show, Les suddenly burst into the studio clad only in underwear and socks. On a similar occasion he set fire to Mary's sheet music. There was never a dull moment.

Shortly after his stint with the Army Air Corps, Gene Autry lured Mary away from Cliffie Stone for his newly resurrected *Melody Ranch* radio show. Sponsored by the Wrigley gum company, the CBS Sunday-evening program cleverly combined music and comedy with a smattering of drama, which usually centered around the gallant cowboy hero himself. Never a star maker, Autry dominated the thirty-minute broadcast. But for Mary it was still an honor and privilege to win one of the coveted slots on the immensely popular variety show.

In late September 1946, Autry brought his annual World Championship Rodeo to New York's Madison Square Garden. In addition to a full range of entertainment from his regular radio troupe, he promised Big Apple denizens the thrill of "the largest outdoor show presented indoors," daring bronco busters, bone-breaking steer-riding contests.

"Come see the living steaks," the rodeo barkers teased a city still suffering the effects of the wartime meat shortage. Unable to resist the spectacle, New Yorkers of course turned out in full force, making Autry's thirty-three-day engagement one of the Garden's most profitable shows ever.

Mary, however, couldn't have cared less. All she wanted was to get back to California. She hated New York's bone-chilling fall weather, and worse, she missed her family. "Why doesn't someone write to me?" she pleaded in a letter to her parents before returning to L.A. in early November. "I'm awfully lonesome."

She also pined for Les, who was in the midst of his Club Rounders gig in Hollywood. By then, the sorry state of his tattered marriage was an open secret. When Mary finally began making nightly visits to the club, Les introduced her to such show-biz pals as Groucho

Marx, Pat O'Brien, and the Andrews Sisters. Then there were all the extraordinary guitarists who stopped by to admire his freewheeling performances. Mary's circle of friends was expanding well beyond the crooning cowboys she had grown up with. It was heady stuff for a little hillbilly singer from Pasadena.

By the middle of 1947, the couple apparently found it increasingly difficult to remain apart. Les snuck away from home for overnight outings with Mary as often as possible, and she occasionally rendezvoused with him on the road. But it was still unacceptable for them to travel together openly, even among some of the musicians. Indeed, the Andrews Sisters had no idea Mary sometimes shadowed their road tours. "I couldn't figure out where Les was always disappearing to," Maxene later said. "I knew he wasn't running with the boys."

In fact, Les's days of running with the boys were numbered. Within a few short months his life would revolve entirely around Mary and hers around him.

Chapter 14

DOWN
FOR THE COUNT

January 1948 was brimming with promise. Les had just signed an exclusive long-term agreement with a young, aggressive recording company, and "Lover," his first solo single (since Rhubarb Red's 1936 Montgomery Ward outing), was on its way to record bins all over the country. Meanwhile, back in Wisconsin, Les's father and brother were teaming up to open a tavern, a cozy brass-railed watering hole across from the Waukesha & Western railroad depot that would remain in the family for more than twenty years.

As soon as the ink was dry on the Capitol contract, Les jumped into his shiny Buick Roadmaster convertible—purchased in part with proceeds from the Andrews Sisters tour—and headed for ice-slicked Wisconsin. Before departing, though, he left dozens of masters with Capitol, including "What Is This Thing Called Love," another multidimensional guitar instrumental that label executives correctly assumed would make the charts. He also left his wife and children. In their place he took Mary, the tavern opening providing a perfect cover for the couple to slip out of town for a while.

Once he got to Waukesha, Les tried to keep Mary in the background. He couldn't conceal her presence from his father for long, though. Now a churchgoing Presbyterian who had settled into a twenty-two-year marriage with a Waukesha-born nurse, George berated his son for running off with a "homewrecker," conveniently overlooking his own history of extramarital dalliances. But Les apparently made peace with his father in time to help celebrate the opening of the Club 400, pulling together a bunch of boyhood chums for a down-home jam. Among the specially invited guests were several of Les's old bandmates. Together they played for hours for friends and neighbors sipping drafts at the tavern's handsome oak bar.

Les, of course, assumed his accustomed role of leader of the pack, the big shot. "He thought I was playing my drums too loud, so he quit on me and made me drum all by myself for five minutes," remembered Cullen Casey. "I could have killed him. That was the night he said, 'I'm going to have a record out soon that's going to revolutionize the whole industry.'" A few days later the guitarist brought a copy of "Lover" to Waukesha deejay Mig Figi and told him the same thing.

Life for Les Paul was sublime.

Then disaster struck. On Monday afternoon, January 26, 1948, while he and Mary were driving back to L.A. on Route 66, their car careened out of control on the Sante Fe overpass near Davenport, Oklahoma. The Buick convertible skidded off the road, crashed through the wooden guard rail, and plummeted twenty feet into a frozen creek bed. For years Les told the press he had passed out at the wheel, suffering from a raging fever brought on by a severe cold. But local reports clearly indicated that Mary was driving the car, though she had identified herself to authorities as Iris Watson.

As Les later recounted the story: "I was so sick I was lying down on the front seat, listening to the weather forecast. They were saying how treacherous the driving was because of all the snow and ice. All of a sudden I heard Mary scream. When I got up I saw the car was going sideways. We were going up a steep ramp onto a bridge. I got the car straight momentarily, but then it started skidding sideways again and I could see we were going to bust through the rails and go over. So I put my arm around Mary's head to protect her face."

A speaker ripped through the soft canvas roof, and the couple followed. According to Les, they lay for several hours in the snow some forty miles outside Oklahoma City before being discovered. Both were eventually taken by ambulance to the Robertson Hospital in Chandler, where they received emergency treatment. Then they were removed to Wesley Hospital in Oklahoma City.

Miraculously, Mary suffered only a cracked pelvis and a few minor injuries. She was able to cast off her crutches and resume touring with the Sunshine Girls in a matter of weeks. Les, on the other hand, once again came close to death. In addition to puncturing his spleen, he broke his nose, collarbone, and pelvis and fractured six ribs. Worst of all, his strumming arm was shattered in three places, his elbow joint smashed to smithereens. "My arm," he later said, "looked like a bud vase with a bunch of stems hanging out of it. It was swollen three times its normal size."

Despite excruciating pain, he somehow managed to remain lucid throughout the ordeal. Before leaving the Chandler hospital, he calmly instructed the emergency crew to get in touch with his old friend Ken Wright, the organist he had worked with in Sunny Joe Wolverton's band sixteen years earlier. Ken, who lived in the Oklahoma City area, was standing outside Wesley Hospital when the barely conscious guitarist was lifted out of the ambulance. Looking up from the stretcher, Les muttered, "Gee, Ken, you look awful. What the hell have you been through?" Then he passed out cold.

Dr. Robert Knight, who happened to be a longtime Les Paul fan, was also waiting. Dr. Knight worked himself into a state of total exhaustion that frigid January evening, piecing the guitarist's shattered right arm back together. But the unspoken consensus among the hospital staff was that Les Paul would never play the guitar again. His condition worsened after he contracted pneumonia. A single cough sent spasms of pain coursing through his body, making him cry out in agony. Ken Wright tried to rally his spirits with news that Walter Winchell had written a touching piece about the crash

"*I* knew he was going to be the best," said Evelyn Polfuss, pictured here with her son in the early 1960s, and again in March 1988, when they were jointly honored by the city of Waukesha on Evelyn's one hundredth birthday.

Courtesy of Waukesha County Museum Collections and Mary Alice Shaughnessy

Mary Alice Shaughnessy

$\mathcal{L}$es used a variety of customized instruments, including the Log and this headless aluminum guitar *(both pictured at left)*, before switching over to Gibson's new Les Paul solid-body *(below)* in 1952. However, in early 1961, the company overhauled the design and introduced what was eventually called the SG series, displayed *opposite right* by Les and Mary in the early 1960s with Les's son, Gene, who briefly joined their act. Introduced in 1971, the Les Paul Recording model *(pictured opposite bottom with Les at his home in 1988)*, was among the first Gibson instruments with pickups designed by the guitarist. Now, with more than forty variations based on several models carrying his name, Les Paul is widely regarded as the most successful endorser of guitars in history. Sought by collectors the world over, some of his vintage guitars (those made between 1958 and 1960) can fetch up to $60,000, though the average is $25,000.

Courtesy of Wilbur Marker

*M*ary Ford, née Iris Colleen Summers *(standing, center)*, with family, circa 1941, when her father, Marshall, a Nazarene minister, hosted a religious program with his wife and children on Pasadena's KPAS.
Courtesy of Bob Summers

*T*aking a cue from Hollywood's honey-haired glamour girls, Mary bleached her long curly locks. Her *Barn Dance* appearances with The Sunshine Girls at one time included her younger sister, Carol *(foreground)* and Vivian Earles. Horse tricks were a favorite of the *Barn Dance's* live audience.
Courtesy of Bob Summers

*T*he Sunshine Girls *(Mary stands center)* were a popular attraction on KNX radio's *Hollywood Barn Dance* in the mid-1940s. Two decades later Foy Willing *(far left)* played a disastrous role in Mary's tumultuous split from Les.
Courtesy of Bob Summers

In the summer of 1948 Les and Mary debuted together at the Club "400," the Polfuss family tavern, which still stands in downtown Waukesha. It was Les's first public performance since his nearly fatal car crash eighteen months earlier. His boyhood chum Warren Downie played bass.

Courtesy of Mary Alice Shaughnessy and Waukesha County Museum Collections

The trophy room in Les's sprawling Mahwah, New Jersey, home is crammed with honorary plaques and statuettes. But the most touching momento is this unframed 1949 wedding picture with Mary, which rests against one of the tattered Army boots Les wore when the couple met in the summer of 1945. Mary later had the boots bronzed.

Mary Alice Shaughnessy

MOCKIN' BIRD HILL
(TRA-LA LA TWITTLE DEE DEE DEE)
Words and Music by **VAUGHN HORTON**

Sincerely
LES PAUL *and* **MARY FORD**

Les and Mary went from being relative unknowns to superstars in 1951, the year they scored nine hit records, including "Mockin' Bird Hill."

The couple cheered up a patient at Waukesha's Memorial Hospital in the early fifties, just before Les retired this modified Epiphone for his new gold Gibson Les Paul, which he also altered electronically to suit his taste. The steel plate bolted onto the top of his guitar gave it a solid-body sound.

Courtesy of Waukesha County Museum Collections

$\mathcal{M}$ary's younger sister, Carol *(right)*, joined the act in 1950 and then married Wally Kamin *(far right)*, Les and Mary's bassist. The foursome often crisscrossed the country for months on end, but Les never allowed Carol to emerge from behind the curtain, where she accompanied Mary's vocals to simulate the multivoiced sound of the famous couple's disks.

Courtesy of Waukesha County Museum Collections

$\mathcal{L}$es and Mary played the Chicago Theater in 1952, shortly before the Eisenhower/Stevenson presidential election, but the couple's fans cast their ballots early.

Courtesy of Wilbur Marker

𝓜ary was a love-smitten twenty-six-year-old when she and Les started climbing the record charts in 1951, but ten years later the sparkle in her eyes—and in her marriage—had faded.

𝓜ary Ford made a halfhearted attempt to salvage her show business career after leaving Les in 1963, but abandoned the pursuit after remarrying two years later.

𝓗aving lapsed into a diabetic coma that lasted two months, fifty-three-year-old Mary Ford died in 1977. Engraved on her burial plaque was the title of her favorite song with Les, which means "Go with God."

Mary Alice Shaughnessy

in his nationally syndicated column. But Ken failed to mention that Winchell suggested that Les was dying.

"I was at a crucial point," Les later said. "It came to a decision to fight or give up, and I damn near called it quits. It was just like everybody says. Whether or not your mind has just been conditioned from the time you're a kid that there is a God, I don't know. I know it sounds stupid now, but I saw a long tunnel. Standing at the end bathed in light was a figure with outstretched arms, saying, 'Give up the pain and come with me.' I'm sure there have been a lot of other people who have been near death, just hanging on to a ledge by a thread like I was. But when I opened my eyes and saw all those nurses and doctors buzzing around me, I decided I had to gather enough strength to beat it."

Ironically, now that he was down for the count, Les Paul was getting more exposure than ever. Dave Garroway was one of the first deejays to break "Lover" and "Brazil," released on February 23, four weeks after the crash. The popular Chicago NBC radio personality, who later became the founding host of television's *Today* show, helped generate a tremendous amount of excitement over Les's new Capitol disk. He played both sides several times a day, heaping them with unqualified praise.

Though other music aficionados liked the cuts, some were genuinely mystified by Les's "New Sound." *Down Beat* mistakenly credited Capitol's engineers with overdubbing his single-string solos: "They have come up with a finished platter that sports as many as eight distinct voices, counting four-way harmony on the lead and various countermelodies, running hither and yon. Listen to these sides and then try to figure how the devil they do it!"

Metronome was equally confused: "Capitol's heralded 'New Sound' consists of five Les Pauls. The fleetest of present-day guitarists has dubbed one sound track over another, playing bass, drums, rhythm guitar, claves, and solo guitar."

Variety, however, wisely refrained from speculating on how the disk was made, commenting instead on its overall impact: "Compared to the practice many record companies used prior to the disk ban of cutting musical background and inserting vocals, the latter was child's play." "Lover" and "Brazil," the entertainment trade predicted, "are on their way to hitdom."

Indeed, by the end of the month, "Lover" reached No. 21 on the *Billboard* charts, with "Brazil" trailing close behind in the No. 22 spot. The disk soon became a hit in Great Britain as well. *Down Beat* lauded his outstanding performance with Nat Cole on a newly released Jazz at the Philharmonic recording that included parts of the July 2, 1944, concert in Hollywood. Then there was the *Billboard* report that Capitol and Universal were engaging in a bidding war over fifty Gene Austin masters that Les had produced in his garage studio just a few weeks before the accident.

Ken Wright brought a radio to the hospital so Les could hear his first solo hit on the air. But the ailing guitarist was simply too ill to take an interest. "It meant nothing to me," Les later said. "I couldn't sleep. I couldn't eat. It took me hours just to get through a bowl of cereal in the morning. But I promised myself I'd finish the damn thing if it took all day. They'd bring me lunch and I'd still be eating my breakfast."

He remained bedridden for at least eight more weeks, reading as much as his concentration allowed during waking hours. But then he had to face some of the grim possibilities that stretched before him. What did the future hold for a guitarist in danger of losing an arm? How would Capitol behave in the aftermath of the accident? How much longer could he carry on the painful pretense of his failing marriage? How would Mary react if he was permanently disabled? And perhaps the most important question of all: when would he regain control over his life? No small issue for a man accustomed to mastering everything about him, people and objects alike.

Strong enough to travel by mid-March, Les was shipped to Good Samaritan Hospital in Los Angeles, where a new medical team performed more extensive operations. Awaiting surgery, he overheard two doctors hotly debating alternative treatments. One was determined to save the arm; the other doctor insisted they amputate. "There was a silence in the room while I took in the full meaning of this," Les wrote in *Reader's Digest* nine years after the episode. "Amputation would mean the end of my career and all I had worked for. Lying there, I seemed to be swinging backward through time—to an old ditchdigger who played a battered harmonica and whose counsel had brought me what success I'd had. I could see his grizzled face, hear his words. 'I'll tell you what,' I said to the physician nearest my bed. 'Let's not say we can't save the arm till we prove we can't. Okay?' "

The doctors finally decided to graft bone from his leg to his arm and rebuild his shattered right elbow with a metal plate, removing the threat of amputation. Before the delicate surgery began, though, they asked Les how he wanted his arm positioned. For once the metal plate was set in place with seven tiny Phillips screws, his elbow joint would forever remain unbending. "Just point it toward my belly button so I can play," he casually replied.

When it was over, the dazed patient was dressed in a rigid plaster cast that enveloped the top half of his body like an overstuffed white sweatshirt. He enjoyed full range of motion in his left arm, which was left free, but the right was frozen from that day forward at almost a ninety-degree angle. He spent the next two years shuttling between specialists in Oklahoma, Memphis, Los Angeles, and Rochester, Minnesota.

In the interim, however, he enjoyed a steady stream of visitors at his Curson Avenue home. One day Bing Crosby dropped by with an extraordinary get-well gift: an early Ampex reel-to-reel tape recorder, based on a model brought to the United States from war-torn Germany by engineer Jack Mullin. At Les's instigation, Crosby began using a prototype of Mullin's machine in 1947 to prerecord his Philco radio programs. Now the singer could escape the rigid schedule of live broadcasting and host his shows at a far more relaxed pace. Shortly thereafter, Crosby Enterprises became the worldwide distributor of Ampex tape recorders, which turned out to be an extremely lucrative business arrangement. "The only reason I got mixed up in that deal was because of Les," Crosby told Bill Putnam years later. The Ampex he gave Les, which retailed for $1,500, was apparently Crosby's way of saying thank you.

Les's recovery was productive, despite the impediment of the bulky plaster cast. He read scores of electronics manuals and dreamed up new instrumental arrangements. "The inside of my head became a private long-playing record storing up music against the day I could pick up my guitar and actually play it," he said. With the help of a few friends he concocted a brace that held his guitar in place so he could begin the arduous task of retraining his crippled right arm. "He was not going to let that accident stop him," recalled longtime friend Wally Jones. "At first he didn't have any movement at all in the arm. He had to learn to play all over again, make it all come from the wrist. But his playing gradually improved through sheer determination."

Along the way he picked up another lifelong friend. Zeke Manners, an immensely popular hillbilly radio star turned deejay, single-handedly generated a massive Les Paul letter-writing campaign from his Los Angeles radio station. "This man has broken almost every bone in his body," Manners told his listeners, whom he bombarded with repeated spinnings of "Lover" and "Brazil." "His elbow has been knocked clean off, and he may never play again." Zeke's emotional appeal brought in more than five thousand sympathetic missives, which he promptly turned over to the grateful guitarist.

By the summer of 1948, Les was ready for a little kindness from strangers. Finally acknowledging the utter impoverishment of her marriage, Virginia packed her bags and the two children and returned to Chicago. Zeke stumbled into the middle of the Pauls' domestic upheaval, perhaps even unwittingly playing a minor role: "The first time I ever spoke to Les, he invited me to his house. He only lived about eight blocks from me, so I walked over. He was still in his big body cast. Virginia was living there with the two kids, Rusty and Gene. After talking for a few hours, I was getting ready to go home and Les said, 'Let me walk you to the corner.' I said, 'You're crazy,' but I finally gave in. 'Okay,' I said, 'but just to the corner.' When we got to the corner, Les points to a tavern called the Red Coach and says, 'Let's go have a beer.' So we go in and there was this gal in the corner. It was Mary. So Les goes over to sit with her and they talked for a long time. Four weeks later, I go back to his house and there she is, washing his clothes, scrubbing the floors. I look at Les and he doesn't say anything. He just laughs."

However, some of Les's friends who sympathized with Virginia failed to see the humor in the situation. "Les had a supreme ego," said one engineer who had visited the couple's home on several occasions. "Everything in the world centered on what he wanted to do. And anything or anyone who got in the way would go down under the onslaught because the supreme ego had to be satisfied no matter what. Les got the most from everybody he could and then moved on when he found somebody who could give him something else."

Mary's father was even more irate, although he choked back his anger in her presence. It wouldn't have mattered anyway. Les and Mary were hopelessly in love, which was blatantly apparent to anyone who spent a moment with them. The near-fatal accident and seemingly endless recovery period only made them closer. Mary was Les's constant and solicitous attendant. The time they spent together on Curson Avenue—before the pressures of show business began to bear down on them—was the closest the couple would ever come to experiencing a happy, uncomplicated family life.

Between April and December 1948, Capitol released three more Les Paul singles, including such bromidic bombs as "The Swiss Woodpecker," "The Man on the Flying Trapeze," and "By the Light of the Silvery Moon." The most commercially successful of the lot was "What Is This Thing Called Love," which actually surpassed "Lover" on the charts and in record sales. But by then, many critics had already tired of the "New Sound." "It's hard to admire Les's mechanical versatility more than once," carped *Metronome*, "because it really doesn't provide good music."

Believing his new recording artist had run the overdubbed-guitar gimmick into the ground, Capitol's Jim Conkling encouraged Les to abandon his single-handed approach to making music and form another band. But Les wasn't quite ready to retreat back into a conventional studio format. The year-long recording ban of 1948, which excluded singers, greatly enhanced the public's tastes for vocal music. So Les decided to try overdubbing with a female vocalist.

Although he loved the lush sound of Mary's voice, he had pigeon-holed her as "a hillbilly singer, a lightweight." He wanted a vocalist with more vibrato, more guts. Among those he claims to have auditioned are Kay Starr, Rosemary Clooney, and Doris Day (all of whom deny any such auditions took place). In any case, he finally decided to give it a whirl with his lover. "Mary couldn't sing hot," he said, "but she was completely unaffected and this was a tremendous asset."

According to Les, Capitol turned down the couple's first joint effort, "Night and Day." Finally, in May 1949, the label released "Until I Hold You Again," a doleful tune featuring a supple trio of Mary's voices. Perhaps to discourage deejays from playing the flip side, Les backed the ballad with an inane hillbilly romp called "You Can't Expect Kisses from Me," on which he plucked banjo and sang with an atonal chorus of unknowns. But to no avail. Between its sad lyrics and Mary's tear-jerking delivery, "Until I Hold You Again" sank under the weight of its own pathos.

Though their debut disk was largely ignored by record buyers and deejays alike, the couple were on the brink of a radical change, in both their professional and personal lives.

Chapter 15

How High
The Moon

The summer of 1949 had an inauspicious start.

Though eighteen months had passed since the car crash, Les's life was still in an uproar. While everyone else was out celebrating the Fourth of July, he was passing another uncertain night in the Mayo Clinic, one of the country's most famous research hospitals. His now-deformed right arm was finally freed from the last in a series of gradually smaller casts. But he still had to undergo another round of examinations to see if he needed surgery on his back.

Throughout the ordeal, Mary had never left his side. "I sure hope they accomplish something here," she wrote her parents from the clinic. "Everything is so undecided that I have no idea when we'll be home. If they fix Les's back so he can work, we'll be here a few months yet. If not, we'll probably be home, or go to Memphis, Tenn., to have it operated on."

In fact, Les decided to postpone the surgery and remain for a few weeks in Waukesha, where he hoped to work his withered right arm back to life. The family tavern was an ideal place for his post-accident debut before a live audience. One of the first people he called was boyhood chum Warren Downie. Les and Warren hadn't played together since the Independence Day parade in the late 1920s, when Les's "Red Hot Rag Time Band" was hauled through the streets of Waukesha on the back of a flatbed truck bedecked with red-white-and-blue bunting. Warren plucked a banjo and donned a dress and lady's straw hat for that occasion; now he was a well-regarded guitarist/bassist who worked with orchestras all over the Midwest.

From the outside, Club 400 resembled an old-style grange hall, a rustic two-story building on a quiet tree-lined street near the heart of town. On the inside, though, it looked like any other smoky neighborhood saloon, except for the stairway with shiny brass rails leading to a dozen or so tables where all the regulars sat. To create a homey atmosphere on the makeshift stage he created for his son's opening night, George put a lamp on top of a pile of beer cases he had pushed together and covered with a sheet.

Surrounded by friendly, familiar faces, Les and Warren tuned up for their first set. The only thing missing was a rhythm guitarist. Les, however, greeted the audience with his usual nonchalance. He told a few stories and joked around with Warren. After playing a couple of standards on his customized Epiphone, though, he decided the two-piece band sounded a little too thin for his taste. Suddenly he pulled Mary out of the crowd and thrust a guitar into her hands.

Though she had done countless radio programs and experimental recordings with Les, Mary had never performed with him in public. Her métier was country, not pop music. "I don't know the words to all the songs you're playing," she protested. But Les was insistent. He called out chord changes while his musician friends jotted down lyrics on coasters. Mary fell in like a road-tested pro. As the trio began picking up steam on more familiar tunes like "Pennies from Heaven," "Bye, Bye Blues," and "Sentimental Journey," her shyness melted away entirely. She strummed and sang with vigor, her honey-blond curls pulled off her youthful, radiant face with a barrette. "Isn't she great?" Les remarked to the audience, more as a statement than a question. He could see that the crowd adored her. Before the evening was over, he decided to make her a permanent part of his stage act.

Even flinty Evelyn Polfuss found Mary irresistible. "Mary was the only person I know who got along with my mother," Les later remarked. "No matter how sarcastic mother got, no matter how hard she came after her, Mary just ducked and came back with a very nice compliment." The sweet-faced girl from Pasadena also left a lasting impression on Warren Downie, who sometimes invited her and Les to his home for a nightcap after an evening onstage. "My little girl wasn't sleeping very well at the time, so Mary used to carry her around the living room hour after hour to soothe her," he said. "She was very maternal."

Although George's attitude toward her had softened considerably, he disagreed with Les's decision to make Mary part of the act. "Dad thought she was too frail to keep up with a roughneck like me," said Les. "I just told him that I knew nobody could do what we could do as a team." Both men were right. While Les and Mary undoubtedly shared a combination of skills that could surpass anything they had done individually, *nobody* could keep up with Les's frenzied pace. But he couldn't see that at the time. His head was too full of dreams.

Encouraged by the enthusiastic reception the trio received at his father's saloon, Les booked a few more dates at a small club on the south side of Milwaukee. When those proved to be similarly successful, he moved on to Chicago. Dave Garroway, the deejay who had played such a prominent part in breaking "Lover" and "Brazil" onto the charts nineteen months earlier, helped him land a two-week engagement at Chicago's prestigious Blue Note jazz club, beginning Monday, August 22. Best of all, the gig paid $1,000 a week.

The place was packed on opening night. Les Paul jazz fans were there. A coterie of Rhubarb Red hillbilly enthusiasts showed up. And the front-row tables were lined with reviewers from *Down Beat, Newsweek, Variety,* and the Chicago dailies. Some of the Blue Note regulars, however, must have thought they had walked into the wrong place. Instead of the finely attired performers they were accustomed to seeing in their cherished jazz club, they beheld Les in a pair of baggy, wrinkled trousers, Warren in an open-neck sport shirt, and Mary in a plain black dress. They gaped in astonishment at Les's squirrely mixture of straight melody, jazz, and all-out hillbilly corn." Reported *Down Beat:*

"Paul and his group looked like a contingent from the WLS *Barn Dance,* and their relaxed friendliness, like a breath of fresh country air, put the at first unnerved audience at ease, then entranced them. ... Les's socks were bright multicolor plaid, which were clearly visible when he kicked off his shoes while playing hillbilly numbers. Don't get the wrong idea. Mixed in with the fun was some fine music. 'How High the Moon' and 'Lover' were not neglected, nor tunes such as 'Out of Nowhere' and 'Blue Skies.' There were no set arrangements on the things they played. Paul says he prefers doing each tune differently each time. One song segues into another, and Les thinks nothing of stopping in the middle to say hello to a friend or to joke about what he and his group are doing."

Les's screwball stage antics didn't always sit well with Warren, though. One night the sober-minded bassist was deep into a solo when Cullen Casey strolled into the darkened club. Without warning, Les suddenly kicked off his loafers and hollered: "Somebody just came in from my old hometown!" Then he broke into a rousing chorus of "Chicken Reel." Everyone but Warren thought it was a hilarious bit of slapstick. "Warren took his music very seriously," said Casey. "After the night was over, he came over to me and said, 'That s.o.b.' He was mad."

The truth is, Les would do *anything* to get a laugh from the crowd, even if he had to upstage or embarrass his bandmates, which he often did. It was nothing personal. It was just showbiz. He did it all the time. He liked to think of it as being spontaneous. Mary, his most patient and enduring musical partner, would soon discover that she would always have to play straight man to his joker.

Of course, everything Les did onstage was calculated to produce a specific effect. The homespun patter and casual clothing, for instance, were "all based on our being natural," he told *Newsweek* on opening night at the Blue Note. "We perform like we're singing in the bathtub." Unfortunately, Frank Holzfeind had something else in mind when he hired the Les Paul Trio. It was hard to tell which the jazz club owner hated more: Les's down-home garb or his affection for three-chord hillbilly tunes like "Wreck on the Highway," an old Roy Acuff twanger.

As Les tells it: "We got fired the very first night. There was a pay phone at the edge of the bandstand. You couldn't make a call without everybody hearing what you were saying. Well, Holzfeind gets on the phone with my agent and says, 'You got one helluva sense of humor to send a hillbilly trio in here. The place is full of cowboys. This guy's a goddam comedian, a lounge act.'

"I told Holzfeind that I heard everything he said, then I ran over to the press table and got down on my knees. I kidded with them, saying, 'Please be good to us. We just got fired as it is.' The audience cracked up. I didn't care. I knew we were good."

By the end of the evening Holzfiend apparently came around as well. In between novelty numbers he could see why Les was reputed to be "a musician's musician." But Les made it abundantly clear to one reporter that night that he was no jazz snob, that he was now seeking a larger following: "Never try to educate people," he said. "I let them show me what they want. One thing I want to be sure of is that John Q. doesn't think I'm on Cloud No. 9 all the time."

Although Les was scheduled to return to L.A. in September for another operation, he and Mary moved on to a string of dates in Detroit, St. Louis and New York City. It was time to let the world know that Les Paul was back with a vengeance. Warren, however, felt that touring with a relatively unknown trio was far too risky for a man with a family. He was replaced at the end of the Blue Note run by Ed Stapleton, a Chicago bassist who would work with Les and Mary off and on for the next several months.

In the meantime, Les suffered another crushing blow. He and Mary were in the midst of an engagement in New York City when they received word that his father had died suddenly, stricken in his home on October 2, 1949, with a cerebral hemorrhage. Les arrived in Waukesha two days later, just in time to see George's body interred in the Prairie Home Cemetery.

Ralph was left with the tavern, Les with only a few poignant memories. But the guitarist took comfort in knowing that he and his father had enjoyed a heart-to-heart conversation just a few weeks earlier. George painfully acknowledged for the first time in his life that he had been an inattentive father. The sixty-seven-year-old Polfuss reached back twenty years, regretfully recalling how he refused to give his young son $2.50 for a special harmonica. "A quarter yes, two and a half dollars no," George said at the time. "But if I'd only known!" he later lamented.

Les buried his grief in work, work, and more work. The Les Paul Trio appeared all over the Midwest—Rock Island, Illinois, East St. Louis, South Milwaukee, anyplace that would hire them. Unfortunately, Les's strumming arm still hadn't fully recovered. Sometimes it swelled up and started to throb in the middle of a set. The audience had no idea he was in pain, though. He'd simply tell more stories or encourage Ed Stapleton to take longer bass solos.

He couldn't afford to stop anyway. His medical bills had gobbled up all his savings. He and Mary were broke. "There were times when we got pretty hungry out there," Les remembered. They were forced to stay in second-rate motels that ranged from bad to worse. One freezing night in rural Ohio a snowstorm drove them into a flophouse "that used newspapers for sheets, had an outdoor bathroom and an awful wood stove we were afraid to use."

But the couple seemed to roll through the rough times. "They were head over heels in love," recalled former deejay Bob Maxwell, who did a live broadcast of their combo around this time from Detroit's London Chop House, a cavernous restaurant in which performers had to compete with clattering dishes and the roar of a lively dinner crowd. "It was touching to watch them. He stared at her, practically salivating, and she looked at him like she couldn't believe he was real. You could feel the heat across the room."

They played games in the car to stave off boredom during the long, tedious drives between gigs. "Mary's ear and my ear were pretty well matched," Les once said. "We'd be out in New Mexico somewhere and we'd tune in to the hum of the motor. I'd say, 'That's A flat.' She'd say, 'It's A.' So we'd pull out the guitar and give it a strum to see who was right. She was something else."

Just as Mary made a conscious decision to shed her country-queen mantle, Les finally abandoned all pretense of being a jazz player. The couple now met firmly in the middle of the musical road. But it was really Les's show. He did all the talking onstage, he chose all the music, and Mary didn't seem to mind at all. Live performances helped Les decide which songs to record. When he found a tune that people consistently applauded, he'd sometimes stop playing halfway through to ask if it should be done faster or slower. Then he'd wax the arrangement that got the greatest applause. Tepidly received tunes, of course, were ditched altogether.

Touring the heartland made Les believe more firmly than ever that he had to "please the freight payers" if he wanted to be a serious commercial proposition: "The people you're playing for work all day. They don't go to music schools and study harmony. They pay their dough, they come, they listen. If they don't understand what you're doing, they walk out. What are you supposed to do, tie 'em to a chair with a rope while you explain you're performing great music?"

Certainly not in the kind of gin joints that he and Mary were playing, like the Red Rooster in Detroit. One night in the middle of a set, five mobsters wearing hats in brim-down underworld fashion trooped across the floor in front of the bandstand en route to their table. Unable to resist a crack, Les leaned into the mike, and asked, "Whadda you guys looking for, a hat rack?"

After calming five bruised egos, the manager rushed over to the wisecracking guitarist and blurted out, "Whadda you looking for, a cement overcoat? First thing you need to know is those types have no sense of humor!"

By December 1949, Les and Mary were back in Milwaukee, booked into Jimmy Fazio's Town Club, a real listeners' nightspot. They now had a devoted Milwaukee following, including Dr. George Miller and his wife, Bertha. Like Les, George was an electronics buff. He used to bring his Magnecorder to the club to record the couple's act, then invite them back to his home to listen to the tape. The Millers'

children were crazy about the two entertainers, especially their youngest son, Steve, who later became an outstanding blues-rock singer and guitarist.

George sometimes brought his boy to the club to see Les and Mary perform their oddball mix of pop and country standards: "That's where I first heard hillbilly music," Steve Miller later recalled. "Les and Mary used to make fun of it. They'd sing cowboy harmonies that just killed me. They sounded so good.

"Les was great to me, too. I was a shy kid, so he'd calm me down by showing me his guitar. Over the years, he taught me how to sing in a studio, entertain a crowd, and promote records. But I fell in love with Mary. She was soft and sweet and had a beautiful, beautiful voice, that sort of languid, Southern sound. I remember her in a cowboy outfit and I wanted to be a cowboy more than anything in the world."

Les and Mary were in the midst of their engagement at Fazio's when they finally decided to plunge into marriage. Dr. Miller dropped by the club one afternoon and administered their blood tests while they sat on a stack of beer cases in the stockroom. They were married a few days later without fanfare at Milwaukee County Court (not in the bar, as Les has claimed in the past). The fifteen-minute ceremony was performed at three o'clock on December 29, a chilly, sun-washed afternoon. Mary wore a dark, high-necked dress and a single white flower in her hair, Les a plain suit. Judge Robert Cannon officiated, and the wedding vows were witnessed by the Millers and Ed Stapleton. No members of the family were present, though, not even Les's mother or brother, who lived less than fifteen miles away.

Four or five hours later, the bride and groom tuned up their guitars and went back to work at Fazio's, where the regulars helped them celebrate their midafternoon marriage. There was, of course, no thought of a honeymoon. "We hope to throw a big party next week when the rest of our friends in the music business will be available," Les told a reporter that day. "We're not going to take any vacation."

The couple returned to L.A. in mid-January. Shortly thereafter Les replaced bassist Ed Stapleton with Wally Kamin. Formerly with Art Van Damme's band, Wally used to jam with Les in a bowling-alley cocktail lounge in Chicago during the early 1940s. By all accounts, he was a lovable, good-natured man, but his craving for the bottle alarmed Mary. In a rare moment of assertiveness she threatened to end her professional relationship with Les if he hired the bassist. However, Les called her bluff and brought his freewheeling pal into the fold. Wally, in turn, was willing to do anything to please his new boss, and he eventually won Mary over with his relentless enthusiasm. One day, while helping to record Les's self-penned single "Walkin' and Whistlin' Blues," he pulled on a pair of heavy work boots and walked in circles around the couple's tiny tile bathroom to create a vivid sound picture of a man casually strolling.

In between gigs at small nightspots around Hollywood, Les continued to cut scores of experimental disks in the garage studio. He was so pleased with the pristine sound wrought by his constantly improving audio equipment that he briefly considered expanding his recording business. He even printed up fliers and recruited his friend Wally Jones to demonstrate some of his freshly minted ten-inch disks to people in the industry.

But Les lost interest in the venture before it got off the ground. One thing remained constant at his Curson Avenue home, though— it was always stuffed with musicians and engineers. Whenever Les added a new gizmo to his sound system, he'd ask one of his friends to lie in front of the speaker for hours at a time to listen for tone variations while he twisted the knobs in the control room.

Through it all, Mary continued to be Les's faithful servant. According to Les, she sang when he wanted her to sing and whipped up vats of macaroni and cheese to feed the hungry hoards, sometimes inviting her younger sister Carol to stay at the house a few days a week to lend a hand.

The couple's personal and professional lives became even more intertwined when they began making radio shows together for NBC, *The Les Paul Show with Mary Ford*. The fifteen-minute radio program, prerecorded on transcription disks and broadcast every Friday night on Los Angeles's KFI, was packed with music and sketches created by Les and Mary. The couple's amiable on-air chats sometimes included friends who just happened to drop by, like radio veteran Zeke Manners, who played Ed McMahon to Les's Johnny Carson.

But the show generally cleaved to one formula: Mary singing as she performed her household chores while Les tried to get some crazy new sound out of his instrument. During one episode, he pretended he had built a gas-powered guitar. "Your electric guitar is going to be awfully hard to beat," Mary warned.

"I'm going to go down in history with this thing," he answered, before turning on the gas and sending himself into a make-believe dream world, simulated by some of his special sound effects.

Les's radio transcriptions and experimental disks from this period reveal his dogged perfectionism. Dissatisfied with one take, he'd improvise something entirely new on the next, playing the same tune over and over again until he got it just the way he wanted it. Mary's innate gift for music shone through as well. She played pulsing rhythm guitar and effortlessly conjured up five-part harmonies off the top of her head. But she often ran out of steam before her tireless husband. When her patience ran out too, said Les, she retreated to the kitchen to make more macaroni and cheese—or to have a good cry.

That's when Les concentrated on his solo instrumentals or his own radio show. Other times he sought the company of his engineer friends. "I spent a lot of time at Les's place doing electronic work on his guitar or amplifiers," said Wally Jones. "When I wasn't over there, it was quite common for him to come to my house. We'd work in my garage till the wee hours of the morning while my wife and Mary sat in the dinette, waiting for us to finish. At the end of the night, Les'd say, 'That's it, I've got it.' But the next night the phone would ring at eleven o'clock and he'd be right back here, wanting to make another change."

During this period, Les began seriously experimenting with his Ampex tape recorder. Although he had succeeded in producing remarkably clean overdubs with his custom-made disk cutter, he knew he could overdub on tape with even greater fidelity. All he had to do was strum along with a guitar solo he cut on one Ampex and simultaneously record both parts on a second Ampex. Unfortunately, there was no way he could afford another tape machine.

Groping for a solution, Les went straight to the source, Jack Mullin, the brilliant audio engineer who was largely responsible for introducing Hollywood to high-fidelity magnetic tape recording (and later videotaping). At the time, Mullin was also engineering Bing Crosby's weekly Philco show, the country's first tape-recorded radio program. One night, after appearing on the show with Mary, Les laid out his dilemma for Mullin. By the end of the evening, the two men had devised a method for overdubbing on the Ampex, which involved adding a second playback head.

But the modified Ampex had one distinct drawback. If Les made a mistake in, say, the twelfth overdub, he'd have to record the first eleven all over again. In other words, one small mistake could cost a day's work. With the disk-to-disk recording method, he could simply go back to the last good disk and redo the part. But he felt the advantages of overdubbing on his customized tape recorder outweighed the disadvantages, even if it put him and Mary under far greater pressure. "It made us real pros," he later boasted.

Beyond fidelity, the Ampex offered greater portability. Les could easily pack up and carry the boxy tape recorder like a piece of hand luggage. Now all he needed was a portable mixer. For this he turned to Wally Jones: "Les wanted to continue recording the radio shows when he and Mary went out on the road, so he asked me to build him a small mixer. Some portable ones were available at the time. They were used for remote broadcasts, ballgames, things like that. But they were unsuitable for Les. He had certain ideas about what he wanted in sound, certain inputs, connections, and so forth."

In honor of his resourceful friend, Les called his new toy the Wally Box. About fifteen inches long and eight inches square, the mixer was powered by an old Gibson amplifier and fitted with a leather strap for easy over-the-shoulder carrying. It also had guitar, microphone, and headphone inputs so Les and Mary could cut disks in their hotel rooms without disturbing the other guests. The mobile recording studio, roughly the size of a few suitcases, soon became the talk of the industry—and the source of several of the couple's hit records.

From the day Les signed his contract with Capitol, he exercised un-precedented control over his career. At a time when disk executives typically dictated every move their artists made—from the material they recorded to the tempos and sidemen they used—Les functioned as his own A&R man. Not only did he choose and arrange all his own songs, he pioneered previously unthinkable methods of producing and engineering his own disks. At first Jim Conkling couldn't even get the guitarist to come into the Capitol office. "He'd just play me stuff over the phone. Then he'd send in the finished masters."

But Les's unique blend of musical craftsmanship and technical virtuosity still wasn't setting the record-buying public on fire. "His records were too fast, too spectacular," Jim recalled. "Musicians raved about them, but other people didn't catch on." Jim advised Les to "come up with something your grandmother could tap her foot to."

That discussion, said Les, inspired his first hit in more than two years. One afternoon, while he and Mary were recording "Crying," a song they cowrote based on the chord changes to "Bye, Bye Blues," Zeke Manners burst into the garage, his face red with excitement. Oblivious to the fact that he was interrupting a recording session, he pulled his cigar out of his mouth and held up a handsome new accordion. "You gotta hear this thing," he exclaimed. Without wait-ing for a response, Zeke plopped himself down on a chair in the middle of the studio and launched into a fast-paced rendition of "Nola," an old piano novelty number popularized in 1922 by band leader Vincent Lopez.

"Hey, what is that?" Les asked from his pantry-size control room. "I like it." He walked into the studio, picked up one of his hollow-bodied Epiphones, and began plucking out the melody as Zeke's fingers flew over the keys. Lying in bed that night, he resolved to make "Nola" his next release, although he decided to slow down the tempo to satisfy Conkling. Too excited to sleep, he wandered into the garage and came up with a technically uncomplicated arrangement before daybreak.

After hearing "Nola" just once, Capitol's sales department unanimously agreed it was going to be a summer hit. They were right. Released on May 15, 1950, the upbeat instrumental climbed to *Billboard's* No. 9 spot by the third week in June and soon became Les's best-selling single. The disk made a big splash in Great Britain as well. England's *Melody Maker* said: " 'Lover,' the first multi-guitar recording attempt issued here in July 1949, created a mild stir; but when 'Nola' was released exactly a year later, the public became Les Paul conscious."

From that date forward, Les and Jim had a running joke. Whenever Les delivered a new disk to the Capitol office for release, the record executive asked, "Will Granny be able to tap her foot to it?"

Les and Mary now toured extensively, making frequent appearances on Dave Garroway's Chicago-based radio show and on Jack Hersh's Prudential Insurance program. Around this time, Les decided he and Mary should find a place to live on the East Coast. Hollywood had been good to him. He had worked and played with some of the biggest names in show business, made a few movies, scored a major recording contract, and married the girl of his dreams. But there was no longer enough work there to sustain him and his new bride comfortably. Television, which was gradually killing off live entertainment, was largely centered in New York City. So that's where Les wanted to be.

By 1950 there were more than a hundred TV stations in thirty-eight states, and more being born. Many of Les's colleagues from radio—Ed Sullivan, Milton Berle, and Freeman Gosden and Charles Correll (a.k.a. Amos and Andy)—were hosting or starring in their own weekly TV shows. Even his old pal Zeke Manners moved to New York and made the crossover. Why not Les Paul and Mary Ford?

All the couple had to do was finish up a few gigs in the Midwest and continue traveling east. Les drafted Wally Kamin and Mary's younger sister Carol to help them make the move. So, shortly after he and Mary left Los Angeles for their heartland engagements, Wally and Carol headed for the Big Apple in a station wagon loaded with luggage and audio equipment.

Wally Jones's Los Angeles home served as command central. At the end of each day, Wally Kamin called collect and asked for Les Paul. Les, of course, was never there, so there'd be no charge for the call. But the ongoing telephone contact helped Wally Jones keep Les apprised of his bass player's cross-country progress—and all at minimum cost, which is the way Les liked to do *everything*.

The two couples finally met in Cleveland and headed for New York together. After nearly two days of driving without stop, the weary travelers pulled up in front of the Two Pigs Meat Market on Northern Boulevard in Jackson Heights, Queens, Les's old New York City neighborhood. He pointed to a set of windows above the butcher shop and led the entourage up a flight of stairs.

Mary took one look at the cramped $40-a-month apartment and nearly burst into tears. There was no phone. There wasn't even electricity. So Les sent Wally Kamin out to pick up a batch of candles to get them through the night. When the lights were switched on a day or so later, though, he made Wally return the remaining candles for a refund. The best the hapless bass player could do was swap them for a load of bubble gum. The couple never did get a phone, though, relying instead on the kindness of the butcher, who bellowed upstairs whenever they got a call.

Dick Linke, Capitol's East Coast promotion manager, was stunned to hear that Les and Mary had driven across country with all their recording gear: "It was almost like pioneers going east instead of west. Hillbilly heaven. I couldn't reach them by phone, so I went over to see them as soon as they got settled. I took one look at their setup and I says, 'Jesus Christ, what is this?' They were all jammed into this little apartment. There were boxes everywhere!

"I didn't realize how pretty Mary was—or how wild Les was. He lived an uninhibited life-style. Les listened to nobody but Les. His family, his work, his pleasure were all wrapped up in one. There was no separation. He would go eighteen, twenty hours a day, record all night, and get to bed at five in the morning, and he expected Mary to do the same."

Jackson Heights was an ill-conceived choice for a man who planned to make a good portion of his living from homemade recordings. The densely populated working-class neighborhood abutted La Guardia Airport, which had grown considerably since Les had lived in the area a decade earlier. The roar of airplanes overflying the guitarist's apartment ruined more than a few disks. Then there were the other tenants in the building, who complained about his and Mary's round-the-clock recording schedule.

They had occupied a basement apartment in the same area briefly during an earlier tour, but even then they never entirely escaped disgruntled neighbors, who would pound on the plumbing pipes if the music was too loud. As the hour grew later, Les often threw a blanket over Mary's head both to block out unwanted noise and to muffle her singing. One day Carol persuaded them to record her favorite song, "How High the Moon." A jazz anthem for years, the standard had already been waxed by such well-known artists as Stan Kenton and Benny Goodman. Les himself had often performed the upbeat tune, first on radio with his own trio, then with the Jazz at the Philharmonic gang—and much more recently with Mary. In fact, the husband-and-wife team had been testing various arrangements of "How High" before live audiences since they began working together the previous summer.

Once he got the first take down, Les called his friend Zeke Manners, who was now living on Riverside Drive in Manhattan. "You gotta get over here right away," he implored. "I got something you gotta hear."

For the next several hours, Zeke and his wife, Bea, sat quietly in Les and Mary's homemade studio—each wearing a set of headphones—and listened to the couple's work in progress. "It must have been a hundred and seven degrees there," Zeke later recalled.

"I think they did at least six takes of the thing. Les cut the rhythm track first. Then he laid down all the countermelodies. The son of a gun had worked out the whole arrangement in his head, and it sounded great. He was so happy when he finished that he cut another song on the same machine, with me playing accordion and Mary singing."

Darkness was beginning to give way to dawn before Les finally turned off the tape recorder. By then he had laced "How High the Moon" with several intricate electric guitar and bass lines. Mary contributed a lively chorus of harmonies as well as the singular sound of her pulsating rhythm guitar (though to this day Les refuses to give public credit to Mary's splendid strumming on this or any of their other joint recording ventures).

In any case, Les's hard-swinging, multilayered arrangement of "How High" offered a glistening sound that was uniquely his own. The total number of overdubs: twelve, which was absolutely unheard of at the time.

Confident he had created a disk that would make the recording industry stand up and take notice, Les rushed to the phone that night and called Jim Conkling at his home in California. Although it was already past two on the West Coast, he kept the record executive on the phone for at least two hours. When words apparently failed to convey his triumph, he held the receiver next to his record player. But Conkling remained noncommittal.

The pair met face to face a week or so later. "I told Les it was a sensational arrangement," Conkling remembered, "the best I had ever heard. But I said, 'You have to understand, every jazz artist is making "How High the Moon." There are so many copies of that song on the record-store shelves, the dealers are going to say "Forget it. We can't get rid of the ones we've got." ' So I refused to let it out." (Capitol, in fact, had at least twenty-three different versions of the song in its vaults.)

Les knew that Conkling was making a big mistake. But there was little he could do. Apart from Glen Wallichs, the head of the disk company, Conkling was the only man at Capitol authorized to release a new pop single. Unwilling to give up, the guitarist needled

Jim for the next several months. In the meantime, Capitol released another Les Paul/Mary Ford record: "Goofus" (reputedly the first overdubbed instrumental Les made on tape), backed by "Sugar Sweet," which featured a vocal duet by Mary. Although the single was largely ignored by the critics, "Goofus" climbed to No. 21 on the charts by the end of October.

Finally, between December 1950 and February 1951, the Paul/Ford team scored big with a couple of hillbilly-flavored hits: first with "Tennessee Waltz," then with "Mockin' Bird Hill," the only song Capitol ever asked them to record. In Les's mind, this twofold victory sounded the first shot in a head-to-head competition between his wife and Patti Page, a more established singer who had put out a couple of vocally overdubbed records of her own.

Blessed with a voice that exuded the same easy country charm as Mary's, Patti hit No. 1 with "Tennessee Waltz" about a month before Les and Mary's disk started climbing the charts. "People were walking into stores to ask for Patti Page's 'Tennessee Waltz' and walking out with ours," Les later said. The confusion might have played a part in the couple's record reaching No. 6 on *The Hit Parade* by the end of December.

Eight weeks later, however, they beat out Patti's version of "Mockin' Bird Hill" by a few days. "It may be a successful gimmick, but it can't keep up forever," one *Metronome* reviewer said of the newest Paul/Ford collaboration, which boasted a quartet of Mary's voices. "Les Paul's multiplying guitars and Mary Ford's ditto vocals have been milked for all they are worth; now is the time for both to use their considerable talents in a musical way again." But the public obviously thought otherwise. "Mockin' Bird Hill" quickly became the second-largest-selling disk in the country.

Les now felt he had the sort of ammunition he needed to persuade Jim Conkling to release "How High the Moon." He approached Conkling at a party in early 1951 at the home of Glen Wallichs, the president of Capitol. "Jim, please," Les pleaded. "We're almost No. 1 and Patti Page is on our rear. We want to put one out that nobody can touch."

"If it's 'How High the Moon,' forget it," Jim replied. "It's a musician's song. And it's got the most ridiculous lyrics I've ever heard. I'm telling you, it's not going to go."

A few weeks later, however, Conkling reversed himself: "I got a call to run Columbia Records, which meant I'd leave Capitol in March. Les had never stopped pushing me to put out 'How High the Moon,' and he finally wore me down. It was one of the last records I scheduled before leaving Capitol. But I told Les, 'I still think you should have made another record. I just hope that it will sell.'

"I had a similar situation with Nat Cole," Conkling added. "I wouldn't touch 'Mona Lisa.' At first Nat didn't like it either. He thought it was a dumb song. But after he played it around the house a few times he said that even his dogs were beginning to go for it. The only reason I finally put it out was because the two fellas who wrote it were such nice guys. But I was sure that neither song was going to make it.

"Well, 'How High the Moon' became one of Capitol's biggest sellers of all time, up until the Beatles came along. It was not only a big hit, it stayed on the charts forever. I laugh about it now, but at the time it embarrassed me to death. Over at Columbia, they kept saying to me, 'How long is this tune going to be No. 1?' "

By April 21, 1951, less than a month after its release, Les and Mary's commercialized version of "How High the Moon" and "Mockin' Bird Hill" had captured the No. 1 and No. 2 spots respectively on *The Hit Parade*. It was an unprecedented popular-music success, two resounding hits by relative unknowns hitting simultaneously—and hard.

Les Paul and Mary Ford were in.

Chapter 16

Introducing America's Musical Sweethearts

The widespread recognition Les had craved for years now came his way easily, casually, almost as a matter of course. But then he had many powerful friends to help turn the floodlights of fame his way. Foremost, of course, was Bing Crosby, who invited Les and Mary to perform on his Hollywood-based radio program on March 21, 1951, just a few days before Capitol released "How High the Moon."

The promised appearance that night of Judy Garland probably lured even more listeners to Crosby's popular network variety show. But the radio host introduced the husband-and-wife team first, calling special attention to Les's secret recording technique: "I'd like to present two sensational performers. They have some terrific records I'm sure you're all familiar with, 'Tennessee Waltz,' 'Mockin' Bird Hill' . . . and now a brand-new one called 'How High the Moon.' It has an unusual sound, folks, so I don't want you to miss a single note of it."

Using prerecorded background vocals and guitars, Les and Mary tore through a high-octane version of the tune, duplicating their sparkling performance on the Capitol single. Moments later, Crosby stepped up to the microphone to join the couple on "Mockin' Bird

189

Hill." He promised that he and Mary would sound like a chorus of six (supported, of course, by the same offstage overdubbed tape recording that had fattened up "How High the Moon"). But Les tried to create the illusion that the backup voices were going to come from a mysterious electronic device he had invented: "I'll just run you through the Les Paulveriser and you'll sound like Fred Waring and the Glee Club."

"Good," Crosby replied, happily playing along with the ruse. "Les will do about eighteen guitars and we'll really wrap it up. Incidentally, I think we'll dedicate this number to the Music Operators of America, the jukebox folks, who are now in convention at the Palmer House in Chicago," Crosby added, giving the couple an additional plug.

"How many hear us in Chicago?" Les asked with more than a little coyness.

"Lester, dear boy," answered Bing, "this show goes coast to coast."

"Well I'll be darned, Mary, we're in the big time."

Meanwhile, back on the East Coast, Les's old pal Jim Moran, now lord of his own wildly offbeat Madison Avenue public relations firm, dreamed up an unconventional plan to launch "How High the Moon." Since his tenure as Fred Waring's public relations chief, Moran had run up a journalistic record of high jinks that had in all probability made him more famous than most of his clients. Among the puckish press agent's widely reported exploits: persuading Waring to lead a prize-winning bull through Plummer's patrician china shop on New York's Fifth Avenue (to prove that the orchestra leader was clumsier than a bull in a . . .); curling his lanky six-foot-two frame around an abandoned ostrich egg until it hatched twenty-six days later (to advertise the 1946 comedy flick *The Egg and I,*), and selling an icebox to an Eskimo (to advance the cause of the National Association of Ice Advertisers, then battling the onslaught of electric refrigerators).

Compared to his previous publicity stunts, then, Moran's idea for promoting Les and Mary's latest disk wasn't *that* preposterous. A champion kite flier, he decided to loft a huge custom-made kite emblazoned with the legend "How High the Moon" over New York's sprawling Central Park. He insisted the kite be sturdy enough to support human cargo—a midget, that is. First he had to find a trusting midget to go along with the lunatic scheme, though. Plastering posters all over Times Square—long a magnet for misfits and glamour seekers alike—Moran quickly found his man.

Accompanied by a fleet of assistants, he and the midget drove to an open field in northern New Jersey, where they practiced with the kite for the better part of an afternoon. "As soon as I got a lot of drag on the kite," Moran remembered, "I hooked a little drop seat onto the line and the midget climbed on. The only problem was that he started to spin as soon as I got him airborne. So I made a little tail to keep him headed into the wind."

Several days later, with a dozen or so friends from the media in attendance, Moran prepared to sail his manned kite above a grassy expanse in Central Park known as the Sheep Meadow. "I had about thirty people there to help me get the thing aloft, because it was so big and heavy. The midget was all set to climb into the drop seat and take off when this big Irish cop comes by and tells me that he'll put me in jail if I persist. So I says, 'Why can't we fly him over the park? He's willing.' The cop says, 'Suppose he falls and hits a ballplayer?' Well, that was the end of that. But the reporters took the ball and ran with it anyway. We got what we were looking for: lots of ink."

Les and Mary, eager to build on the momentum of their early hits, were busy formulating a wide-ranging publicity campaign. "We got down to work as soon as they were ready, which was right away," remembered Dick Linke, who managed the couple's press and travel affairs for Capitol until 1955. "Les found a perfect foil in me. He knew I'd work my head off for Capitol—at no cost to Les Paul. But he was a joy to work with, because he just couldn't get enough of it. I never had to prod him to do anything. In fact, he played ringmaster. He snapped the whip and everybody jumped, regardless how they felt."

Consequently, in the spring of 1951, Les and Mary visited more than fifteen hundred disk dealers and deejays in less than three months. No record retailer was too small, no radio station too obscure. If they spied a lone transmitting tower shining through the desert night as they drove along the highway, they'd point their car in the direction of the dim illumination and drop in for an unscheduled visit, bearing gifts of freshly cut vinyl.

Sometimes the couple encountered deejays who seemed immune to the Paul-Ford school of charm, like the one in Philadelphia who tried to give them the brush-off when they unexpectedly turned up late one night in his studio. The disk jockey figured they'd go away if he ignored them long enough. But they simply planted themselves on the floor outside his control room until he dug up one of their disks and gave it a spin.

After a while, Les began compiling dossiers on his hosts, noting their birthdays, their favorite foods, perhaps even the names of their wives and children. Then he'd transfer the information to five-by-seven file cards so that it would be handy for return visits. He dazzled more than a few deejays and dealers with his phenomenal memory.

"I must have traveled to at least thirty cities with Les and Mary," said Linke, who went on to become a major TV producer and personal manager to the stars. "Les had an insatiable appetite for driving. It was nothing for him to drive from New York to Chicago nonstop. We did that several times, them in the front seat, me in back. He and Mary were so much in love they didn't seem to mind the long drives. But they almost had to put me away. All the hand holding and kissing was sickening. I used to tell them I was going to put a towel over my head if they didn't knock it off."

At Linke's suggestion, the duo began hosting cocktail parties for the press and other music-industry people. These affairs soon became the hottest ticket in town. "We'd bring all the sound equipment along and put on shows that knocked these guys out," said Linke. "They had never seen another artist make this kind of effort to reach out to them. You were lucky if you could get performers like Sinatra to visit the biggest deejays in town. Not Les and Mary.

No matter how big they got, they'd go anywhere, do anything to get people to buy their records."

By May 1951, "How High the Moon" was the most requested number on radio—both here and abroad. The song's sprightly rococo arrangement appealed to widely different musical tastes. In the United States it became the first single by a white act to reach the top of the rhythm and blues charts, and in England it became a consistent front-runner on British Broadcasting's weekday-afternoon radio program *Housewife's Choice*. It also sank deep into the heart of a generation of budding musicians from Eastern and Western Europe, Japan, South America, and elsewhere abroad.

"Les Paul was the first person to turn me on to the guitar," Rolling Stone Bill Wyman wrote in his autobiography forty years later. " 'How High the Moon' had terrific verve, proof at last that pop music had something more than love songs; that it could provide stylish instrumental inventiveness."

"It sounded like it came from another planet," remembered *Miami Vice* theme composer Jan Hammer, an elementary school student in Czechoslovakia when he first heard the tune in 1951.

"I was intrigued with the way Les would double his guitar and stack Mary's voice," said A&M Records cofounder and trumpet star Herb Alpert, who as a teenager spent countless hours in his own West Hollywood garage studio trying to capture Les's "New Sound."

There was, however, a cell of hard-core jazz purists who were less than enthusiastic about Les's super-slick treatment of the oft-recorded standard. "Take off your hats, gentlemen, the national anthem is no more," complained critic Jack Tracy in the April 20, 1951, issue of *Down Beat*. "All 'Moon' needed was to have a Les Paul version of it to kill it for all time. It is not for tender ears."

Others, like *Metronome*'s Barry Ulanov, lamented the sleight of overdubbing that led to Les's "downward path" to commercial success: "This isn't the kind of gimmick that dies out with one or two or even half a dozen successful records. It is not, on the other hand, a trick that can bask forever in such high esteem. That's where the musician enters and—however temporarily—the clown departs. Other gimmicks and tricks have come and gone in records and with

them their nervous operators; not so Mr. and Mrs. Paul. Les has still
got the fleetest fingers among guitarists and one of the best jazz
beats. . . . Remembering the sound of Les's V-Disks, recalling the
quality of his jazz trios, it's hard to know which to cheer more, the
success of these records, which has brought his charm and wit, extraordinary skill and beat to every jukebox in the country, or their
eventual failure, which might bring back a great soloist."

But by this stage in his career, Les regarded criticism as one of
the condiments of success. He had steeled himself against the slings
and arrows of professional reviewers, recalling the condescending
manner with which some had described the Andrews Sisters' act,
which he thought was terrific. Besides, skyrocketing record sales
clearly indicated that the public loved the music he and Mary were
making, and that was all that mattered to him at the time.

In fact, within twenty-two weeks of the release of "How High,"
he and Mary scored several more international hits—"Walkin' and
Whistlin' Blues," "Josephine," "I Wish I Had Never Seen the Sunrise," "Just One More Chance," "Whispering," and "The World Is
Waiting for the Sunrise." The couple's total record sales: four
million.

Tom Morgan, an erstwhile jazz saxophonist who began peddling
disks for Capitol in 1951, remembered: "I never had any trouble
selling Les and Mary's records. No matter where I went—record
stores, radio stations, jukebox places—everybody just wanted to
know how many copies I could get them."

To get maximum mileage out of one cut before releasing another,
Les devised an elaborate system to keep tabs on his records' weekly
Billboard chart positions. "We had immaculate timing," he later
boasted. "As soon as one disk was coming down, the other was on
its way up."

He also obsessively monitored other hit makers' progress on the
charts, which drove Dick Linke crazy: "I used to tell Les, 'Forget
Patti Page, forget Perry Como. Don't set your sights on twelve different artists—why they're doing better than you or not doing better
than you.' He was diffusing his energy, trying to man too many
different battle stations at once."

If he was, it hardly showed. The August 25, 1951, issue of *Billboard* announced that Les and Mary were the only artists in music history to simultaneously hold four spots on that publication's Best Selling Pop Singles chart, establishing a record at Capitol for consistency in hits. Incredibly, many of these cuts, as well as scores of others, were recorded in hotel rooms on Les's custom-built portable equipment, an unheard-of practice then or now. "We grind 'em out like hamburger," he proudly crowed to *Time* magazine.

Just a few weeks earlier, Les persuaded Capitol to draw up a long-term contract that included Mary Ford. After all, with the exception of "Lover," "What Is This Thing Called Love," and "Nola," the Les Paul titles that fell into the best-selling category all featured his wife's shimmering harmonies and propulsive rhythm guitar playing.

The record company, however, "was very much against signing Mary," Les later claimed. "They just wanted me to continue giving her credit as vocalist," as he had on their first eight singles together. However the announcement of the couple's joint contract in Capitol's July 1951 newsletter indicates that Les finally got his way. Before signing the agreement, though, he insisted Mary relinquish the right to use her stage name if they broke up.

Their new recording contract secure, Les and Mary soon embarked on a seemingly endless round of tours that eventually brought them to every U.S. state except Hawaii, as well as to Europe, Japan, and South America. To simulate the sound of their multiple recordings in concert, they enlisted Wally Kamin and Mary's younger sister Carol, who soon became Mrs. Kamin. Wally played string bass onstage while Carol sang backup vocals from the wings. Nearly inseparable for the next six years, the foursome bunked under the same roof and traveled to gigs in two automobiles that sagged under loads of luggage, instruments, and sound equipment—Les and Mary in a sedan, Wally and Carol in a station wagon.

"I did all the secret work," Carol later said, recalling one performance when she was hidden on a scaffold over the men's rest room in an unfinished rented hall in Olympia, Washington, where they were performing for a cerebral palsy benefit. "I could hear everything that was going on below me."

Happily, the act quickly graduated to more upscale venues. In May 1951 they broke audience attendance records at the Hotel Golden in Reno. They then moved on to the Thunderbird in Las Vegas, where they drew even larger crowds. The following month Les and Mary staged their first major showcase at San Diego's Pacific Square Ballroom. Their act, now built around a fast-paced montage of their hottest disks, retained its folksy flavor, both in appearance and in choice of material, including a Ma and Pa Kettle–like parody of "There's No Place like Home."

From the Pacific Square Ballroom stage, Les came across as a cracker-barrel philosopher, often referring to his shapely twenty-seven-year-old wife as Mom. One night a gang of Hollywood record executives, bookers, and agents came down to San Diego to see the couple's new show. "The Gestapo," Les called them. "They wanted to know why Mary and I sat down when we played," he later recalled. "I said 'Look, it makes it more intimate.' But they didn't see it."

That's not to say their act wasn't laced with some highly choreographed entertainment. Les worked out a stage bit in which he traded increasingly complicated guitar solos with Mary. The routine came as a complete surprise to the couple's fans, who had no inkling that Les's shy, velvet-throated partner was also a prodigiously gifted instrumentalist.

Les would feign bewilderment when Mary echoed his first few licks with ease. Then he'd pick out a run at breakneck speed, grinning and winking at the crowd to signal his confidence that she would fall on her face. When it became apparent that she was going to replicate his fancy finger work, though, he'd take a swipe at her strumming hand or rip the plug out of her electric guitar. "The whole thing was planned down to the last note," said Les, "but the audience loved it because it looked like it happened spontaneously."

By the middle of July, Les and Mary were primed to appear for the first time as headliners on what was left of the vaudeville circuit, theaters that now interspersed live entertainment with Hollywood feature films. In between viewings of *Showboat* at Chicago's Oriental Theater, the couple topped a bill comprising a trio of trick cyclists, a comic, and the Sherman Hayes Orchestra. They did six performances on weekdays—the first beginning at 10:30 A.M., the last at 11:30 P.M.—and eight on Saturday and Sunday.

During breaks, Les chatted with backstage guests while Mary wrote letters to her family or freshened her makeup for their next performance. Then there were the media interviews, in which Les, of course, did all the talking. He and Mary were lucky to get four hours of sleep a night. But at least they were now being richly rewarded for their unsparing work schedule, lining up dates that promised to pay between $10,000 and $18,000 a week.

Not that there weren't a few bumpy spots along the way. Uncharacteristically nervous during their Oriental Theater debut, Les turned to Mary in the midst of one performance and asked: "Think we're gonna make it, Mom?" Meanwhile, off in the wings, the stage manager playfully kissed Carol's neck, doing his best to make Mary's pretty backup singer giggle halfway through a song. Naturally the audience wondered where the disembodied voice was coming from. But Les went out of his way to conceal Carol's supporting role in the show. The way he figured it, the more mystery surrounding Les Paul and Mary Ford the better. Poor Carol never did get a chance to step out from behind the curtains to soak up some of the applause she'd had a hand in creating.

On August 9, the act left Chicago for a two-week engagement at the Capitol Theater in Washington, D.C., playing to sold-out houses every night. "It's been a long, long time since the big F Street house has teed off a new vaude bill to the jam-packed aisles the disk stars drew," *Variety* reported. "When the couple segued into their top successes like 'Mockin' Bird Hill' and 'How High,' the rafters rang with mitt action not heard here since the good old days of '43 and '44."

Later that month Les and Mary wandered into even greener pastures. "The amount of 'extra money' that hot disk artists can earn, and the sources from which the money can come, is currently being demonstrated in a highly interesting way by the Les Paul–Mary Ford team," *Billboard* reported of the couple's foray into radio advertising, reputedly the first by a big-name act. "In addition to the money being earned by the disk duo on record sales and personal appearances, manufacturers of various products are ready to swell the earnings of Mr. and Mrs. Paul by paying large sums for radio commercials, using the multiple-dubbed guitar and voice sound familiar to millions of people."

Hired in mid-August to create three one-minute jingles for Rheingold beer at $1,000 per spot, the pair waxed parodies of such well-known tunes as "There'll Be Some Changes Made," "Whispering," and "After the Ball," all of which were recorded on the run in hotel rooms. "I got a better echo by putting Mary and a mike in a bathroom," said Les.

Though none of the jingles took more than fifteen minutes to make, the beer company was well pleased with them. Deejays got such a kick out of the bouncy, multilayered jingles that they played them almost as often as the couple's hit records. Concert audiences howled for "the Rheingold song," and Capitol's sales department was flooded with calls from record dealers for the spots. Within two months, the couple was besieged with similar offers from other manufacturers, some willing to pay up to $10,000 for nationally broadcast commercials.

Eager to capitalize on Les and Mary's snowballing celebrity, Rheingold took out full-page ads in several New York City dailies to announce the couple's October 1951 debut at the Paramount, the same Times Square theater where Les had worked with the Andrews Sisters in 1946. This time he and Mary were opening for pop star Frankie Laine, the same cherub-faced singer who had auditioned in vain for a spot in Les's Hollywood trio seven years earlier. To make matters worse, Frankie was getting paid ten times more than Les and Mary combined.

"Frankie was real big at the time," Dick Linke later said. "We knew that he was going to get all the publicity if we didn't make an extra effort to get Les and Mary's name out there. So we did *every* disk jockey in the city. But because we were opening for Frankie, we promoted him real hard too. We came off smelling like a rose."

Les and Mary had no trouble filling the 3,700-seat theater with their own fans. Mary, however, was nearly overwhelmed by the thought of playing in what was still reputed to be America's premier pop music palace. She was much more at ease in intimate night-clubs, where she could wear comfortable clothes and tie back her hair with a ribbon. The idea of squeezing into a tight, frilly gown and performing in front of a New York crowd sent her into a fit of white-knuckled terror.

On opening night, halfway through their second performance, she came down with a severe case of nerves, which intensified after she saw a young woman in the front row point in her direction and say, "Look at her. Her knees are shaking like mad." Mary held herself together long enough to finish the set. Then she fell apart. Les begged her to go back out for their next show. He promised to buy her a new mink coat. But to no avail.

Finally Carol, who closely resembled her sister in visage and voice, climbed into Mary's strapless, pastel gown: "I had to stand in for her with Les for the next two appearances. It was so traumatic. I was scared to death. After I finished my performance, I didn't remember a thing about what I had done onstage."

As the week wore on, however, Mary calmed down, bolstered perhaps by the thumbs-up notices in the press: "Laine Falters but Les-Mary Pace Strong Para[mount] Bill to Whirl Finish," *Billboard* headlined its review of the show. In fact, the couple were so much more enthusiastically received than Laine that the Paramount eventually reversed the program order, insisting that the pop star open for them.

While Les's advanced studio techniques made waves within the recording world, guitar makers all over the country hotly debated the merits of manufacturing electric solid-body guitars. The controversy over who was responsible for this revolutionary instrument continues today. For years Les has shrewdly perpetuated the myth that he invented the solid-body guitar. But in the August 1991 issue of *Guitar Player* magazine, Tom Wheeler, one of the country's foremost guitar experts, outlined a more likely scenario: "No one knows for sure who invented the electric Spanish solid-body guitar. There is not even much consensus concerning the criteria establishing the event. Did it occur when someone strung up a lap steel with six strings at standard pitch? Or when someone else stuck some frets on an electric Hawaiian guitar? Besides, simultaneous development by independent builders—each with diverse inputs, resources, and influences—is more likely than a straight-line evolution traceable to a single, hallowed First One.

"The issue of who came first, while fascinating to some and historically important, sometimes obscures an essential fact: It was Leo Fender who put the solid-body on the map. . . . He first developed a process by which solid-bodies could be profitably manufactured on a large scale; thus in a very real sense it is Clarence Leo Fender who is the father of the solid-body guitar."

Indeed, traditionalists in the industry—Gibson, Gretch, Harmony, Kay—kept a wary eye on this upstart Fender. But they secretly regarded his "crudely crafted" instruments with contempt. "We didn't think it took a lot of skill to build a plank of wood that made a shrill sound," said Ted McCarty, then president of Gibson. That biting, electric sound, however, was precisely what appealed to the latest crop of young guitarists. Country-western players eagerly embraced Fender's new solid-bodies, which had longer lasting sustain and a sharper treble tone than their old hollow-body electrics. And they could boost the volume much higher without getting feedback.

Convinced by 1950 that solid-body guitars were here to stay, McCarty instructed Gibson's R&D department to get busy designing one of its own. Several months later his team of engineers turned out a viable prototype. Instead of the usual nineteen or twenty frets, it had a neck with twenty-two frets attached to a single cutaway mahogany body equipped with two single-coil P-90 pickups. The top was carved in a slightly convex shape to conform to earlier Gibson models, and to discourage knockoffs, since other manufacturers lacked the equipment to carve tops in a similar manner. The prototype was smaller than the company's typical electric hollow-body—so it wouldn't be too heavy to cart around onstage—but McCarty thought it sounded terrific.

The only thing he had to do now was figure out how to market the newfangled instrument. That's when he thought of Les Paul. Les had not only been a vociferous early proponent of amplified guitars, he also was now one of the country's most highly acclaimed players. An official endorsement from him would go a long way toward legitimizing the latest addition to Gibson's famous line of instruments, which the conservative fifty-five-year-old company was quite frankly nervous about.

In the fall of 1951, McCarty flew from Kalamazoo, Michigan, to New York to show the prototype to Les. By then the guitarist and his wife had fled to the mountains of Stroudsburg, Pennsylvania, about a hundred miles northwest of the Big Apple. Driven out of the city by bothersome neighbors and the roar of La Guardia air traffic, the couple rented a rustic two-story hunting lodge, which they shared with Wally and Carol, who continued to serve as loyal aides-de-camp both on- and offstage.

Only eight miles from Fred Waring's Delaware River resort, the hideaway belonged to erstwhile bandleader Ben Selvin. A wooden balcony hung over the living room, where Les set up a makeshift recording studio next to a baby grand once owned by former Selvin sideman Tommy Dorsey. Now, completely isolated and free of distractions, he and Mary could work unfettered from dusk till dawn. A crowing cock usually signaled the end of their recording sessions.

First McCarty met with Les's financial adviser, Phil Braunstein, in New York City. Later that day, the two men set out by car to find the remote mountain retreat. They drove for what seemed like hours through blinding rain before arriving in Stroudsburg. It was pitch-dark. After eating dinner in a hash house at the foot of the mountain, they phoned Les, who sent Wally down in the station wagon to guide the pair through the winding roads to the lodge.

After exchanging a few pleasantries with the Gibson president, Les pulled the solid-body guitar from its case and picked out a few tunes. His eyes lit up. Moments later he called his wife, who was resting upstairs, inviting her to strum a solo or two. "Mary," he said, "they're getting awfully close to us. I think we should join them."

Negotiations dragged on through the night, fueled by several pots of fresh coffee. Finally, by dawn, Les, McCarty, and Braunstein hammered out an agreement, which they celebrated with a hearty breakfast of bacon and eggs. Written on a page and a half of ordinary stationery, the renewable five-year contract stipulated that Les would receive a royalty for every solid-body instrument Gibson produced. He, in turn, was required to play only Gibson instruments in public. Failure to do so would result in the forfeiture of Gibson earnings.

At Braunstein's urging, McCarty agreed to set up a sinking fund so Les could postpone paying taxes on the Gibson royalties for at least the next five years. The government, Braunstein reasoned, was already siphoning off a hefty chunk of his client's rapidly rising income.

Regarding the design of the new Gibson solid-body, Les had only one substantial suggestion. He wanted the company to utilize a trapeze-type tailpiece with a cylindrical bar that he had recently developed: "I wanted the strings to go over the bar, so you could get that muting sound that I was well known for."

Other than that single modification, the first Les Paul guitar was entirely the creation of Gibson's R&D department. As Les tells the story, though, he was the one who persuaded the company to name the new solid-body model after him, which was an unintentional stroke of genius on his part: it ensured that he would remain a force in the music industry long after his recording career was over and ultimately immortalized him in the eyes of many young guitarists who otherwise would never have heard of him. Nearly forty years later, he wrote in the foreword of Tom Wheeler's book *American Guitars,* "I'm so identified with the Les Paul electrics that sometimes a kid'll come up and say, 'Hey, you're a real person, not a guitar.' "

By the end of 1951, Les and Mary had risen to dizzying heights. They were now appearing regularly on network TV favorites like *I've Got a Secret* and *What's My Line,* and had racked up more Top 10 hits for the year than Bing Crosby, Frank Sinatra, and the Andrews Sisters combined. Best of all, they wound up in a photo finish with Patti Page for top-selling recording artist, selling more than six million disks since the beginning of January.

Les, of course, was energized by these hard-earned triumphs. But Mary was already beginning to show signs of exhaustion, telling one Capitol staffer she was in the market for "some sort of pill that would produce a nice, logy, lazy feeling in Les." But there was no chance of that. His adrenaline was pumping so hard he would have been resistant to its effects anyway.

Chapter 17

"Vaya con Dios"

Les and Mary reportedly earned $500,000 by the end of 1951, roughly one hundred times more than they made the previous year. Though never one for conventional status symbols, Les went out and bought the longest, widest, flashiest set of wheels he could find: a gleaming two-tone-green Caddy, which told the world that he and Mary had finally arrived. But the luxurious car was also a practical choice: from now on, "Mr. and Mrs. Guitar" were going to spend most of their waking hours on the road, crisscrossing the country in an automobile stuffed with instruments and audio equipment. At least the spacious new Cadillac Fleetwood would help them do it a little more comfortably.

Then came the woodland retreat in Mahwah, New Jersey, a simple seven-room stucco house when Les bought it for $10,000 in late 1951 or early 1952. Nestled in northern Jersey's gently rolling Ramapo Mountains, the secluded haven teemed with birds, cottontails, and deer that fed on the tender shrubs and dandelion greens covering the seven-acre spread. The smell of blooming lilacs and white dogwoods filled the air, and the soothing sound of church bells echoed from the valley below.

The house was far too small to comfortably accommodate Les and Mary and Wally and Carol, who were still an integral part of the stage act. But Les had big plans for the place. With extensive renovations under way, Les and Mary hit the road. They kicked off 1952 with packed houses at Ciro's, the swank movie-colony hangout on Hollywood's Sunset Strip, then moved on to theaters and nightclubs from San Francisco to Syracuse. Their accommodations, however, were considerably better than the fleabag motels they had been forced to stay in the previous year: when they played Harrah's in Lake Tahoe, the management gave them the keys to a seven-room house and a Rolls-Royce.

In between concerts were countless promotional appearances on TV and radio and at benefits and record sales meetings. By then Les already had been voted the country's top guitarist by the readers of *Down Beat* magazine, and he and Mary had been named the most popular stars on disk by eight hundred leading deejays. It was impossible to spin your radio dial and not hear several different stations playing the couple's electrified work-over of the oldie "Tiger Rag," which was first popularized in 1918 by the Original Dixieland Jazz Band.

They returned to the New York Paramount on June 19, 1952, for a two-week engagement—this time supported by a full-size orchestra—and as the main attraction. On opening day, Les unveiled his new Gibson Les Paul, which had a single-cutaway mahogany body and neck, two Gibson-designed pickups, and a gold top with ivory-colored trim. Les boasted about the extraordinary range of special effects his handsome new solid-body was capable of producing, shamelessly exaggerating, as usual. But at least one reviewer took him at his word. Describing the Paramount show, *Variety* gushed: "The powerhouse platter team display sock stage savvy by giving the pewholders the same sound they project on records via a specially constructed guitar that gives the echo-chamber effect. . . ." Some who saw their backstage equipment, however, insisted that Les fattened his sound with prerecorded background music (which Les denies to this day).

In any case, he and Mary drew crowds wherever they went. Arriving at the Chicago Theater a few weeks later—just as the Eisenhower-Stevenson presidential race was coming to a full boil—the couple were greeted by scores of fans waving placards emblazoned with slogans like "Vote for Les Paul and Mary Ford."

Before leaving Chicago, the couple agreed to sit for one of Leonard Feather's famous musical "blindfold tests." As usual the *Down Beat* writer played ten different contemporary disks. Then it was up to Les and Mary to identify the musicians and grade them on a scale of one to five, one representing the lowest score. Surprisingly, out of a group of such well-known artists as Ella Fitzgerald, André Segovia, and Miles Davis, Les correctly named only three: Ella, Peggy Lee, and Coleman Hawkins. Among those he missed: Django Reinhardt!

"Who that is would be hard to say," Les commented after hearing Django's up-tempo "Impromptu." "If you were there in person at this particular jam session, you might get enthused. But when you listen to it cold like this, it doesn't strike me as proving an awful lot. . . . This is more an exhibition-type thing. Trying to prove something, I guess. I'd give it a two."

He also failed to identify Miles's distinctive bebop horn on "Budo," the final selection in Feather's blindfold test. While acknowledging that he was bewildered by bebop in general—"I don't get the message a lot of times"—Les added a few sage comments about Miles's disk in particular, which had been released three years earlier: "There's a place in the world for that type of music, and it's very well done. It's very progressive. I think it's great because it's going to be a stepping-stone to the future. . . . Someday we are going to find that music incorporated and it's a good thing. But I don't think I could listen to five hours of that record. I'm afraid I would become very nervous. It's nervous music. In fact these are very nervous times."

Indeed they were. Joseph McCarthy, the Republican senator from Les's home state of Wisconsin, was conducting a no-holds-barred witch-hunt for Communists in the United States, sifting through the staffs of the State Department and Voice of America as well as the stages of Hollywood and Broadway, which he considered hotbeds of Red subversion. Korean War–inflated food prices were so high that Eisenhower used them as a campaign issue. And Malcolm X, recently inducted into Elijah Muhammad's Nation of Islam, was poised to launch a career as black America's militant spokesman.

But Les and Mary floated high above the political fray. In fact, life for them had never been better. By the fall of 1952, fresh off their $18,000-a-week Chicago gig, they had racked up seven more country-wide hits since "Tiger Rag," the first song Les recorded with his new Gibson solid-body. Now it was time for them to capture an entirely new audience.

On September 3, just hours after cutting their newest disk, "I'm Sitting on Top of the World," Les and Mary made a headlong dash for Manhattan, where they boarded the *Queen Elizabeth* for a leisurely sail across the Atlantic. They were scheduled to begin a two-week engagement at London's illustrious Palladium Theater in twelve days. Neither of them had ever been abroad. In fact, Les later claimed that in the process of applying for his passport, he realized for the first time that he had been born in 1915, not 1916, as he had often told reporters.

Carol and Wally checked into tourist class while their more famous relations moved into fancier digs on the deck above. But that was fine with Mary's sister and brother-in-law. The lazy transatlantic voyage gave the newlyweds an opportunity to get out from under Les's watchful eye for the first time since he had brought them together for the stage act the previous year.

Several days later, two tugs guided the stately *Queen Elizabeth* into its rain-shrouded Southampton berth. Armed with special passes to get aboard the ocean liner, several reporters accosted Les and Mary the moment they stepped out of their cabin. Though running on a dangerously tight schedule, the couple agreed to pose for photographers and field questions from reporters on the deck above before disembarking. Swathed in her prized new mink, Mary was eager to escape the chilly early-morning drizzle. But Les, who shivered in his lightweight suit, acted as if he had all the time in the world for the press, which he usually did. "And they all told me I'd hit a blazing English summer," he joked.

"Surely you've prerecorded some of those backgrounds to solo against in concert?" one reporter boldly asked.

Les just grinned. In fact, the act was prepared to perform without any prerecorded support. The risks of mechanical failure involved in playing against multidubbed backgrounds, he explained, were too great. Besides, he and Mary were flying back to the States and couldn't possibly carry the weight of the extra equipment.

Stepping off the gangway, the couple was mobbed once more, this time by fans as well as journalists. But their British guide anxiously waved a rail schedule in the air and whisked them off to catch the next train to London. As the man herded them through the throng, Les nervously scanned the dock area for Wally, who was supposed to be overseeing the transfer of their baggage and instruments. Instead a stranger was loading the stuff onto a trolley bound for the customs office.

"But Wally . . . " Les protested, looking over his shoulder as he was hustled down the escalator to the rail station.

"Don't worry," a bystander hollered, "I'll find him and get him safely to the Savoy Hotel in plenty of time for the opening." Moments later, the good Samaritan found Les's brother-in-law being pushed along the dock in a wheelchair, bent over in pain with a mild case of food poisoning. But by then the London-bound locomotive was chugging its way north.

To make matters worse, soon after arriving at the theater, Les discovered that half of the band parts for "How High the Moon" had been lost in transit. Fortunately he had a highly competent conductor named Bob Farnon, who quickly worked up new arrangements for the horn and rhythm sections. Les liked the new charts so much that he later recruited Farnon to reorchestrate the rest of his repertoire.

With a couple of free days before the Palladium opening, Les decided to take Mary to Paris to find his hero, Django Reinhardt. Since neither of them spoke a word of French, that was not going to be an easy task. Three years earlier, Django had all but abandoned Paris, retreating to Fontainebleau, some forty miles south, where he passed his days fishing and playing billiards. But the gypsy guitarist loved to wander. He could have been anywhere between there and southern Italy.

According to Les, he and Mary began scouring likely nightclubs and buttonholing every musician who could speak English. They eventually ran across jazz violinist Stephane Grappelli, Django's former Hot Club bandmate. "I haven't seen Django in two years," Grappelli told the Americans. "You'll never find him."

"You wanna bet?" Les replied.

Now the search for his longtime idol became a crusade. It seemed like every gypsy he met claimed to be one of Django's relations. "They were all out to get your money," Les later said. In desperation he tore a couple of twenty-dollar bills in two and gave half of each bill to two gypsy cabbies who seemed to know a lot about the Reinhardt family. "You get the other half when you find Django," he promised.

Les finally found a Frenchman who led him to one of Django's real cousins, a guitarist performing at a cozy, dimly lit *boîte* called the Romance. "He sure played guitar," Les later recalled, "and I took a turn myself. But most important of all, he had Django's phone number. I knew it could not be as simple as that. Django had many things—but I was certain that a telephone was not one of them. I was right. The number belonged to a café near where Django lived."

Nevertheless, the gypsy guitarist got the message that Les was eager to see him. Next morning he rushed up to Paris, just in time to jump in a cab and ride to the airport with Les and Mary. "He was a very warm, emotional man," Les later said. "He cried his heart out because he felt nobody appreciated his music anymore. I pleaded with him to come to the States. I told him that I worshiped him and that I'd do everything I could to see that he got the recognition that he deserved."

That dream, however, would never come to pass. Django died at the age of fifty-three of a stroke eight months later, on May 16, 1953.

DJANGO WAS 43   born 1910

Les and Mary debuted at the Palladium on Monday, September 15, 1952, before the Queen and several other members of the royal family. Nearly a quarter of a century later, in the February 1975 issue of Britain's *Guitar* magazine, journalist/guitarist Ivor Mairants recalled the concert: "It was obvious that, even minus the multitracking, Les was an extremely resourceful player, using every effect his guitar was capable of producing: slurs, pull-offs, hammer-ons, pizzicato, pulled strings, and the tremolo arm."

That night Les had to be even more resourceful backstage. As he later recounted the story, he and Mary were hosting a rip-roaring celebration in their dressing room when someone knocked on the door and announced the imminent arrival of the Duke of Kent, who was a big fan of Hollywood. The unexpected news brought a surge of panic to the crowded compartment. One of the guests, a famous American actress, had apparently passed out dead drunk on the couch. With a few helping hands, Les gingerly laid her limp body on the floor of the walk-in closet, where she peacefully reposed while the duke exchanged show-business gossip with his new American friends.

At one point, the nobleman turned to Mary and exclaimed, "I sure like that noise you make." Noticing a deep furrow forming over her brow, he explained that the British commonly referred to music as noise and that the remark was intended as a compliment. Les, however, didn't need to be reassured that he and his wife were hot. With characteristic swagger he later told *Vogue* magazine that the Palladium "audience reacted like you'd poured kerosene on them."

In between concerts and public appearances, Les combed the city for audio equipment and Mary dashed off excited missives to America. A September 24 postcard to her parents showed her and Les shaking hands with a jovial-looking middle-aged gentleman, the star of the popular British TV series from which Les had culled his latest instrumental hit, "Meet Mr. Callaghan." "Just a line to let you know we're having a great time over here," Mary wrote. "Kiss all the kids for us."

When she and Les and Wally and Carol returned to the States, they settled into their new Mahwah, New Jersey, home, which was still in the midst of expansion. Les, of course, had insisted that the construction begin with a studio of his own design. He wanted it to be big enough to accommodate his ever-expanding line of recording equipment and instruments as well as a "clients' booth," editing room, a bar, and television cameras. Nearly one thousand square feet when completed, the recording facility was equipped with a noiseproof ceiling, a glass-enclosed control room, rock-wool-insulated double walls (built at odd angles to reflect sound), and garage-style doors to make equipment deliveries easier.

In one corner stood a handsome full-size jukebox, which provided more than just an atmospheric touch to the newly created studio. Les understood that many people heard his disks for the first time on a jukebox, so that's the way he wanted to hear them—before they reached the public. He also set up a radio transmitter that allowed him to listen to his freshly cut disks on his car radio. (A similar monitoring practice was later adopted by Motown's Berry Gordy, Jr.)

The tiny Mahwah retreat eventually became a monument to the "New Sound," with four state-of-the-art studios and a two-story, three-thousand-cubic-foot echo chamber carved out of an adjacent mountain. During the winter it looked like a Christmas-card picture: a sprawling snow-covered mansion of redwood, fieldstone, and stucco lit by multicolored flood lights. The inside was even more impressive. A stone fireplace the size of a walk-in closet warmed the twenty-foot-high Western-style family room, which abutted a four-hundred-square-foot oak-and-birch-paneled living room that was rarely used.

Les and Mary slept in a forty-foot-long master bedroom with a semicircular wall of windows overlooking their private woodland. But then they didn't spend too much time in that part of the house. When they weren't tooling around the country in their fin-tailed Caddy, they were working in the studio, usually from midnight to four or five in the morning. Les preferred those sleepy hours because there was much less chance of extraneous noises turning up on the recordings, either man-made or natural. "But," he once said only half jokingly, "if it's a bird with a dainty trill, I leave him in the record. Maybe I'll get credit for another new sound."

He set up an intercom system and scattered tape recorders and connecting microphones throughout the house. As the story goes,

Mary could cut vocal tracks in the studio with her husband, or in the kitchen by herself. Les thought that was so clever that he often invited newspaper and magazine photographers to shoot her in front of the sink in a frilly apron, singing into a microphone as she washed dishes. But friends thought his constant effort to merge his personal and professional life was beginning to border on obsession.

"Les was driven by his own force, but I'd say it was a self-destructive one," said Dick Linke, the couple's Capitol publicist. "There was no separation between his work and pleasure. He'd brag about staying up eighteen hours a day, every day, and he expected everyone to keep up with him. He'd record all night, then call me the next day and say, 'Wait till you hear the new mix, Dick!' If I heard that once, I heard it a million times."

The problem was, Mary simply didn't have the constitution to withstand this physically punishing regime. A steady diet of high-calorie, low-nutrition food—frequently the only kind available to those on the road—didn't help either. Mary's parents expressed concern about her health in a letter to Carol around the end of 1952, to which Carol replied: "As I probably told you, Mary is taking iron and liver and B1 pills and she looks wonderful now, so please don't worry."

Unfortunately, when dietary supplements failed to keep Mary's energy from waning, she began reaching for something else: vodka. Les later claimed that Mary had an alcohol problem from the day they met, that she always had a bottle hidden somewhere in the dressing room or the house. "She had to have it to stand up and fight," he said. But her family and friends insist that the drinking came later, with the pressures of success.

Mary eventually came to rely on the bottle, which further sapped her strength. Les, however, could consume copious amounts of beer without ever slowing down. He often bragged about how he could work for days without going to bed, and Mary backed up that claim, telling her sister Esther that he sometimes needed sedatives to fall asleep.

Les's urge to dominate everything and everyone around him naturally extended to the couple's finances. Although he and Mary both had worked extraordinarily hard to achieve success, he exercised sole control over their bank account. While freely dipping into their now considerable fortune for studio equipment—by July 1953 the tab surpassed $60,000—he was maddeningly tightfisted about everything else. Former Gibson president Ted McCarty said, "He was tighter than the bark on a tree."

There was, of course, no household help. Carol and Mary handled all of the daily chores and secretarial duties, while Wally served as audio engineer, driver, and all-round handyman. It wouldn't have been so bad if Les's idea of economy had been confined to tearing paper napkins in half and buying toilet paper by the case. But Mary had to beg for money to get her hair done or to buy clothes for the act, which drove the couple's personal manager mad. "Mel [Shauer] thought they should pay more attention to their stage presentation, but Les always fought him," said Mary's older sister Esther.

Accordingly, Carol sometimes skimmed a few bucks off the top of the grocery budget for Mary's threadbare wardrobe. Once, while cleaning the house, Carol discovered a wad of cash that Les had taped beneath a piece of furniture. When she was sure he had forgotten all about the hidden booty, she insisted that Mary go out and buy a new dress, which Mary then said was on loan from Carol.

Despite the mounting stresses and strains in their private life, though, Les and Mary still found pleasure in the waves of adulation that washed over them in public. When they appeared in Hollywood's Christmas parade in December 1952, they happily waved to fans from the top of Capitol's three-tier float, which featured three other artists on the label: Bozo the Clown, comedian Yogi "Yingle Bells" Yorgesson, and singer Dottie O'Brien.

Capitol salesman Tom Morgan, who had done scores of in-store promotions with the guy who normally played Bozo, was forced to fill in that day for the ailing actor. "I felt pretty foolish, running around the float and doing Bozo's routine," recalled Morgan. "Les and Mary didn't pay much attention to me, but then what do you say to a clown? But Les invited me to visit with them a couple of days later. He was a pretty smart guy. He knew I was a salesman and therefore very important to his career."

In the first six months of 1953, Les and Mary turned out five more big hits, including "Bye, Bye, Blues," "Sleep," and "I'm Sitting on Top of the World." Like most of their Capitol songs, these were old, reliable standards. "Sleep," for instance, had been Fred Waring's theme for decades, and "I'm Sitting on Top of the World" had been a 1926 smash for Al Jolson. Nonetheless Les's high-tech modern arrangements of the tunes made them appealing to a broad age range. Referring to "I'm Sitting on Top of the World," he explained, "The older people enjoy their memories of the song, and since the fifteen-year-olds weren't born when the song came out, they react to it as a new tune. So we reach both ends of the listening audience simultaneously."

Apparently so. According to *Variety,* "I'm Sitting On Top of the World" was the husband-and-wife team's thirteenth *consecutive* release to sell well over 500,000 copies, making them one of the country's most successful recording duos—and reinforcing Les's place in history as a guitarist. "I was fourteen or fifteen when I first heard Les Paul on 'How High the Moon' and 'The World Is Waiting for the Sunrise,'" British rock guitarist Jimmy Page recalled more than thirty years later. "What he was doing on those hits couldn't have failed to influence any guitarist."

By then the couple had become so confident of their status in the recording industry that they allowed labelmate Stan Freberg, a popular satirist, to parody one of their 1951 hits. While Freberg's wacky version of "The World Is Waiting for the Sunrise" didn't come close to the couple's runaway best-seller, it did make it to the No. 23 spot on *Billboard*'s pop chart.

One day in the spring of 1953 the couple stumbled across the song that would eventually become the biggest seller of their entire career. Wrapping up an extended Midwestern tour, they had just appeared at an auto show in St. Paul, Minnesota, and were more than ready to return to New Jersey. Settling into their hotel room for the night, Mary pulled out a sewing kit and sat on the bed to mend one of her stage dresses, while Les turned on the radio and began to pack. Suddenly he heard Anita O'Day charging through an up-tempo arrangement of "Vaya con Dios," a Latin-flavored number the jazz singer had cut for Mercury the previous year. As Les recounts, he dove for the radio and turned up the sound.

"Mary, how do you like that song?" he asked.

"I love it," she replied, "but I don't know what it is."

It happened to be a tune that one of their colleagues at Capitol had recently suggested they record. Les immediately called the station to ask where he could get a copy of the disk. When deejay Merle Edwards realized it was Les, he invited the guitarist to come by the studio to pick up one there. As soon as Les got back to Jersey, he called California and informed Capitol executive Hal Cooke that he and Mary intended to cut "Vaya" for immediate release, although he intended to make their version much slower and simpler than Anita's.

"Did you ever hear of it?" Les asked.

There was a long silence at the other end of the phone.

"We published it," answered Cooke, who wasn't exactly thrilled by Les's sudden impulse to leapfrog over the planned release of his single "I'm a Fool to Care." First of all, Anita O'Day, a singer of considerable skill, had proved that "Vaya con Dios" failed to set the record-buying public on fire. Secondly, Capitol had already pressed half a million copies of "I'm a Fool to Care," and that's what the sales department was geared up to promote.

"Sit on it," Les insisted, now emboldened by his highly publicized winning streak.

Backed by a lively bounce called "Johnny (Is the Boy for Me)," "Vaya con Dios" landed in the record bins on June 1, 1953. However, according to Les, a number of deejays across the country preferred the snappy, upbeat melody of "Johnny" to the plaintive sound of the ballad. "I told my manager we had to fly to seven cities right away to get the disk jockeys to play the other side. He says, 'Are you crazy, trying to knock off your own hit?' But I convinced him it had to be done. One by one we got the disk jockeys to turn over the record. You can't believe how glad I am that they did. 'Vaya con Dios' was the one that put us over the top."

Seductively sung by Mary, the song zoomed to No. 1 and remained on the charts for nearly three months, quickly bringing the
couple's worldwide records sales up to fifteen million. "Vaya" became
so pervasive on radio and in jukebox joints that when Capitol salesman Tom Morgan asked dealers how they wanted their disks
shipped, they typically quipped, "Via con Dios."

Critics praised the ballad's unadorned simplicity. "Les Paul and
Mary Ford have come up with a radical departure from their usual
type of record," reported *Billboard,* "and the result is No. 14 in their
string of consecutive hits.... The subtle combination of voice and
background fully capture the tender sentiment of the song." Three
months later Bing Crosby paid the couple the ultimate compliment
by recording his own arrangement of the tune.

Around this time, Les and Mary's "Bye, Bye Blues" album won
Audio Engineering magazine's Best Popular Novelty Award. Later,
Les was invited to speak before the prestigious Audio Engineering
Society, an audience that included some of the best brains in the
television, recording, and radio industries. "I'm never afraid when I
have a guitar in my hand," he later said, "but to have to get up and
give a speech in front of all these bald-headed inventors that I had
admired for so long mortified me." But of course Les, irresistibly
funny when in performance mode, had the starchy crowd in stitches
within moments of mounting the stage.

Now at the apex of their career, Les and Mary finally crossed over
to TV. In the fall of 1953, they signed a $2 million, three-year con-
tract with the makers of Listerine to host their own daily show.
Slated to begin shooting in their New Jersey home on October 1,
1953, *The Les Paul and Mary Ford Show* was really just a five-
minute commercial. However, it marked another first in Les's career. *Variety* noted that "the deal was the first in which big-name
talent had been signed for this type of saturation campaign, representing a new approach to video film and program advertising."

The program was the recording industry's answer to radio's *Ozzie
and Harriet,* intended to offer a flawless picture of wholesome living

and family values. In truth, Les and Mary's personal life had already begun to unravel. Despite a tremendously overburdened schedule, Les continued to book more work, while Mary begged for some time to let down. They hadn't had a vacation since they started performing together in 1949. And there was no respite in sight, especially now that they had to turn out three dozen Listerine segments in less than fifteen weeks. The tension became intolerable. Mary had willingly relinquished control of her life to Les to advance their careers. But after the first blush of success, their conflicting agendas emerged more clearly. Mary began to resent her husband's dominance, secretly referring to him as Simon Legree, the cruel slave owner in *Uncle Tom's Cabin.*

"Mary was exhausted by all those three-day drives between L.A. and New York. She was too frail for that pace," said Dick Linke. "But Les couldn't get enough of it. He'd try to break his own record, like a racecar driver. As it was, Mary didn't like performing because she always got so nervous. But she was in love with Les, so she'd do anything he said. I used to say, 'Les, you have incredible success now. You can pick and choose jobs. You'd better lay off Mary or she's gonna snap. She's like a walking time bomb.' But Les would say, 'She's used to it. She loves it.' And I'd say, 'How do you know?' and he'd say, 'Just trust me.' But I don't know another woman you could have pushed that way."

Wally and Carol also were tiring of their supporting roles in the Les Paul show. "Sometimes," said Carol, "he'd walk into the kitchen while me and Mary and Wally were having a good time talking and he'd say, 'What is this, a ball park?' He didn't mean to be mean. He was just all German, all work. That's the way he grew up."

Other times he was just plain unpredictable, taking off without explanation at four or five in the morning and staying away for a couple of days. Eventually, said Carol, Les and Mary and she and Wally agreed to have Friday night meetings to air out grievances, but to no avail. Toward the end of the summer of 1953, Carol and Wally decided to pack their bags and move back to California. Their planned departure plunged Mary into a state of turmoil. To her, family meant everything, unlike Les, who preferred to maintain a chilly distance from just about everybody. Mary's chances of maintaining her emotional equilibrium were slim without the sheltering love of her sister Carol.

Nevertheless, she regained her composure in time to begin filming the Listerine show. John Mack, a young English sound engineer from New York's Fordell Films, came down to Mahwah to help pull together the first thirty-five programs. His job entailed editing dozens of Les and Mary's hits to fit the show's five-minute format. (Contrary to Les's later claims, the songs were lip-synched, not recorded live.) There was so much to do in so little time that Mack temporarily moved into the couple's home, bunking in a bedroom above the studio. There he remained for three months. Like everyone else, he had to adapt to Les's nocturnal schedule, filming and editing almost around the clock. They never took time out for dinner; they simply ate while they worked.

But Mack was so enamored of Les Paul that he didn't care. "I was flabbergasted when I got the job because he and Mary were *really* big stars. I had my own recording studio in London when I heard 'Lover' for the first time. I never dreamed there was so much technical trickery involved. I thought Les could really play that fast. Consequently I was completely daunted by the task of editing his tapes, and he was truly horrified by some of my edits. I invented a whipping boy, a rubber frog named McAllister. Every time I made a mistake I'd hit the frog and say, 'I'm sorry, McAllister blew it.' Other times when I made a mistake, Les or Mary would look at me and ask, "Is McAllister messing up again? And I'd say, 'No, it was me that time.'

"I had a lot more academic training in engineering than Les, so we'd pick each other's brains. But he could always ferret out what he needed to know to get the job done. And his ears! He had an unbelievable capacity to hear distortion that no one else could pick up. Sometimes there'd be a loose connection and he'd be the only one to notice. We'd tear the system apart and find out that he was right. He'd put on this country-bumpkin cover and introduce himself as Roddy Potts when he ran into people who came on too technical. But I found him terrifying because he had an intellect so far ahead of mine."

The Les Paul and Mary Ford Show premiered on network TV on October 12, 1953, and was edited for radio a few weeks later. These "five-minute musical films," as *Variety* called them, were closer to commerce than art. The couple had just enough time to do one or two tunes and two Listerine commercials—and those were sandwiched between other commercials. Nevertheless, five days a week, Les got to strum the gleaming gold six-string that bore his name on national television, which made him an even more powerful force in promoting the instrument.

A month after the program debuted, *Metronome*'s George Simon wrote: "What Benny Goodman did for the clarinet, Harry James for the trumpet, Tommy Dorsey for the trombone and Coleman Hawkins did for the tenor sax, Les Paul has done for the guitar. He has brought it into such prominence that it has become an almost newly discovered instrument for many people, as well as one with which musicians can make more sound, and more money than ever before."

Meanwhile, Mary continued to prod her husband to slacken their work schedule. She loved recording. She simply had grown tired of viewing life through the windshield of a car. The issue became moot in April 1954, two months before her thirtieth birthday: Mary discovered she was pregnant. She had showered other people's children with affection for years. Now she eagerly awaited the arrival of one of her own. She'd have to wait until July before she could call off the endless nightclub and disk-jockey stints.

But Les made sure "she didn't stagnate." Indeed, he and Mary were working on a new recording in their Mahwah studio the day their baby girl was born. She arrived on November 26, Thanksgiving Day, at Valley Hospital in Ridgewood, New Jersey. Lamentably, she was a month premature, and like many preemies she suffered acute respiratory distress. Two days later the five-pound infant was placed in a portable incubator and rushed by ambulance to St. Vincent's Hospital in Manhattan, where she underwent a futile operation to correct her breathing difficulty.

Initially, the surgery appeared to have given the baby some relief, so her death at one-fifteen the following morning was a shock. Mary, however, was the last to know. According to a statement by the couple's press agent in the early edition of the November 30 *New York Post,* Mary was still at Valley Hospital and "would not be told of the baby's death until later today." Through some grotesque lapse in communication, though, Perry Como, who had often featured the husband-and-wife team on his network TV show, inadvertently broke the horrific news to Mary when he called the hospital to express his sympathy.

Too distraught to attend the funeral service at a nearby Nazarene church, Mary never laid eyes on her newborn child. "She cried on the couch for days," said her sister Carol, who had returned to live with Les and Mary earlier that year. "The baby's death destroyed her."

It also delivered the first in a series of devastating blows to Les and Mary's career.

Chapter 18

ROCK AND ROLL IS HERE TO STAY

In no shape to resume the rigors of touring, the couple left for Europe around the middle of December. Mary needed a complete change of scenery to soften the aftershock of the baby's death. But rest and relaxation were the last thing on her husband's mind. Finding the notion of taking a vacation entirely foreign, Les scoured the continent for new instruments and recording gear, dragging his grief-stricken wife from one factory to another.

The first stop was Spain, where he searched for an acoustic guitar. Then he and Mary moved on to Switzerland, Germany, Holland, and Sweden to shop for microphones and other audio equipment, scouting for new songs along the way. "The fact is," Les told *Melody Maker*'s Paris correspondent at the time, "the best recording equipment is really a combination of the products of several countries."

Les and Mary faced far more intractable problems when they returned to the States in early 1955. Rock and roll had put down roots like some unruly jungle creeper, first in the wildly exuberant music of Cab Calloway and Louis Jordan and later in the earthy sounds of blues stalwarts like Big Joe Turner, who introduced the rock classic "Shake, Rattle and Roll" in August 1954. The early-fifties charts had been governed by wholesome, white performers like Doris Day, Teresa Brewer, Perry Como, and, of course, Les Paul and Mary Ford. Sweetly melodic and above all inoffensive, pop music was tailored to reflect the taste of a growing white middle class, which was enjoying the fruits of postwar prosperity.

But behind the calm facade, dark fears and ugly undercurrents troubled the nation. Federal anti-segregation legislation set the white South against the black South, spawning racially motivated lynchings, church bombings, and assassinations. At the same time, Joseph McCarthy's unremitting campaign against the "Reds" destroyed the lives of hundreds, perhaps thousands, of innocent Americans.

While their parents sat home watching McCarthy's nationally televised hearings, American youngsters were lining up at theaters across the country to see *The Wild One,* a Marlon Brando movie about a motorcycle gang that terrorizes a small town. "What are you rebelling against?" one of the townspeople asked Brando. "What've you got?" he replied.

The following year, *Blackboard Jungle* and *Rebel Without a Cause* discharged even more potent volleys in Hollywood's first round of anti-establishment films. Rebellious young voices were raised in the publishing world as well. In the fall of 1955, a San Francisco–based beat poet named Allen Ginsberg burst forth with the *Howl* heard round the world, galvanizing an underground movement on the West Coast, while the *Village Voice,* one of the country's first alternative newspapers, was being launched on the East Coast.

Radio spread the gospel of dissent far more quickly than all the other media combined. Bored with the numbingly sentimental pop fare of the musical mainstream, teenagers began tuning in to radio stations that featured a more exciting sound: rhythm and blues.

Alan Freed, a white deejay who was particularly partial to black harmony groups, began playing R&B on his Cleveland, Ohio, radio station as early as 1951, using the term "rock and roll" to hide the music's black origins. Other disk jockeys gradually followed Freed's

lead. The next year, a small-time country-and-western band from Chester, Pennsylvania, hit the ground running with a curious mixture of R&B and country swing. Bill Haley and the Comets attracted enthusiastic crowds up and down the East Coast throughout the early 1950s. Then, in early 1954, after cutting three relatively successful disks for the Essex label, Haley was signed by Decca. He proceeded to turn out a string of hits, including a cover of Joe Turner's newly released "Shake, Rattle and Roll" and a foot-stomping, hip-rolling single called "Rock Around the Clock."

Though "Rock Around the Clock" climbed to the No. 23 spot on the charts by the end of May 1954, nobody could have predicted the pop-culture upheaval that would follow ten months later, when Haley's self-penned rocker played behind the movie credits of *Blackboard Jungle,* a melodrama about slum-hardened high school kids. In one memorable scene, an embattled teacher tries to reach out to the rowdies in his class by spinning some of his cherished jazz records. But they mock him and his music, smashing the disks to bits.

The symbolic rejection of traditional values was not lost on *Blackboard*'s youthful viewers, most of whom sat through repeated showings of the movie. The moment they heard Haley's "Rock Around the Clock" on the soundtrack, many stood on their cushioned seats and danced; others ripped the chairs from their bolts and hurled them across the theater.

The adolescent frenzy cut across class boundaries. After the movie played in Princeton one night, a mob of rowdy university students went on a post-midnight rampage through the streets of the upper-crust town, leaving broken windows and burning trash cans in their wake. The dean was summoned from his bed to lead his unruly charges back to their Ivy League roost.

Alive with stinging, electrified guitar runs and a biting back beat, "Rock Around the Clock" was not only the biggest hit of the year, it jolted an entire generation into a new orbit. Raggedy guitar bands popped up all over the country, and they all dreamed of becoming overnight stars and making a fortune like Haley.

Anyone could cut and press five thousand disks for as little as $1,200. Consequently, hundreds of small mom-and-pop recording

operations sprang up from coast to coast to meet the demand. While
the major labels looked upon this youthful racket with contempt
and prayed for its quick demise, these new little companies were
busy changing the face of American popular music.

By the end of 1955, more than half of *Billboard*'s Top 30 were
either R&B records or covers or R&B material. The following year
Sam Phillips's Memphis-based Sun label struck gold with Elvis Presley; the Chicago Chess brothers turned Chuck Berry and Bo Diddley
loose, and New Orleans launched Fats Domino and Little Richard.
The rock revolution brought a whole new dimension to stage performances as well, with its crazy costumes, wild haircuts, and un-
intelligible "leerics."

Les had managed to shift into pop music after the bebop players
overtook jazz, but rock and roll left him stranded. He understood
the appeal of bobby-soxer sweethearts like Connie Francis and Bobby
Darin, but he was completely baffled by the rising wave of rock-and-
roll stars. In place of talent, he complained to one Boston deejay,
"they have nothing but a streak of luck. At the end of a recording
session the engineer says, 'We have to redo it 'cause it still sounds
human.' "

"People like me and Crosby were confused," he later explained,
"because everything we had learned was just thrown out the window.
The music world had taken a different shape and I didn't know what
to do about it."

He had no intention of quietly slipping into obscurity, though.
Lester Polfuss had grown up with the sound of applause in his ears.
He needed it to breathe. "Mickey Mantle can bash five hundred balls
over the fence," he once said, "but it doesn't mean anything if the
crowd's not there to cheer him on." It was the same with Les: without an audience, he didn't exist. He and Mary still had their own
five-minute TV and radio show, but they no longer could depend on
getting the kind of radio saturation they had enjoyed in previous
years. Teenagers were expropriating the airwaves, abetted by program directors who compiled playlists based on the charts. Therefore
Les felt that personal appearances were now more important than
ever.

Although still emotionally fragile, Mary agreed to do a fresh round of radio-station visits in the summer of 1955 to promote their newest release, "Hummingbird," a medium-tempo tune that cleverly counterpointed her lazy, country-inflected vocals with Les's mechanically sped-up guitar picking. Boston was one of the most important markets in the country to crack. The town was packed with record-hungry college students and deejays who had built sterling reputations on their ability to pick hits. If Joe Smith, Bob Clayton, Ed Penny, or Norm Prescott got behind a new disk, it was destined for Hitsville.

Consequently, recording artists of every description scrambled for the privilege of appearing on Boston radio. The station waiting rooms often looked like Grand Central, crammed with record-company salesmen, performers, and independent promotion men (who were just beginning to carve a niche for themselves in the music business). Rumors of widespread payola only heightened the competitive tension.

Capitol salesman Tom Morgan had just been transferred from L.A. to Boston a few weeks before Les and Mary's arrival. Still unfamiliar with his new territory, he wasn't sure how to drive to some of the local stations outside the city. Nevertheless, he set aside all the work he had planned for other Capitol artists and blocked out two full days to personally shuttle the couple around town. They were two of the most unpleasant days of his life.

"I got the company station wagon and met Les and Mary at the airport," Morgan later recalled. "I had appointments set up with all the major disk jockeys, but in between, when we didn't have appointments, I thought we could catch some of the smaller stations. I knew Les was very aggressive and that he'd want to catch those little guys, too. Mary was the sweetest little thing. She seemed so delicate. I remember trying to be extra warm toward her because she seemed like this fragile little bird. Like if you weren't careful, you'd crush her. But Les was a very tough guy. He was critical of me from the start because I didn't know the Boston area better."

A heated argument broke out between the two men after Morgan got lost looking for a radio station north of the city. There was nothing on either side of the road but acres of marshland. Les accused the salesman of bluffing his way through the job and threatened to report him to his Capitol bosses back on the West Coast. With that, Morgan angrily offered to turn the car over to Les, saying he'd find his own way home.

Unable to endure the bickering for one more instant, Mary finally intervened. But by then she'd had enough of both men. She told Morgan to drive her back to the Statler Hotel before going on to the last scheduled stop of the day: WORL in downtown Boston. "We got to the station early," Morgan remembers, "so we went to a little bar and had a beer. We weren't too happy with each other, though. Here I was a Capitol Records manager and him a big star and we wouldn't pay for each other's beer."

Ironically, the electric guitar that Les had done so much to popularize was becoming the instrument of his professional doom. The rock revolution, detonated by the raw-edged, guitar-based sounds of Bill Haley, Chuck Berry, and Bo Diddley, was inexorably altering popular music for all time. Les and Mary's sweet sound and down-home stage patter were simply too quaint for modern tastes. "Hummingbird," which climbed to the No. 7 spot on *Billboard* charts by July 1955, was their last big-selling single, despite continuing TV and radio appearances nationwide on their Listerine shows and on *Standby with Bob and Ray*.

Les and Mary both started showing serious signs of strain. He was becoming increasingly nervous and moody, especially during recording sessions, and Mary piled on extra pounds. While he held court for visitors, regaling them with Crosby and Andrews Sisters stories, she silently remained in the background. One day in the mid-1950s, Capitol A&R men Voyle Gilmore and Dave Dexter dropped by the couple's isolated Mahwah home. Les, said Dexter, flipped into performer mode as soon as he and Gilmore walked through the door. "Watch this dog!" Les exclaimed, as he poured a full bottle of beer over the shiny parquet floor in the family room. "He's magical."

"The dog came running over and lapped up all the beer," remembered Dexter. "Les laughed and slapped his thighs and said, 'Isn't that great?' But Mary never said a word. She just watched from a corner and rolled her eyes." Other times she withdrew entirely. Les claims she eventually began holing up in their bedroom, sometimes for days at a time. One night he tried to get her to come down to the studio long enough to record "Allegheny Moon." When all else failed, he threatened to give the song to Patti Page, Mary's biggest competitor. "You do that," snapped Mary.

Esther Williams later described her younger sister's behavior as passive resistance. "Les promised Mary she could retire from the road when she turned thirty. He said nobody would want to see her then anyway. So she turns thirty and puts on forty pounds. I think she was trying to make it a self-fulfilling prophecy. She didn't care how she looked."

Les was beside himself. He brought his wife to one doctor after another, trying to recover the sweet, malleable girl who "would have stood on her head for me." The truth is, Mary was already lost to him—and he to her. But neither of them was ready to acknowledge that the pall cast over their fading career had also enveloped their marriage, which was based on going up the ladder of fame, not coming down. The situation hardly improved when Mary tried to lose weight, first with reducing shots—from which she contracted hepatitis—then with diet pills. Her moods grew more volatile and unpredictable.

No matter how hard she resisted, though, Les always managed to drag her back out on the road, sometimes with disastrous results. In February 1956, the husband-and-wife team played at the Moulin Rouge on Sunset Boulevard. A gang of Les's old Hollywood friends, including Art Partridge and Vern Carson, showed up on opening night. "When they walked out on stage," said Art's wife, Holdie, "they looked like poor people. Mary's outfit was embarrassing. She was wearing this tight satin dress that was years out of date and too tight because she had gained so much weight. Everybody in the audience was kind of shocked by the way they looked. We were embarrassed because hardly anybody clapped.

The engagement was canceled after the third day. Les was very upset."

Two months later he and Mary returned to Los Angeles to celebrate the opening of Capitol's now-famous circular thirteen-story building on Vine Street, just half a block north of Hollywood Boulevard. It was fitting that Les and Mary attend the party at the Beverly Hills home of Capitol boss Glen Wallichs. Their multimillion-selling hits had helped build his company's flashy new headquarters, which had been designed to look like a towering stack of disks.

"If you think we're a Cinderella story," Mary said that night, "then Capitol has been our palace." Nevertheless, rumors of the couple's departure from the label for Columbia had been swirling through the industry for some time. Asked by a reporter that evening if there was any truth to the story, Mary offered little more than artful evasion: "Whatever we do in business has nothing to do with our personal friendship."

Les and Mary's plummeting record sales did little to quell the rumors. "In all my time in the music business—and it's been more than five decades—Les Paul fell faster than any other artist I can remember," said Dave Dexter. "For a few years, everything Les and Mary did was a smash hit, but all of a sudden it just stopped. Voyle Gilmore would issue the records that Les wanted out there, but nobody bought them. It was just as abrupt and inexplicable as anything that ever happened in the music business. It didn't just taper off, the way it did with Crosby and hundreds of other artists, it just absolutely stopped. Everybody started running around Capitol asking, 'Why aren't Les's records moving?'

"Of course, that was when rock-and-roll mania began, although we didn't realize it at the time. We had no idea that Presley was going to be as big as he was. We were all big-band people. We eventually hired a couple of young producers who went out and signed all this junk, hoping to get Capitol in on this craze, but nothing really worked until we got the Beatles."

Les's commercial prospects as a recording artist waning, he returned with a vengeance to his other preoccupation: electronics. He'd always had a hand in the making of his records. During the

1940s he had built his own disk-cutting lathe to create miraculously crisp overdubbed instrumentals. By 1950 he had figured out how to cut even cleaner multigenerational recordings on tape with a single modified Ampex. Later he used two off-the-shelf Ampexes to achieve the same effect, bouncing sound from machine to machine.

One day in 1954, though, while taking a break from filming the Listerine TV show, he came up with a better idea. What would happen if he electronically stacked eight of these recording units? If it worked, he could cut several separate parts on discrete tracks with absolutely no loss of sound quality. It would be like having eight tape recorders in one.

After Westrex rejected the idea, Les commissioned Ampex's Special Products Division to build a prototype. The West Coast–based manufacturer had already developed multitrack taping for instrumentation data recording. These seven-channel machines were used by the military to simultaneously record the various physical phenomena of, say, an airplane in flight. Channel one recorded wing vibration, channel two airspeed, channel three skin temperature, channel four engine RPM, and so forth.

Making the leap from multitrack data recording to multigenerational music was a little more complicated. First of all, the Ampex engineers had to devise a means by which the record head would act as both a record and playback head (later known as Sel-Sync), thus enabling Les to listen to one track while simultaneously recording on another—without even a fraction-of-a-second time delay. Then Les had to hire additional engineers to design and build a mixing board to accommodate the eight-channel recorder. "You never saw such a nightmare in your life," he later said. "I sat around my dining-room table with Ampex's top engineers and we mapped out all the problems and licked them one by one. I'm sure many ulcers came out of that first machine."

By the summer of 1957, the Ampex custom Model 300-8, or "the Octopus," as Les called it, was fully operational. With this sophisticated equipment at his command, he became a space-age sculptor of sound, capable of laying down up to eight different tracks, which then could be individually reverberated, multiplied, filtered, equalized—or rerecorded if necessary. But others in the industry were slow to see the virtues of this technological leap. Fellow musicians viewed multipletrack recording with alarm. "We saw its potential to put players out of work," said veteran studio musician Don Butterfield. Record company executives, on the other hand, thought it was too costly. "They didn't want to go to the expense of retraining their entire engineering staff to work wih this untested device," said Mitch Miller, then head of Columbia's pop division. "Besides, why did you need it if you had fine artists and stereo tape that you could edit if you wanted to take out a phrase? No one was looking to correct one note. The studios were not ready, at that price, to take the eight-track on as a minor tool."

Former Atlantic recording chief Tom Dowd thought otherwise. Up till 1957 he had been using a two-track Magnecorder to produce the likes of Ray Charles, the Drifters, and Big Joe Turner. If he wanted to overdub, he had to bounce between two machines, or even trickier, two tracks. But tape noise made that method of recording undesirable. Dowd generally recorded the work of each artist from beginning to end three or four times, then, like other producers, sat down with a razor blade and splicing tape to perform small miracles of plastic surgery, patching together the best performances. But, he adds, "I could only cut at the beginning or end of a phrase where no one would notice the splice. It was very hit-or-miss."

As soon as the young engineer heard about Les's new eight-channel recorder, he knew he had to have one. Persuading Ahmet and Neshui Ertegun—the Turkish brothers who owned Atlantic—to drop nearly $11,000 for the revolutionary machine was another story. "They looked at me like I was crazy," Dowd remembers. "But after I told them we would be able to deploy the sound of a whole band over five or six tracks, with a couple of tracks to spare if we wanted to change anything or add something later, their eyes bugged out."

By the end of 1957 Dowd had his own Model 300-8, the third off the line at Ampex (Les and a French film company got the first two). "Now, after everyone went home," he said, "I could go over two or three takes of each song and say, 'This solo is great, but I gotta mix down the rhythm track to make sure they match.' All of a sudden, I was sending the office acetates of rough mixes two hours after the session."

Engineers from other recording studios often visited Atlantic to watch Dowd work his multitrack magic. But they didn't routinely begin using the eight-track until the mid-1960s, nearly a decade after the one Les commissioned. Then they quickly graduated to machines capable of handling scores of tracks.

Meanwhile Les continued to create new electronic toys. Sometime around 1956 he devised a remote-control gadget for his guitar that would allow him to manipulate the taped accompaniment he used during performances. He mounted the little black box below the tailpiece of his guitar and called it the Les Paulveriser, though he had used that name as early as 1949 to obliquely describe the tape system itself.

As Les recounts it, an invitation to perform at the Eisenhower White House gave him the first opportunity to test the remote device before a live audience. But then he had to bring along an engineer to oversee the eight hundred pounds of audio equipment it hooked up with backstage.

"My God, you're not going to take all that stuff down there, are you?" Mary fretted.

"That's just what I'm going to do," Les answered.

"Well, you'll do it without me."

"You mean you're going to turn down the President of the United States?"

As usual, Mary gave in. The only time she and Les nearly lost their cool was when Vice President Nixon needled them to ask Mamie if she had any requests. The prerecorded accompaniment dictated the order of their songs. They worried that the First Lady would ask for something outside their repertoire. By sheer luck, she selected "Vaya con Dios," the next song on the tape.

Les later used the "Paulveriser" to play even more elaborate tricks on his audience, calling forth Bing Crosby's disembodied voice for a round of playful conversation, or to accompany Mary on a chorus or two of "It's Been a Long, Long Time." While some critics were delighted by the novelty, others greeted it with derision. "Les Paul, Mary Ford, and eight hundred pounds of tape equipment are currently at the Fairmont's Venetian Room," wrote one San Francisco reviewer. "With the couple 'mugging' many tunes, we're moved to wonder why they don't just play the tapes and be done with it."

Les and Mary produced their last mildly successful record for Capitol in December 1956. "Cinco Robles," a Spanish-flavored waltz, reached No. 35 on the *Billboard* charts before dying. But the rest of their disks for the label were greeted with indifference. Oddly enough, Les laid part of the blame for their failure on his own creation: the eight-track. Back in the old days he and Mary were forced to pour every ounce of concentration into their recording sessions, because one mistake could cost hours of additional work. With this state-of-the-art overdubbing method, though, they could keep redoing individual parts until they got them right, which he ultimately felt destroyed creative tension.

In fact, by the time the eight-channel recorder was up and running, Les and Mary's music was already outdated by the gritty sounds of Elvis, Chuck, and Little Richard. Berry Gordy, Jr. had already launched Motown, and Buddy Holly's Peggy Sue was a household name. According to Les, Capitol wanted him and Mary to take a stab at producing more rock-oriented material. But he "felt that was the wrong way to go, that we'd certainly lose the audience we already had. So we gracefully went our own way."

Their last single for the label, released in February 1958, included a sorrowful ballad called "Small Island." Its lyrics offered a heartsick appeal to a lost lover, but they could have been addressed to Les and Mary's shrinking audience.

Chapter 19

MR. AND MRS. GUITAR
GO SOLO

On July 7, 1958, after interviewing the couple on his CBS radio show on the arts, Columbia A&R man Mitch Miller signed Les and Mary to a two-and-a-half-year recording contract. Les found a kindred spirit in Miller, who regarded rock and roll with the same degree of contempt as he did. Four months earlier, Miller had given a thunderous speech to the First Annual Popular Disk Jockey Convention at Kansas City's Muehlebach Hotel. His address began on a civil note, but quickly descended into a fiery tirade in which he accused the deejays of subverting American popular music. Industry insiders called it Miller's Gettysburg Address.

"Gathered under this roof," the record company executive intoned, "are a great many men of fantastic skill, taste, and imagination. You caused radio to jump out of bed and click its heels a few years back, while the public was dressing for a funeral. You made radio once again a vital force on the American scene, a source of first-rate entertainment, and—best of all—you made it pay.

"But what's been happening in the last year or two? To say that many of you have grossly mishandled this great, fat money maker, radio, would be understating the case. . . . You carefully built yourselves into the monarchs of radio and then you went and abdicated—abdicated your programming to the corner record shop, to the eight-to-fourteen-year-olds, to the pre-shave crowd that makes up twelve percent of the country's population and zero percent of its buying power, once you eliminate ponytail ribbons, popsicles, and peanut brittle.

"The kids write the records, perform them, and pick the ones you play," he continued. "I've got an idea. How about sub-teenage disk jockeys, salesmen, and station managers? Then you can all take time off for a well-deserved rest."

Some deejays apparently agreed with Miller's dire assessment of the industry, posting a copy of his speech on their studio bulletin boards for all to heed. Others were outraged. "My records got banned on a lot of stations because I told the deejays they were pandering to twelve-year-olds," Miller later claimed. "I didn't say they shouldn't feature rock and roll. My argument was that they were only playing one line on the musical spectrum. I proved that people were still interested in hearing other kinds of music when I came up with the sing-along albums, which were every bit the antithesis of rock and roll. We sold twenty-two million copies."

Miller hoped he could do the same for the recordings of Les Paul and Mary Ford. He believed Les's groundbreaking work with the electric guitar and in the studio made him a visionary. Like the executives at Capitol, he gave the musician total control over his own product: "Les just handed over the masters and we put them out. He created his own sound, which was impossible to imitate."

One new artist at Capitol, however, came reasonably close. Sitting in their kitchen one evening in 1959, Les and Mary heard a multi-layered guitar record on the radio. "Listen to that, Mary," Les sniffed. "Everyone is copying me." He became even more annoyed when he heard the name of the artist: it was Mary's youngest brother, Bob Summers. An avid Les Paul follower since childhood, Bob had begun noodling on Mary's old Martin at the age of eight. He cherished the recordings his famous brother-in-law left behind in the Curson Avenue garage. "I just lived and breathed Les's music," said Bob. "It was hard to duplicate his sound on record because you had to have a guitar, a studio, and the right kind of equipment. But I had all three, and I worked at it day and night."

Les and Mary released their first single for Columbia on July 28, 1958, just three weeks after signing with the label. "Put a Ring on My Finger" was a perky little number Mary could have performed on Gene Autry's *Melody Ranch* radio show a decade earlier. The echo-laden flip side, "Fantasy," had more of a rock feel than anything they had done together in the past, but not enough to attract younger listeners. The most noteworthy thing the disk earned the couple was a trip to Manhattan District Attorney Frank Hogan's office.

On December 4, 1959, Hogan questioned Les and Mary and three other recording artists, including Bobby Darin, about their appearances on radio programs hosted by disk jockey Alan Freed, who recently had been fired from two New York City stations for allegedly accepting bribes to promote selected records. Les and Mary had turned up on the deejay's show the previous year to beat the drum for "Put a Ring on My Finger." At the D.A.'s office, though, Les insisted he and Mary were paid union scale for the engagement and had never given a dime to Freed or any other deejay.

During this period the couple led a relatively quiet life. They remained strangers to their neighbors, but made a lot of friends at the Mahwah police department, especially after volunteering to perform for several policemen's balls. In the summer of 1958, they played for the boys in blue at a little roadhouse on Route 17 in Ramsey, New Jersey. Guitarist Bucky Pizzarelli was among the four hundred or so people who crammed into tiny Club 17 to see "Mr. and Mrs. Guitar" perform.

Unfettered by the "Paulveriser" and other electronic gimmickry, Les handled his instrument with the same matchless grace and zest that had caught Bucky's ear seventeen years earlier, when Bucky used to run home from school to listen to the guitarist on Ben Bernie's Chicago-based radio show. Mary's facility with the six-string, however, completely took Bucky by surprise: "She was supposed to be doing these little throwaway bits, just filler, but she was playing brilliantly."

Toward the end of the evening, Les invited Bucky to sit in for a couple of tunes and apparently liked what he heard. A few days later, he invited the younger guitarist to his Mahwah studio to play rhythm on a recording he was producing for a husband and wife harmonica duo called the Mulcays. Les often encouraged musicians to drop by the house for impromptu recording sessions, especially if he thought their playing had spirit. That was his idea of fun.

Mary derived greater pleasure from family life. Now approaching thirty-four, she was more determined than ever to have a child of her own. In April of 1958, after repeated attempts at pregnancy failed—and after lobbying her husband for months—she and Les assumed custody of a week-old baby girl, whom they named Colleen, like the infant daughter they had lost four years earlier. Then, on October 7, 1959, much to everyone's surprise, Mary gave birth to a son, Robert.

Mary managed to persuade Les to cut down on bookings while both children were still infants. But after getting a two-year extension on their Columbia contract in February 1961, the couple returned to a full touring schedule, traveling up to thirty-six weeks a year. Once one of the most highly paid acts in the country, they now played smaller venues—everywhere from New York's Latin Quarter and Chicago's Edgewater Beach Hotel to Milwaukee's Holiday House. Then there were the Army base tours, which took them from the far-flung corners of Alaska to West Germany.

During the summer they became regulars on the state fair circuit, which was anything but glamorous. They usually dressed in trailers next to the stage. Once they fled in the middle of a performance, after Les's sound system knocked out two of the fairground's main speakers. "It was our crowd," he told a New York columnist. "We could do no wrong. But after those speakers blew I was left standing in the middle of an outdoor stage with this dead hunk of guitar in my hands. What did I do? I had the audience rise and sing 'The Star Spangled Banner.' While they were singing, we ran out the back."

Les's weekly performances at Fat Tuesday's in New York City resurrected his career *(left)*. Since debuting there in March 1984, he has attracted legions of devoted fans, including such rock stars as Steve Miller *(below, facing camera)*; Billy Idol *(below, left)*, and Rick Derringer *(bottom)*.

Mary Alice Shaughnessy

Mary Alice Shaughnessy

Leo Manolis

Mary Alice Shaughnessy

Jazz man George Benson *(left at center, with photographer Leo Manolis)* has traded solos with Les at Carnegie Hall—and at Fat Tuesday's. In 1988 the Russian rock group Stas Namin *(below)* presented Les with a balalaika at the club, where the guitarist often signs autographs at the bar *(bottom).*

*I*n April 1988 Les presented Paul McCartney with a left-handed Les Paul Custom guitar. Author Mary Alice Shaughnessy was there to record the event.

David McGough

*L*es met Beatles' producer George Martin in 1988, when the guitarist was inducted into *Mix* magazine's Technical Excellence and Creativity Awards Hall of Fame.

Mary Alice Shaughnessy

*T*ony Bennett *(left)* dropped by the Hard Rock Cafe to croon a tune for Les's seventy-second birthday party in June 1987, which attracted dozens of other stars, including English rock guitarists Jeff Beck and Jimmy Page *(center)*, and jazzman Al Dimeola *(bottom, far left)*, who sat in for a few tunes with Les and Jimmy.

Nick Elgar/London Features

Nick Elgar/London Features

Nick Elgar/London Features

𝒯n 1988 Les was inducted into the Rock and Roll Hall of Fame, along with the Beatles, the Beach Boys, the Drifters, the Rolling Stones, the Supremes, and Berry Gordon. Les accepted his award from Jeff Beck *(left)* and Atlantic Records chief Ahmet Ertegun *(far left)*, who proclaimed, "Without Les, it is hard to imagine how rock and roll would be played today."

Robin Platzer

𝑅ockin' the rafters at the Rock and Roll Hall of Fame's traditional end-of-the-evening jam session, Les bellied up to the front line with *(from left)* Jeff Beck, Dave Edmunds, George Harrison (standing in front of Mick Jagger), and Bob Dylan.

Robin Platzer

𝒯n the mid 1960s Les recorded an unreleased instrumental version of Paul Simon's "The Sounds of Silence." The pair met two decades later at the Rock and Roll Hall of Fame.

Robin Platzer

On August 18, 1988, Cinemax Sessions filmed *Les Paul: He Changed the Music*, an all-star tribute to the guitarist featuring a diverse roster of stars, including Eddie Van Halen *(above)*; B. B. King *(below)*, Waylon Jennings and his wife, Jessi Colter *(opposite, top)*; and Rita Coolidge *(opposite, center)*. Jon Bon Jovi showed up for the postproduction bash *(opposite, bottom)*.

Mary Alice Shaughnessy

Robin Platzer

Mary Alice Shaughnessy

𝓛es Paul's version of the joy of cooking

Courtesy of Richard Lieberson

By Les's own admission, the relentless demands of touring were harder on his wife than on him: "Lots of times we'd have a six-A.M. radio show. I could walk into the station with my hair standing straight up on end and the deejay would say, 'I look a mess when I get up in the morning, too.' But he'd turn to Mary and tell her she looked like Miss Prune. That meant she had to get up at four-thirty in the morning to put on her makeup and get her clothes together, so she wouldn't go to bed."

Not that she didn't complain. Mary felt increasingly torn by the burden of being the beautiful, perfectly coiffed songstress the public demanded and the attentive mother Colleen and Bobby needed. They had millions in the bank and in real estate holdings, she argued. Why did they have to leave their children in the hands of a governess seven or eight months a year? As always, Les put his professional life above his family. Performing was his aphrodisiac. He did it for love, he told her, not for money.

According to Mary's sister Carol, Les often reminded his wife that people paid to see him, not her. But his behavior suggests he was afraid he'd fail without Mary: he was reluctant to put together a solo act or start a group of his own. Mary, on the other hand, was apparently worried he'd run around with other women. At least that's what he told her he'd do if she forced him to work by himself: "I said, 'You know damn well I will. I'm not about to sit in a hotel room and think about it. I'm gonna go out and have a ball.' "

As a compromise, they sometimes brought the children with them, converting the backseat of their big white fin-tailed Caddy into a portable nursery. Colleen, who went along more often than her infant brother, relished these road adventures. The preschooler got to play with all sorts of farm animals at the county fairs and to eat as much Howard Johnson's pumpkin pie as she could hold. And people fussed over her, telling her she looked like Shirley Temple. At night, as her parents drove from one engagement to another, she gazed at the stars from her tiny, padded berth beneath the Caddy's rear window. Later she slept on the floor behind the front seat, using the bump in the middle of the floor as a pillow. When she tired of traveling, her parents put her on a plane to New Jersey, where their manager, Gray Gordon, met her at the airport.

In the meantime Les maintained contact with his two oldest sons, Rusty and Gene, who periodically lived with him and Mary. In the fall of 1961, shortly after recording an album for Columbia with Gene, Les began incorporating the seventeen-year-old boy into the act. "Father and Son" was never released, but the aspiring drummer performed with Les and Mary on numerous occasions over the next two years. He even posed for publicity shots with them. Though the same age when he made his debut on the road as Les had been, Gene was much shier than his extroverted father. Some even described him as withdrawn. To give Gene a reprieve from the adult world, Les's longtime friend Peg Ray always invited other teenagers to her Arizona home when the threesome passed through town. "He seemed lost, not close to his dad, not close to Mary. He was just there," remembers Mary Vinger, whose father, Harold, often invited the family to bunk at his Wisconsin farm.

In fact, life was difficult for all three of them. "Mary was just so goddam tired all the time," said Harold Vinger. "She was fading fast." The strain was showing on Les as well. In October 1961, he and Mary returned to Waukesha to perform for the opening of the newly built Catholic Memorial High School gymnasium, where they shared the stage with an archer, a judo team, and a dog act. After the show, the couple met several of Les's boyhood chums at the Club 400, his brother Ralph's tavern. Cullen Casey regaled Mary for an hour or so with tales of her husband's youthful exploits, which she drank in with fascination. But when she tried to bring Les into the conversation, he stormed off in a huff, casting a shadow over the rest of the evening.

The couple frequently stopped for layovers in Kalamazoo, Michigan, Gibson's headquarters until moving to Nashville in August 1975. Mary and Colleen always stayed at Gibson president Ted McCarty's home with his wife, Ellie, while Les spent hours on end at the guitar factory. "When he walked through the door, you were on Les Paul time," recalls Wilbur Marker, Gibson's former quality-control director. "He was a nut on string action and insisted on trying every conceivable string gauge. He'd say, 'Try this, try that.

It will only take a minute.' Those were his famous last words. But you stayed until his stuff was done, no matter how long it took."

More often than not, the taskmaster rewarded Gibson's twelve hundred employees with a private recital. Ted McCarty tried to persuade Mary to come down to the factory to sing a few songs, but she'd always refuse, preferring to remain at his home with Ellie and Colleen. The respite never lasted long, though. Late one night the two couples were chatting in McCarty's living room when Les suddenly jumped up and announced that it was time to go. "What do you mean, 'Time to go'?" the Gibson president asked. "It's nearly midnight. You can't be thinking of driving back to Jersey now."

"Oh sure," Les answered. "We'll be there by morning."

McCarty was alarmed not only by the lateness of the hour, but also by the condition of Les's tires, which as usual were nearly bald. "He thought they were good enough until they blew out," said McCarty, whose concern for the family's safety was heightened by his awareness of Les's propensity for driving at top speed. Unable to persuade the guitarist to stay till morning to buy a new set of tires, McCarty called a friend who owned a nearby tire store and talked him into selling Les four new Generals right then and there. Within an hour or so, the Paul family was hurtling over the darkened interstate toward New Jersey.

Mary longed to move back to California to be near her family again, an idea Les consistently rejected. So she was thrilled when her sister Carol came to New Jersey for a visit in August 1961. But the reunion failed to disperse the clouds looming over the Paul/Ford household. "Les was his usual ornery self," Mary wrote her parents a few days after Carol left. "I was miserable the whole time and still am for that matter. I just don't understand him at all."

Every time she and Les appeared on Jack Paar's *Tonight Show,* though, they acted as if they were still smitten with each other. The NBC-TV host was so captivated by the couple that he invited them on his late-night talk show several times a year during the early 1960s. He loved Les's outrageous tales almost as much as

Mary, who laughed long and hard at each telling, no matter how often she had heard them. "You know what you two are?" Paar asked the couple on the show one night, "You're nice, old-fashioned, homey, kind of vaudeville folks, the kind you don't see anymore."

Les, of course, did most of the talking, reciting stories that continue to crop up in his act today. One night he recounted the time he and Mary checked into an Atlantic City hotel under the name Mr. and Mrs. Lester Polfuss to avoid being detected by fans: "About an hour later the phone rings and the fella says, 'Is this Les Polfuss?' I say yes, and he says, 'Can I speak to Mary Fordus?'" The crowd laughed uproariously. Problem was, Les repeated the same story on another Paar broadcast, except the setting was Brazil.

One night in January 1962, Mary unexpectedly took the floor: "We had our twelfth anniversary on December 29th, and a friend of ours sent us a dozen roses. His card said, 'One rose for each miserable year.'" The remark, which elicited a collective gasp from the studio audience, was meant to be a joke, but it was read differently by those close to the couple, except Paar.

Paar invited Les and Mary to his home the following Christmas, then celebrated New Year's Eve with them in Mahwah a few days later. Fascinated by their topsy-turvy life-style, he showed his TV audience a video clip of the couple's two-year-old son, Bobby, togged out in a diaper and yellow cowboy hat, drumming on a set of pots and pans in the kitchen well past midnight. "Les and Mary record until three in the morning, then sit around and eat popcorn," he told the viewers.

Shortly thereafter, in January 1963, the couple left the States for a two-week engagement in West Germany. Mary sent her family a postcard that indicated she had recovered some of her early enthusiasm for performing: "We're having a ball, but working very hard," she wrote. "I have a lot to tell you when I get home."

Indeed, something certainly was brewing in the Paul/Ford household. The following month, the couple put their sprawling Mahwah mansion on the market for $149,000. They distributed an elaborate four-page flier with nine interior and exterior shots of the seven-acre wooded retreat. But more significantly, they also offered Les's recording equipment for separate purchase.

Nobody knew why they were abandoning their home of eleven years—or where they were going. Les simply told the *Bergen Record* that he and Mary planned to spend "considerable time making personal appearances." Though they failed to sell the house, they did go back out on the road. After performing in Cocoa Beach, Florida, in February, they returned to New York for a March 1 appearance on Jack Paar's new variety show, then left seventeen days later for a string of engagements out West and in Alaska.

Everything seemed fine to their friends back East when they returned in June—which is why their separation came as such a shock. Bucky Pizzarelli had been with the couple just a few days earlier, when they dropped into the Little Ferry, New Jersey, nightclub where he was working with his jazz trio. Les often sat in on Bucky's gigs, but that night he and Mary remained quietly seated at the bar.

During a break, Bucky persuaded them to attend a big bash the next day at his mother's Paterson, New Jersey, home. He promised that lots of other musicians would be there, including a couple of Les's favorites, Bucky's banjo-playing uncles. After the guests stuffed themselves on spaghetti, chicken, and homemade Italian cheesecake, Bucky invited the musicians in the crowd to jam. Les borrowed Bucky's classical guitar and Mary happily strummed away on a ukelele.

"It was a wild day, a lot of fun," remembers Bucky. "Les and Mary took home a big package of food, and my wife made plans to get our kids together the next time. It seemed like a day or so later we read in the paper that Les and Mary split up. We didn't have a clue before that. My mother called me and said, 'What's going on?'"

In fact, Mary had been trying to break out of the marriage for the past year. One night several months earlier, after she and Les had a violent fight in a Chicago hotel room, she managed to slip away from her sleeping husband and fly to L.A. But he persuaded her to return within a few weeks. Later he threatened to take the children away and leave her penniless, as if she had no legitimate claim to the millions they had earned together. Finally, not even those admonishments could hold her. On June 19, 1963, Mary fled their Mahwah home with little more than the clothes on her back, leaving the children behind. The next day she called her oldest sister from the Los Angeles airport.

"When Mary got off that plane," remembered Esther, "she looked at me and said, 'Esther, I don't know who I am anymore.' She wanted attention, not the kind she was getting onstage as Mary Ford. She wanted personal attention, as a woman. She was still little Colleen underneath."

Mary temporarily moved into Esther's El Monte, California, home, where Les plied her with late-night phone calls that sometimes lasted till dawn. How could the only woman he ever really loved do this to him? Hadn't he made her a star? Hadn't he given her a luxurious home? But none of the usual arguments worked. On July 9, Mary filed for a legal separation, charging Les with cruelty and failure to support her. Shortly thereafter, a Los Angeles County Superior Court judge awarded her a $5,000 monthly alimony payment, pending the outcome of the trial.

Bitterly hurt, Les struck back at Mary with a ferocity that stunned even her. On October 30, after having his wife tailed for weeks by private detectives, he slapped her with an ugly countersuit, accusing her of being a drunk, a negligent mother, a deserter, and an adultress. He named two Los Angeles men as her lovers—Foy Willing, the cowboy crooner with whom she had had a brief fling twenty years earlier, and Donald Hatfield, a childhood sweetheart.

Though he later dropped the adultery and desertion charges, Les claimed in court that Mary had caused him "shame, anguish and humiliation" since 1956. Turning to their professional life, he said she "constantly made arrangements for tours and performances and then canceled out at the last minute or became so intoxicated or hysterical that she could not perform." All of this "malicious conduct," he added, including her charges of physical abuse, "practically ruined his health." He asked for a dissolution of their marriage and custody of the children.

During the next fourteen months, sordid details of Les and Mary's divorce case cropped up in newspapers on both coasts, stripping the couple of the wholesome, down-home image that had taken years to cultivate. In the meantime, they each tried to launch independent careers. One of the first people Mary contacted after returning to the West Coast was Dick Linke, who by then had gotten out of the record business and into personal management. "Mary was lost," he recalled. "She didn't know what to do, where to go, or how to get started. One day she called and asked me to drive out to her sister's house. The place was full of kids, so we went to a little tavern down the road where we could talk. She wanted me to manage her. I told her I didn't think that was a good idea because I was friends with Les. When we got back to her sister's house, I told her I thought we were being followed from the time I arrived. She said, 'Oh, don't worry about him. He's just one of Les's guys.' "

Mary eventually turned to Foy Willing, despite objections from her family, who thought the former cowboy crooner was out to make a fast buck off Mary. Foy talked her into creating a knockoff of the Les Paul/Mary Ford act with her brother Bob, complete with taped accompaniment. The pair recorded a promotional record for the Ford Motor Company—a reprise of Les and Mary's hit disks—and eventually expanded their stage act to include Mary's younger sisters, Carol and Eva, as backup vocalists, and Eva's husband, Red Wooton, on upright bass. The family act enjoyed successful engagements at several nightclubs in Reno and Hollywood and even gleaned a favorable review from Walter Winchell. But Mary called it quits after Bob tired of being a Les Paul stand-in and soon thereafter abandoned the entertainment world forever.

Bereft of her home, her belongings, and, worst of all, her children, Mary was sucked deeper and deeper into a vicious circle of depression and alcoholism. One day Esther looked her square in the eye and said, "Mary, *you are killing yourself.*"

So? Mary replied.

Nobody could reach her.

On December 19, 1964, a few days after a New Jersey Superior Court judge granted Les an uncontested divorce on grounds of extreme cruelty, Mary told a *San Gabriel Valley Tribune* reporter, "What I mainly want now is to get my children back and spend the time with them I never could when Les and I were traveling thirty-six weeks a year."

The show, of course, had to go on—with or without Mary.

With numerous bookings well into the next year, Les found himself in an untenable position. The children's German-speaking governess, Marie Neuenhaus, could continue to replace Mary at home. But finding someone to replace her onstage was a daunting prospect.

Les eventually discovered an unemployed actress who lacked Mary's musical talent, but had much more sex appeal. Joi Lansing was a robust twenty-five-year-old blonde who emulated Marilyn Monroe and Jayne Mansfield. A product of the MGM school of talent, she proudly publicized her voluptuous measurements (39-23-35), but later wished she had not: "Being blond and curvy was kind of a mixed blessing. I was always known as the glamour girl and categorized only as that. It was very limiting and I was held back by my image."

But that image is what gave the fledgling actress her first big break in show business. After spotting her in Los Angeles in the mid-1950s, a writer for *Love That Bob* created a special part for her on the prime-time TV show. For the next five years, Joi portrayed a coquettish model named Shirley Swanson. The program was a hare-brained sitcom, but it eventually helped Lansing launch a respectable career in movies and on the stage.

In the interim she found herself on the road with Les Paul. Though Joi had a pleasant enough voice, she was no match for Mary Ford. Les only brought her onstage long enough to warble through a few of his and Mary's more popular ditties. Predictably, "Tiger Rag," with its "Here, kitty, kitty; here, pussy, pussy" vocal refrain, was a staple of the new act.

"Joi was never intended to replace Mary," Les later remarked. "Nobody could ever do that. I could have added a guy, or a dog. I just thought I needed variety."

His mother thought he needed his head examined. Evelyn met the come-hither blonde when the pair stopped at her Waukesha home on their way to an engagement at Wisconsin's Jackson County Fair. "My mother almost fell over when she saw Joi," Les later remarked. "She gasped." His new partner drew even more stunned reactions at the fairground. Les's old friend Harold Vinger helped book the date, and Harold's son, Donald, gladly offered to shuttle Joi between the hotel and the venue. "You should have seen the Lutheran Ladies' Auxiliary, behind their little cookie stand, when they got an eyeful of Joi," Donald remembered. "She definitely did *not* look like a local. She had this long, flowing blond hair and she was wearing a white sheath dress the likes of which had never been seen in puritanical Jackson County. It looked like she found a dress that fit just right, then asked for one two sizes smaller. After she sang, all these young guys came up for her autograph. She leaned over the stage and had cleavage clear to her navel. They're still talking about it today."

According to Les, Joi lasted about a year. Then he found a tall, dark-haired singer named Arlene Carrol, whom he claims to have discovered in a Newark, New Jersey, nightclub called Chez Charles. By then his son Gene was a regular part of the act, which featured an hour-long set of his old hits, as well as tricks with the Paulveriser. The trio played in the Grand Heights NCO Club in Tokyo in June 1965. "In one of their funniest bits," reported *Stars and Stripes,* "Arlene opens her mouth to sing and out comes Bing Crosby's voice."

In a peculiar twist of fate, Les ran into the man who decades before had taught him a tune called "Lover" and set him on the road to stardom. Joe Wolverton had been cheering up homesick GIs in the Far East for the past three years. Indeed, after countless nightclub appearances all over the world and a few stints in the movies, the bamboo-thin minstrel had found a home away from home on America's far-flung military bases in the Pacific. Now here he was in Japan, face to face with the scrawny little redheaded picker he'd plucked thirty-three years earlier from the backwater of Waukesha, Wisconsin. "When I went to Les's hotel," Joe recalls, "he greeted me with a six-pack of beer and a big basket of apples, in honor of the Ozark Apple Knockers."

Later that night, Joe attended Les's show at the Grand Heights NCO Club. In the middle of his set, Les invited his former mentor onstage for a jam, introducing him as the man who "taught me how to play guitar." If it hadn't been for their thinning hair and careworn faces, the impromptu moment would have resembled a scene from the stage of the St. Louis radio station where the pair performed live shows in the early 1930s, with corny one-liners flying and Joe grumbling about "the kid" who slathered his violin chin rest with glue.

For the first time in years, Les relinquished his center-stage position, strumming a few simple chords while Joe ripped through chorus after chorus on lead guitar and banjo. For one brief moment, Les had come full circle. The Tokyo tour was the last of his long career. When he returned to the States, he swore he'd never perform again. "They're playing angry music," he said sadly. "They don't want to hear me anymore."

Chapter 20

LYING LOW
IN JERSEY

The Beatles, the Byrds, the Rolling Stones were now the country's top-selling disk acts. The British Invasion brought an insistently darker tone to the beat-driven sound of the 1960s. The Stones' "Get Off of My Cloud" and the Animals' "We Gotta Get Out of This Place" were positively menacing compared to the up-beat standards that launched Les Paul and Mary Ford into orbit during the 1950s.

Nevertheless, in February 1966, the veteran guitarist took another stab at recording. He cut two solo sides for Columbia, a remake of his own "How High the Moon," and an instrumental version of Simon and Garfunkel's smash of the previous year "The Sounds of Silence." Neither disk was ever released. But Les wasn't ready to drop out of the music world altogether. The way he looked at it, he had one hell of an ear and a state-of-the-art recording facility that could easily compete with the best commercial studios in New York City. He intended to put both to good use.

By then, Phil Spector had become one of the most sought-after producers in the country with his "Wall of Sound," which featured densely layered instrumental arrangements and a myriad of special studio effects. Les Paul was determined to create the "Mahwah

255

Sound." All he had to do was pick the acts, get them down on tape, and wait for the recording contracts to start rolling in.

In a June 1966 interview publicizing his intention to become a talent scout, Les said: "Friends in the business have told me you've got to go to Nashville or Chicago or the West Coast to find new talent. But I think it's right here in our own backyard, in Hackensack and Garfield and Ridgewood. There's no great shortage of talent in this country. In fact there's more than ever. But it needs discovering and developing. We need vocalists, songwriters, and musicians who can do rock and roll, country-western, and jazz."

Consequently, he began haunting little backwater joints along New Jersey's Route 46, places like the Choo-Choo Club in Garfield and the Club Allegro in Lodi, where he claims to have spotted the Young Rascals and Jimi Hendrix respectively. Though he didn't quite understand the appeal of Hendrix's searing six-string, he could see that the young crowd at the Allegro did. "The people really seemed to dig it," he told his son Russ later that night. However, by the time Les returned to the club to approach Hendrix, the wild-haired southpaw had moved on.

The truth is, he wouldn't have known what to do with Hendrix if he had signed him. When it came to hard rock, the fifty-one-year-old guitarist was truly out of his element. He still had an uncanny instinct for predicting changing public tastes in the decades to come, though, as evidenced in June 1966 by his assessment of American pop: "I think we'll see a change to a softer rock-and-roll sound, leaning more toward good music, and an increasing popularity of country-western and rhythm and blues."

In early 1967 he stumbled across Stan Melton, a handsome Ridgewood, New Jersey, nightclub crooner with whom he had more in common. In fact, Les was so certain he'd found a hitmaker in the blond, blue-eyed baritone that he brought in three dozen instrumentalists and a vocal chorus to accompany Melton on "Born Free" and on another inspirational ballad, "One Hand, One World." Les also made determined attempts to launch a solo career for Thumbs Carllile, Roger Miller's nimble-fingered guitarist. But all such efforts met with failure, a condition Les was becoming increasingly familiar with for the first time in his life.

Attempting to recreate the spirit of his youthful past, he often hosted raucous jam sessions that lasted till dawn. He supplied the popcorn, and his guests usually brought the beer. One day in 1966 he invited his old Chicago friend guitarist George Barnes to his home to meet Roger Miller. "Roger didn't show up," George's wife, Evelyn, remembered, "but we stayed till five in the morning. Les and George and a few other musicians jammed the entire time and we drank what seems like ten thousand beers. I can still hear all those cans going 'Pffft, pffft.' "

The party was finally broken up by the Mahwah police, who came in response to a distress call from the Barneses' twelve-year-old daughter. Alexandra was home alone in her parents' midtown Manhattan apartment, anxiously awaiting their return. Remembering the terror she had experienced on several occasions as a passenger in the backseat of Les's old Cadillac, she became fearful that her mother and father were lying dead in a ditch somewhere off rural Route 202. "It wasn't that Les was reckless," Alexandra said. "It's just that his driving would have been better suited to the Indy 500."

Les, of course, was always the center of attention during these get-togethers. When he tired of strumming, he'd dip into his repertoire of stories about Bing, Judy, or Rudy. The only person he refused to discuss was Mary. "The divorce really tore him up," said longtime friend Wayne Wright, who played with singing star Peggy Lee and trumpeter Ruby Braff before forming a trio with Les in the early 1980s. "It took him years to get over it. But he was an awfully strong guy. He loved to philosophize. He'd get into all these deep conversations, talk as long as you could stand to listen. He made it pretty hard to leave. I'd start heading for the door at three in the morning, and he'd run to the kitchen to make some more popcorn, which was one of his delay tactics."

Those with the audacity to nod off during one of Les's post-midnight monologues suffered the consequences. Bob Swartz, an audio engineer who spent several months as a guest at Les's house, abruptly awoke one night to find his right foot burning hot, the remnants of blackened matches poking out from the sole of his boot. Swartz leaped out of the chair, ran into a nearby bathroom, and plunged his smoking foot into the toilet. On another occasion, Wayne Wright fell asleep after downing his share of a case of beer he had split with Les and George Barnes during a late-night recording session. He woke up an hour or so later, his face covered with shaving cream.

Though Les had waged a bruising battle against Mary to win custody of Bobby and Colleen, there was in fact little room in his life for two young children. (Mary's sisters, Carol and Esther, both believed he hoped to use the children as a bargaining chip during the divorce proceedings.) He continued to sleep during the day so he could work or play with his cronies at night. "Sometimes we'd get to wake him up with the intercom," Colleen remembered years later. "I'd push a button to talk to him and he could talk back to me."

For the most part, Marie Neuenhaus, the middle-aged German governess who had been with the family for years, looked after Colleen and Bobby, dressing them in the morning and overseeing their prayers (in German) at night. If she visited her relatives on weekends, she took the children along. Back in Mahwah, recalled Colleen, she whipped up delicious dinners. She always served them on the counter that divided the kitchenette from the den, a large, oak-paneled room with two expansive walls of windows overlooking a steep tree-covered slope. A balcony overhung the twenty-foot-high room, which filled with eerie shadows on moonlit nights, the stuff of children's nightmares.

Late one evening, after everyone else had fallen asleep, Colleen got out of bed to use the bathroom. As she crept along the darkened balcony which led to her bedroom, she thought she saw a figure dart across the den below. Frozen with fear, she remained pressed against the wall until daybreak, afraid to call out for help—or tell anyone of the episode the next day. Barely eight years old, she already sensed she was on her own.

But there were also some happy times at the Ramapo Mountain mansion. Colleen and Bobby took great pride in polishing the cymbals on the drum set in their father's studio, where they put on little skits for him and Marie. During the warmer months, Les occasionally took the children fishing and sometimes pitched a tent in the yard so Colleen could invite her friends over for outdoor pajama parties. He even encouraged his daughter to profit from his bad habits. "Dad used to cuss up a storm," Colleen recalls. "Every time he said a swear word, I got a quarter to put in the little swear box he gave me. I must have emptied that box three times a day."

During Christmas holidays, the governess set up an elaborate Nativity scene in the family-room fireplace, which was nearly tall enough for a child to stand in, and Les laid down track for an electric train that ran around the tree. One snowy Christmas Eve, he sat the children down in front of the floor-to-ceiling windows in his darkened bedroom and instructed them to watch for a surprise in the front yard: "You stay here and don't move until I tell you. Santa will be coming up the driveway soon, because it's too slippery for him to bring his reindeer up the hill." A few moments later, Colleen and Bobby heard the tinkle of sleigh bells and saw a plump, red-suited figure lumber across the white-powdered lawn and slip into the house. A wall of presents awaited them. Later that week, they celebrated the holiday with their mother in a nearby motel room, gathering around a tiny tabletop tree with artificial needles.

To this day, Colleen doesn't know why she and Bobby were abruptly shipped off to California in the summer of 1967 to live with Mary and her fourth husband, Don Hatfield. "I didn't think we were leaving forever," she said. "I just thought it was a vacation." The realization that the California sojourn was permanent was even more traumatic: "Whenever I got upset, I'd find something I had from back East—like the lace socks I wore for Holy Communion—and I'd cry into them."

She and Bobby eventually adapted to the bustling home life they found out West, where they now had four stepsisters. Except for an occasional benefit, their mother had put show business behind her for good, although she sometimes sat in at the nightclub where her sister Esther played organ. For a while, the family closeness Mary had craved for so many years was finally hers. There were potluck dinners with her brothers and sisters during the holidays and all-night poker games with them on weekend nights. Colleen remembers falling asleep to the sound of laughter.

Shortly after sending the children out West, Les traveled to Los Angeles himself. There he found Wally, who had been divorced by Carol years earlier, and the pair tore up the town. As Les later told the story, one night they visited a brothel deep in the hills north of Hollywood Boulevard. While Les disappeared with a young woman into a room above, Wally remained in the kitchen guzzling vodka and brooding over his loneliness.

The following morning, Les found Wally stretched out on the floor, his eyes fixed in a frighteningly lifeless gaze at the ceiling. Although he was certain that Wally was dead, Les called an ambulance. Hearing the siren crisscrossing the hills, apparently unable to find the secluded address, he frantically dialed his pal Zeke Manners.

Zeke, who lived nearby and arrived moments before the rescue squad, recalled the scene with disbelief: "The paramedics come in and one of the guys is staring at Les. Finally, he says, 'Hey, aren't you Les Paul? My wife just loves your records.' They get into a whole discussion about Les's music. It seemed like it went on for half an hour. In the meantime, Wally is just laying there on the floor all glassy-eyed. I was a nervous wreck. There was a bottle of booze sitting on the table and I think I drank half of it on the spot."

Les and Zeke followed the ambulance to the hospital, certain Wally was dying. Fortunately, he was only severely inebriated. A few days later, Les handed his former brother-in-law $1,000 in cash and said: "Either go out and get so goddam drunk that you can't take another drink, or come back to New Jersey and I'll pick you up at the airport." Wally weighed his options and decided to move into Les's New Jersey home, where he remained until his death from cancer in the late 1970s. Zeke moved in too, though he stayed for only nine months: "It was a bad time for Les," Manners said. "I just thought he needed a little moral support."

A few weeks later, in September 1967, Les also invited George Barnes and his family to move into his home. Barnes, whose clipped electric guitar lines graced hundreds of jazz and pop disks before rock and roll drove him from the New York studio scene in 1966, was just barely getting by financially with his wife and daughter in Arlington, Texas. Scrambling for cash, he was attempting to produce a series of mail-order recordings of advanced guitar lessons, some of which required overdubbing. "One day," said his wife, Evelyn, "George ran into technical difficulty with the overdubbing, so he called Les. Les said, 'What the hell are you doing in Texas? Stop fooling around out there and come back here.' "

According to Evelyn, her late husband agreed to play guitar on Les's first stereo recording (all Les's previous disks were recorded mono). Les, in turn, promised to help George produce and market his guitar course. "The boys in school couldn't believe I was living with Les Paul," said the Barnes's daughter, Alexandra. "They called his house the pink palace. Everybody wanted to know what he was about because he was so reclusive."

Alexandra couldn't tell her schoolmates much, though. Following Les's typical pattern, he and her father worked in the studio from nine or ten at night till dawn, and Les slept the rest of the day. However, a collaborative effort between two such strong-willed men was doomed to fail. "Les was very big on one-upmanship," said Evelyn. "There was very little camaraderie between him and George. It was strictly business. George admitted it had been a mistake to go live at Les's house. But we were so broke. It was one of the lowest ebbs in George's life. One day while we were in the car, George said that Les told him he should get a job in a gas station, selling gas. He was devastated."

When *Les Paul Now* came out on the London label in early 1968, it bore no trace of Barnes, and Barnes, who moved out of Les's house a few months later, signed his own distribution deal for the mail-order course with *Billboard*.

In the meantime, Les resolved to reestablish ties with Gibson. He had ended his professional relationship with the guitar manufacturer five or six years earlier, partly because of the waning popularity of Les Paul guitars. In the fall of 1967, however, he offered to sell Gibson the design for his low-impedance pickups, which he insisted were an essential component of his pristine trademark sound.

By then Gibson had drastically reduced its line of solid-body electrics. Although the short-lived folk music revival that had grown out of Greenwich Village's coffee houses was all but dead by the mid-1960s, the guitar company continued to funnel most of its technical and marketing resources into acoustic and semi-acoustic instrument sales. The average age of Gibson's staff—and the staff of its parent company, Chicago Musical Instruments—was fifty. These people had little idea of what was going on in the pop music world, even though some of the most influential rock guitarists in the world routinely played Gibson Les Pauls, which were out of production by 1961.

"When I toured abroad in 1966," the late blues artist Mike Bloomfield once said, "I noticed that all the top European players were using the same cherry Les Paul sunburst model as me. Keith Richards had one, Eric Clapton, Peter Green. I wondered how did they know that this guitar had all the inherent qualities of sustain, volume, and tone that was better than any other possible rock-and-roll guitar at that time. But the word was out."

And it was spreading among aspiring young rockers, who had seen their favorite rock superstars wailing away on old Les Pauls. Led Zeppelin's Jimmy Page was perhaps the guitar's biggest booster of all: "What drew me to the Les Paul guitar was really the overall design of it. The pickups, for instance, were the ones that gave me the most response. They were really powerful and extremely sensitive at the same time, and the sort of stuff I was doing I found to be more comfortable on the Les Paul."

"Les talked to lots of music-store owners who said the kids were willing to fork over two and three thousand dollars for the discontinued models," recalled Bruce Bolen, a longtime Gibson veteran before joining Fender's research and development department. "But Les's head was a step beyond that. He also wanted to get these low-impedance pickups of his launched. One day the company brass called me into the conference room to play this guitar that Les brought in. It had these really weird-looking, humongous pickups. They were his electronics, he designed them. But they were basically built by Wally, whose idea of woodworking was to hog out a portion of the body, push these things into it, and hook them up. But as strange as the pickups looked, Les was definitely on to something new and different. The guitar had a real sparkle on the high end. I could hear why Les liked that sound so much. It was so clean, like listening to a record played back. I told my boss, Marc Carlucci, that it was the greatest thing since bottled beer."

Less than a year later, in June 1968, Gibson unveiled facsimiles of the Les Paul Custom and Les Paul Standard models at a Chicago trade show. Les was in a celebratory mood on opening day, jamming for hours in the Gibson showroom with Bruce Bolen and Homer and Jethro, the famous country-comedy duo. After spending the better part of the evening at a nearby bar with several other tippling guitarists, he and Bolen got a hankering to jam some more. The entire entourage trooped back to Gibson's darkened showroom, removed half a dozen or so shiny new six-strings from their display racks, and cut loose till dawn. A few hours later, the head of Gibson's entertainment department blew his stack when he found the instruments in disarray and empty beer bottles strewn across the room. He tried in vain to get Bolen fired, not realizing that M. H. Berlin, the head of the company, had personally ordered the boys' late-night refreshments.

Over the next several years, Gibson introduced a new selection of Les Pauls, including the Personal, the Professional, the Recording, and the semiacoustic Signature models. Unlike earlier Les Pauls, which had high-impedance pickups created solely by Gibson engineers, these included electronics designed by the guitarist himself. Capable of a wider frequency response and range of harmonics, Les's pickups offered a cleaner and brighter sound than other commercial pickups. And because they could be played through two hundred feet of cable without any loss of signal, they were perfect for the concert stage.

But they also had a few drawbacks. The instruments could barely be heard with off-the-rack amplifiers, which, then as now, were all designed with high-impedance electronics. They required an extra piece of equipment—a preamp—to help them match the power found in high-impedance solid-bodies. Even then they lacked the kick young rockers demanded. They were also far more difficult to master than the typical solid-body guitar. The Recording model, for instance, was equipped with nine different function knobs and switches, including a decade control, an eleven-position switch that tuned and altered treble harmonics.

"You needed tremendous ears and a fairly sophisticated knowledge of electronics to use the Recording guitar," said Bolen, who demonstrated the instrument on Gibson's advertising sound sheets. "It was just too complicated. Most players just want to know how much volume they can get out of a guitar."

By the mid-1970s, Gibson was backing away from Les's low-impedance concept, choosing instead to place greater emphasis on solid-bodies with bizarre shapes and psychedelic paint jobs, like the Flying V and the Explorer. It was a sound business strategy, said Bolen, but Les ultimately experienced this and other decisions by the company as a betrayal.

The failure of his personally designed pickups was simply the latest in a painful series of rejections and disappointments that had marked the past decade of his life, beginning with his acrimonious divorce from Mary Ford. He also suffered from a growing number of physical complaints. In the early 1960s, he discovered he had developed arthritis. "I didn't know about it till I broke my finger onstage," he later said. "Mary and I had this gag where I'd take a swipe at her hand while she was playing. This time she pulled her hand away and I hit the edge of her guitar. The doc told me I had to have a bone graft in my little finger because it was so brittle. It took months to get out of the cast."

Unfortunately the degenerative disease eventually manifested itself in both the guitarist's hands, gradually robbing his fingers of their strength and agility. Then, one night in 1969, a friend playfully cuffed him on the right side of the head and broke his eardrum. It was a terrible blow to a man whose livelihood depended on his ability to hear. "He blew my woofer," said Les. Five years and several operations later, the condition improved, but his hearing remained impaired forever.

One day in January 1972, Les got a call from his old pal Bucky Pizzarelli. Bucky was in a jam. He and George Barnes had been playing guitar duets for nearly a year in the cabaret room of the St. Regis, a posh hotel on Manhattan's Upper East Side. After filling the club to capacity night after night, the duo had a spectacular falling-out onstage: "Their swan set was played not on their instruments but on each other," jazz writer Whitney Balliet reported in his 1975 book *New York Notes*.

Bucky had to find a replacement—fast. Les was an obvious choice. The two old friends enjoyed each other's company, and Bucky "knew all the chords Les loved to hear." In the mid-1960s, they had thrown together a band at the last minute to play a New Year's Eve engagement at a Paramus, New Jersey, nightclub. Trouble was, Les had performed few professional gigs since then. He had played at several Gibson clinics, and he still occasionally jammed with friends. But his arthritis and persistent inner-ear problems left him weak in body and spirit. In fact, the day Bucky called, Les's head was still swathed in bandages from recent ear surgery.

"I'm not in any shape to play the guitar," he sighed.

"But I really need you," Bucky pleaded. "It will only be for a few nights."

"I just don't know if I'm strong enough to make it through a whole night," Les answered. "I'd have to lie down between sets."

He finally agreed to do the date after Bucky promised not to broadcast that Les would be on the bill. "He thought he had lost all his chops, so he wanted his debut to be a quiet little night," remembered Bucky, then both an NBC staff guitarist and a member of Benny Goodman's orchestra. "But the minute he got onstage with the guitar in his hand, he was a different person. He had a great time. Everybody was completely gassed by his playing, which was clear evidence to him that he could still sound great. It was an argument against everything he had been saying about his own playing for the past few years."

He also reveled at the sight of the steady stream of musical heavyweights who dropped by the tiny cabaret room: Count Basie, Benny Goodman, Doc Severinsen, and George Benson, to name just a few. When he saw Benson walk through the door he got so excited he put down his guitar and insisted the younger jazzman take his place on the stage to play a couple of tunes with Bucky.

Les loved the sound of applause most of all, though. "The response was terrific," he remembered years later, "the ovations and yells for 'More!' I realized then how much I missed performing. People were applauding me for the first time in years, and it felt great. It was the start of a whole new thing."

Chapter 21

RESURRECTION

Sometime after the St. Regis date, a Hempstead, New York, teenager raised $1,500 from fellow students to bring Les to the Hempstead High School auditorium. Les accepted the invitation, though he was anxious about performing in front of a crowd of teenage long-hairs. Convinced his music was too tame for this audience, he didn't have any illusions about finding new listeners. However, he had grossly underestimated the power that went along with having his name embossed on a guitar that had appeared in the hands of such rock superstars as Led Zeppelin's Jimmy Page, the Who's Pete Townshend, and the Stones' Keith Richards.

In fact, the Gibson Les Paul helped make the aging guitarist one of the few musicians to bridge the vast gulf between the swing era and rock. "The kids went crazy," Les said of his Hempstead High concert. "Then I got a call to play at a college in Illinois. They stood up and cheered me there before I even played a note. That stunned me."

On August 1, 1974, Capitol issued a new Les Paul/Mary Ford greatest hits album. *The World Is Waiting for the Sunrise* earned a spate of favorable reviews, which encouraged Les to get out there and work more. Unfortunately, in an attempt to recreate the multilayered sound of his old recordings onstage, he continued to use his Paulveriser, even though the remote-controlled device often malfunctioned in mid-performance. He seemed to believe that such electronic enhancements were preferable to the sound of his unadorned guitar.

Les's first major date was in October 1974 at New York City's Town Hall. Bucky Pizzarelli, who opened the show, later joined Les onstage for a few guitar duets, and late-night TV talk-show host Joe Franklin served as master of ceremonies. Although Les did his best to promote the concert—even gate-crashing a press conference the previous day for the city's Country Music Month at O'Lunney's bar—the concert was poorly attended. Nevertheless, a star-struck reporter from *The Village Voice* gave Les a worshipful write-up the following week: "Some of Les's licks and spaces go beyond credibility: even with arthritis in his right hand, his playing is technically flawless."

A few days after the concert, Les and Bucky performed on ABC's *A.M. America,* which made Les even happier. It was his first network television appearance in more than a decade. Driving Bucky back to New Jersey that morning, he barely reacted when a huge panel truck rammed into the side of his Cadillac on the corner of 42nd and Broadway: "The driver was beside himself," recalled Bucky, "but Les just got out of the car and told the guy not to worry about a thing. No names exchanged, no nothing. He just drove home and fixed the dents himself. He was so thrilled that he had just played his guitar for the whole country that he didn't want to be bothered."

Throughout this period, Les continued to promote his guitars. At the end of August 1975, he did a concert for Gibson at San Francisco's Great American Music Hall, his first Bay Area engagement in a dozen years. Except for occasional bass and piano support, Les's only backing was provided by the Paulveriser and his fifteen-year-old son, Bobby, on drums.

Although the rumpled gray suit he wore gave him the appearance of a middle-aged bank clerk and he fingered the same old standards he had been playing since the 1930s, Les was treated like a pop icon by the youthful audience, which gave him a standing ovation at the close of the concert. Thirty minutes later, fans were still filing past the stage, clamoring for a chance to shake hands or exchange a few words with the sixty-year-old guitarist. And he loved it.

"There's an excitement you feel from applause that you can't get from just looking in a magazine and seeing your record is No. 1," Les told the *Los Angeles Times* that night. "It's the same thing when someone walks up to you after the show. I know some musicians who don't like to meet their fans. They want to keep things separate. That's fine for them. But my greatest thrill is when someone likes my music well enough to want to say hello. That's a feeling you can't get from looking at a royalty check."

Two weeks later, on September 10, Les enjoyed an even more enthusiastic reception at London's Excelsior Hotel, the site of another Gibson clinic. There he found an audience of hardened rock journalists and musicians. Accompanied once again by his son Bobby and the Paulveriser, Les delivered what friends call "his $10,000 act," alternating between slow blues tempos and lightning-fast runs, and using the little black box on his guitar to summon Bing Crosby's disembodied voice.

After striking Presleyesque poses for the photographers and taking a break to down a few beers, Les retuned his guitar and invited the younger musicians onstage for an all-out jam. But he guaranteed his own preeminence by leading them through a collection of tunes that were popularized long before they were born. Among those mounting the stage was Steve Howe of the rock group Yes. "Off they went," reported Britain's *Guitar* magazine, "but it soon became clear that Steve was well off his home turf and Les continued to play the balls off him."

With the help of this and other pieces in the rock press—which consistently depicted him as an ageless hipster—Les's image as "the Living Legend" grew. In 1975, Catherine Orentreich, a twenty-six-year-old NYU film student, began making a Les Paul documentary, which she eventually titled *The Wizard of Waukesha*. Drawing on testimonials from young rock guitarists and footage taken at Gibson's Kalamazoo plant, Orentreich emphasized Les's pioneering role in the development of rock and roll.

The hour-long film interspersed old photos and TV kinescopes of Les with casual interviews of the guitarist pridefully discussing his career. One segment showed Keith Richards and Pete Townshend sending a concert crowd into a frenzy with their Gibson Les Pauls. Another featured the late Mike Bloomfield and the McCoys' Rick Derringer lionizing Les. "Les was the person who invented the sound of today's pop records," exclaimed Derringer, referring to the guitarist's early experiments with multitracking recording.

The documentary, which eventually was shown in art cinemas and libraries all over the country, as well as the latest flurry of press coverage, represented another circle completed in the life of Les Paul. Here he was in his sixties, suddenly treasured by a generation of musicians who had nearly drummed him out of the business two decades earlier.

All this adulation from the rock set fed Les's vanity, but trading finely crafted licks with other guitar masters remained the best way to satisfy his soul. On April 23, 1975, he and Bucky Pizzarelli shared the stage at Carnegie Hall with George Benson and classical guitarist Laurindo Almeida. Anticipating an onstage jam session at the end of the concert, Les contrived a way to draw Benson into a cutting contest only Les could win: "Before the concert, I went out and bought one of Benson's records and gave it a good listen. There was one run he did a lot. It seemed to be one of his favorites. Sure enough, he played it and I was ready for him. I answered in harmony, and it just stunned him."

Benson was even more stunned by the condition of Les's woodland manse, which by the mid-1970s bore little resemblance to the immaculately kept home he had shared with Mary. Nearly every room in the house was cluttered with audio equipment in various states of disrepair. There were thousands of tapes, miles of wires, banks of consoles, and stacks of amplifiers. One day, while chatting in his den with Benson, Les left to answer the phone. Waiting for his host to return, Benson began flipping through a stack of trade magazines piled waist-high next to the couch. Suddenly a small piece of paper fluttered to the floor. Stooping over to pick it up, Benson was amazed to see a check from Gibson. He told a friend it was for $50,000. But it was more than likely one of Les's quarterly royalty payments, which, at the time, would have been closer to $10,000. In any case, Benson's eyes widened in disbelief. "Is this for real?" he asked as he handed the check to Les.

"Well, I'll be darned," Les replied, jamming it into his pocket. "I was wondering where that damn thing was. I meant to put it in the bank."

To this day the furnishings and wall decorations in the secluded Deerhaven Road retreat remain the same as on the day Mary fled the marriage. Heavy, fifties-vintage drapes cover most of the windows, making the musty, dimly lit mansion eerily reminiscent of the cobweb-filled home of Miss Haversham, the lovelorn bride abandoned at the altar in Dickens's *Great Expectations.* The elaborate bedroom suite Les once occupied with his former wife is now crowded with hundreds of guitars, which are piled on the bed, on the floor, in the closets, and in the adjacent dressing room.

Though he affects an attitude of benign indifference toward his wealth, Les watches his pennies as if he were a poor pensioner on a fixed income. He alternately drives a rust-riddled Lincoln and an old Jeep and skimps on heat even on the most frigid winter days, rattling around his cavernous home in a heavy coat and hat to fend off the cold. Friends say the only warm room in the house is the studio, where the grand piano is.

His scanty wardrobe is another story. In fact, it once nearly thwarted a long-planned meeting with Paul McCartney. In April 1988, the pair arranged to meet in Manhattan at McCartney's suite in the Stanhope, an elegant Fifth Avenue hotel overlooking Central Park. There Les intended to give the world's most famous southpaw a custom left-handed Gibson Les Paul. But first he suffered a humiliating encounter. Although his net worth probably exceeded that of most of the guests at the posh hotel, Les's clothing sent out a distinctly different impression. For this chilly April morning in 1988, he donned a pair of polyester bell bottoms, a well-worn turtleneck sweater, and a navy-blue zippered jacket—the kind often worn by appliance repair men, except Les's had a couple of grease stains in front.

When he tried to enter the hotel with his son Rusty and friend Clark Enselin, both of whom appeared equally scruffy, he was sent away by a young uniformed doorman. It was a cold, windy day, so the trio sought temporary shelter in Clark's beat-up car, which sat in a metered spot around the corner. In the meantime, the doorman allowed a steady stream of stylishly attired strangers into the hotel without question. But when Les, Rusty, and Clark returned fifteen minutes later, he stopped them once again at the threshold. Finally, much to Les's relief, McCartney's New York publicist, Joe Dera, arrived and escorted the party up to McCartney's room.

After a few minutes of polite introductions, Les handed over the gleaming black guitar. "This is unbelievable," McCartney said as he tuned the instrument for a quick test run. "When you start out, you're dead broke and have to scrounge for money to buy a new guitar, and when you get famous, someone gives you one. Funny, isn't it." Lacking a strap, the erstwhile ex-Beatle hiked his foot up onto the nearest table, rested the guitar on his knee, and let his fingers fly across the fretboard as he graciously recounted how he and John Lennon used to kick off their Liverpool gigs with Les and Mary's versions of "How High the Moon" and "The World Is Waiting for the Sunrise." "That would get the crowd's attention right away," he added. "Everybody was trying to be a Les Paul clone in those days."

In early May 1975, a week after his Carnegie Hall date, Les boarded a plane with his son Bobby and headed for Nashville, where he planned to record an album for RCA with Chet Atkins. Music publisher Roy Horton, whose brother Vaughn wrote Les and Mary's first major hit, "Mockin' Bird Hill," had pestered Chet for months about making a disk with Les. But it wasn't until Horton brought the two together for a jam session at Manhattan's Warwick Hotel that the Tennessee picker finally agreed an Atkins/Paul collaboration would work.

Despite the fact that he had recorded more than a hundred solo albums and had risen through music-industry ranks to become an RCA vice president, Chet was still anxious about going nose to nose with a man he had idolized since childhood. His older brother Jimmy had been Les's friend and triomate for years, but he had met the veteran guitarist only once years before. At the time Chet was a twenty-five-year-old staff musician at KWTO, the Springfield, Missouri, radio station that Les had helped launch in 1933.

One night in 1949, while strumming up a storm during a live broadcast, Chet noticed a stranger staring at him through the studio window. "I thought, 'I'm gonna knock this guy out,' you know, impress him. I played a lot of fast runs and spun out a Les Paul chorus or two, pullin' the strings just like Les. Then the man himself walks in and says, 'I opened this goddam station fifteen years ago.' I almost fell over. I was embarrassed because I had played a few of his choruses. I guess he thought I was a thief."

Now here they were, three decades later, meeting as peers. Carrying his custom-built white flat-top guitar—a prized Gibson prototype from the early 1950s—Les was the first to arrive at the RCA studio. There he ran into songwriter Vic McAlpin, who had collaborated with Hank Williams, Sr., on such country chestnuts as "Long Gone Lonesome Blues" and "I've Been Down That Road Before."

"Hey, man," said McAlpin, pumping the guitarist's hand, "what are you doing in these parts?"

"I'm down here to make an album with Chet," Les replied.

"What are you going to record?"

"Oh, I don't know. We're just gonna wing it."

McAlpin, who thrived on creating harmless havoc wherever he went, leaned toward Les and whispered: "You know what Chet will do to you? He'll get you in there and play all the songs he knows best. Why, he'll pick his ass off and make you sound like a goddam sharecropper!"

McAlpin's admonition was only a joke, but to Les it apparently carried the weight of the Gospel. Chet couldn't figure out why his new recording partner rejected nearly every song he suggested.

"McAlpin told me what he had said to Les two or three years later, right before he died," Chet recalled. "He said, 'Isn't that funny?' That was Vic's idea of a good practical joke. But in the long run, it was actually to my benefit to record Les's tunes, because I probably knew his material better than he knew mine."

The session was delightfully casual, intermittently featuring some of Nashville's best studio musicians: pianist Randy Goodrum, drummer Larry Londin, bassists Henry Strzelecki and Bob Moore, rhythm guitarists Paul Yandell, Ray Edenton, and Bobby Thompson. "We were completely unprepared," Chet said. "It's hard to nail Les down on what he wants to do. He just pointed to the mike and said, 'Hell, turn that son of a bitch on. We'll get it.' "

The duo finally agreed to record a number of songs that Les had performed with Bucky at Carnegie Hall a week earlier. Many had appeared on previous Les Paul disks, including an exquisite reworking of his 1945 hit with Bing Crosby, "It's Been a Long, Long Time." But he and Chet endowed each old standard with new life, embellishing and harmonizing on the melodies as they went along. The Nashville rhythm section provided a tight, swinging foundation and ready audience for the guitarists' ongoing banter, much of it left in the final mix.

Although Les has repeatedly claimed the disk was wrapped up in just a few hours, studio files indicate it was recorded over a couple of days, May 6 and 7, with all but two of the cuts, "Caravan" and "Lover Come Back to Me" done live. Chet thought a few others could have been improved with a little more post-session overdubbing. But, said Les, he was in a hurry to get back to Jersey.

"What'll we do about all those clams?" Chet asked.

"Leave 'em in," Les replied, "Let people know we're human."

The finished disk, simply titled *Chester and Lester,* was hard to categorize. It had a distinct country flavor, but was entirely devoid of country tunes. Instead, it offered an assortment of jazz standards that could easily be found on a Count Basie or Benny Goodman album, including "Avalon," "Moonglow," and "Deed I Do." *Chester and Lester* apparently appealed to fans of both genres, enjoying strong sales right from its February 1976 release.

The artists' personal relationship, however, took a turn for the worse shortly thereafter. A few days before they were scheduled to appear on the *Today* show, Les angrily accused his RCA labelmate of cheating him. "He suspected I was getting paid as a producer, getting more money for the record than him," says Chet. "I wasn't. I was just an in-house producer. But he fussed at me a whole lot anyway. I said, 'Les, I'm Jim's brother; I'm not a dishonest person. How could you think of me that way? You have to learn to trust people.' "

When that attack failed to elicit an admission of guilt from Chet, Les launched another, demanding to know whose idea it was to record all the between-tune patter that helped make the record such a success. "You were being pretty funny, so I told the engineer to put the damn mike up," answered Chet.

"Well, it was my goddam idea," Les snapped.

"Okay, okay, it was your idea. I don't care. What's important is that we made a good record."

After that conversation, though, Chet swore he'd never work with Les again. "Life is too short to put up with all the accusations and everything. Right before we went on the air at the *Today* show, Les looked over at me and said, 'I'm sorry, Buddy.' I guess he felt bad about the way he treated me."

The fact that *Chester and Lester* became both a popular and a critical success apparently helped smooth things over between the two guitarists, at least temporarily. *Down Beat* raved: "It is a vivid, one-volume history of the electric guitar, a bonafide supersession. . . . Every person who claims an affinity for the guitar, musicians and listeners alike, should make *Chester and Lester* required listening."

A year later, on February 19, 1977, Les and Chet walked off the stage of the Los Angeles Shrine Auditorium with a Grammy for Best Country Instrumental Performance. They beat out such country stalwarts as Ace Cannon, Floyd Cramer, and the Marshall Tucker Band, which caused a lot of grumbling among Nashville loyalists, who thought the record should have competed in the pop or jazz category. But Les wasn't about to let that dampen his spirits. The National Academy of Recording Arts and Sciences hadn't initiated the annual awards program until 1958—as Les's hit-making days were winding down—so this was his first Grammy. Backstage, old industry friends and adoring new fans gathered around to shower him with praise. "Man, I idolize you," gushed Peter Frampton, the English rock guitarist/vocalist who had recently scored three chart-topping disks of his own.

For Les, the coveted statuette was proof of his triumph over both the relentlessly youth-oriented music scene that had sent his career into a tailspin and the arthritis that was slowly and cruelly robbing him of his powers as an instrumentalist. Suddenly he was a hot commodity. A few weeks after the Grammy ceremony, *People* magazine devoted a three-page article to the sixty-one-year-old guitarist entitled "Somewhere, There's Music, and Les Paul's Influence Is Still as High as the Moon." The following August the prestigious Audio Engineering Society paid him a special tribute at its hundredth-anniversary celebration of Thomas Edison's incredible talking machine. Then the National Academy of Recording Arts and Sciences inducted Les Paul and Mary Ford's version of "How High the Moon" into its Hall of Fame, along with Rachmaninoff's *Rhapsody on a Theme of Paganini* and Count Basie's "One O'Clock Jump." Meanwhile, Les was inundated by a barrage of concert offers and fan mail. It was almost like the old days.

Mary Ford, by contrast, was living quietly with her husband, Don Hatfield, in suburban Los Angeles. Although she had happily abandoned the road-bound existence she had shared with Les—"We were married fourteen years, but it seems more like fifty," she told a reporter in 1977—she was now burdened with a new set of problems. She had developed diabetes in the early 1970s but failed to give up drinking, which further threatened her fragile health. Several years later her husband's contracting business began to founder, forcing the couple to move into a more modest home on a commercial strip in Monrovia.

By then, she and Les were on friendly terms again. According to Les, she sometimes called him at two or three in the morning, eager to reminisce about their performing days. One night in September 1977, though, she complained to him of blurred vision. A couple of weeks later she was rushed to Arcadia Methodist Hospital in a diabetic coma, induced by an adverse reaction to an insulin injection.

Her family visited the hospital daily, playing her records with Les over and over again, hoping to break through the deadly fog that had enveloped her. But she never regained consciousness. She died eight weeks later, at age fifty-three, on September 30.

After an emotional church service attended by hundreds of mourners, Mary was buried in Forest Lawn cemetery in Covina Hills, California. Her grave marker, embedded in a tree-shaded slope overlooking her beloved San Gabriel Valley, depicted a guitar and the title of her favorite song, "Vaya con Dios," Spanish for "Go with God." Mary, at last, had found peace.

Though he chose not to attend her funeral, Les was badly shaken by his former wife's death. He was also mourning several other long-time friends, including Gray Gordon, his personal manager, Jimmy Atkins and Ernie Newton, with whom he had formed the original Les Paul Trio forty years earlier, and Bing Crosby, who died on October 14, two weeks after Mary. Then there was his son Bobby, who was having personal problems in Germany. Les was still reeling when he left for Nashville in mid-November to cut a follow-up LP with Chet Atkins.

This time the producing chores were handled by RCA veteran Bob Ferguson, not Chet. While that personnel change took care of at least one potential conflict between the two headstrong guitarists, others quickly surfaced. Apparently confused by the time difference between New York and Nashville, Les arrived at the RCA studio at nine in the morning instead of ten, which itself was far too early to suit the perennial night owl. When Chet showed up, Les was in a truly miserable mood. First he made derogatory remarks about the catfish dinner Mrs. Atkins had cooked him the night before. Then he insisted he had caught her cold.

"No, Les," exclaimed Chet, "you can't have a cold the next day; it takes five days. You caught the darn thing in New Jersey and you're blaming us."

Nearly another hour passed before the two guitarists began laying down tracks for "Undecided," the first of three tunes scheduled for the day. By then Les appeared even more tense and jumpy. "The looseness and intimacy implied on the cut is not as apparent in person within the confines of the studio," reported Doug Green, who covered the session for *Guitar Player* magazine (and later became a member of the retro cowboy trio Riders in the Sky).

"Undecided" was left on the cutting-room floor, but "Brazil" and "Somewhere over the Rainbow" made it into the final mix. After hearing the last run-through of "Over the Rainbow" and before turning on the tape recorder, Bob Ferguson encouraged Les to play the opening melody a little longer.

"You talking to me?" Les asked the producer, apparently amazed that *anyone* would have the audacity to tell him how to handle his guitar.

"Yeah, Les. Maybe establish a little more melody before you go into improvisations."

"Is he talking to me?" Les repeated.

Despite his cantankerous mood, the final take of "Over the Rainbow" was exquisite, a tenderly evocative musical exchange between him and Chet. Upon hearing the playback, Les hooted, "Now if that don't grab you by the ass, nothing's gonna grab you."

For once there was a genuine consensus in the room. By the end of the morning, though, Chet was eager to shake his recording partner. He suggested they all break for lunch, but added, "Let's send Les somewhere else. I've had lunch with him every damn day this week."

A few days later, Les felt so weakened by his cold that he could barely leave his bed at Nashville's Quality Inn. At one point he summoned Bill Lawrence, a German-born guitarist who was also known in the industry for his engineering skills. Famous for his electric-pickup designs, Lawrence was driven to compete with Les, but the pair never allowed their rivalry to get in the way of an occasional drinking spree, particularly during Gibson trade shows. This reunion, however, was far more somber.

"Les wanted me to help him with his son in Germany, which I did," said Lawrence. "But he was also very sick and down-hearted. He told me the story of his life. It was the first time I had ever seen him so sincere. He said he was sorry for a lot of things he had done, for the way he had treated certain people, especially Mary."

Though *Guitar Monsters* climbed to the No. 13 spot on the country charts within the first three weeks of its June 1978 release, the album failed to generate the same level of enthusiasm as *Chester and Lester*. To give it an extra boost, the two guitarists appeared onstage together for the first time, playing two sold-out sets at the Bottom Line, New York City's most celebrated rock club.

Amazingly, it was also Chet's performing debut in the Big Apple. He opened the July 6 show solo, later playing with a full backup band. Then Les did his own set, accompanied only by his Paulveriser and a drummer. Les's performance garnered widely divergent notices. "Paul came out and ripped the joint like a hot young rock-and-roller with the old hits," said the *Daily News*. "He was bubbly, outgoing, and full of visual wit and musical charm."

The *Times* offered a far less flattering assessment: "Mr. Paul can hardly be accused of exquisite taste. As a musician (as opposed to an inventor, a technician, or historical figure), he seems pretty provincial these days, accompanied by a flailing drummer and cluttering the textures with needless trickery. . . . But after his solo set, he returned for fifteen minutes with Mr. Atkins and his group, and in those circumstances his own questionable musical style was subsumed into Mr. Atkins's. In that context he showed himself to be a responsive musician and still agile player, and the evening ended in a glow of good fellowship and audience appreciation."

Neither reviewer apparently noticed how annoyed Chet became when Les unplugged his partner's six-string in the middle of the show. "Les was full of cute little tricks like that," Chet later recalled.

That was the last time the guitar duo ever worked together.

The summer of 1980 brought Les earth-shattering news. During the course of a routine medical exam, his doctor told him he had severe atherosclerosis. Apart from a minor episode in the late 1970s when

Les thought he might have had a heart attack, there had been no obvious symptoms, no signs to indicate he had developed this life-threatening disease. He had long abandoned his heavy smoking habit and had even cleaned up his diet, favoring chicken and fish over red meat. Yet the doctor said Les's "aorta was so filled with calcium deposits that it looked like a kitchen sink."

Further tests revealed that several coronary arteries were equally blocked. Quintuple bypass surgery was the only solution, but the doctor refused to operate. Convinced that Les's weakened coronary system couldn't withstand the trauma of such a radical procedure, he gave the sixty-five-year-old guitarist a nitroglycerine prescription and told him to go home and take it easy. A second doctor agreed to perform the surgery, but promised only a 50 percent chance of survival. Thus began the frantic search for a more reassuring opinion. Les finally found a surgeon he trusted at the Cleveland Clinic.

"He kept up a brave front through the whole thing," his friend Wayne Wright later said. "He didn't dwell on his heart problem at all. But I know he was scared shitless. He wasn't sure if he was going to come back from Cleveland."

Accompanied by his son Rusty and a friend, Les checked into the hospital in mid-September 1980. For the first week or so he underwent numerous pre-op tests. But he still found time to roam the corridors and regale fellow patients with ribald stories and off-color jokes. Still restless, he prevailed upon Rusty to buy him a guitar and amplifier. Then he somehow persuaded the medical staff to let him convert the cheerless patients' lounge into a makeshift cabaret. The nurses loaded a portable medicine cart with cake, cookies, and punch, and several patients and doctors even sat in with the guitarist. "I had a built-in audience," he later said. "The inmates had nowhere else to go."

Through an odd coincidence, Les's bypass operation was scheduled for September 30, the third anniversary of Mary Ford's death. His daughter Colleen, who flew in from California three days earlier, noted the date with concern, but was afraid to mention it to anybody else. There was ample reason to fear. The complicated surgery—reputed to be the first of its kind—involved transplanting grafts from Les's internal mammary artery and leg veins into his clogged coronary arteries. When he awoke hours later, he was hooked up to a massive heart monitor and riddled with IV needles and tubes. But at least he was alive.

A few weeks later, the ailing Les called Wally and Eleanor Jones and asked if he could recuperate in their West Coast home. Though surprised by the request, the couple, who had known Les since the early 1930s, immediately agreed to nurse him back to health. On the appointed day, they met their old friend at the Los Angeles airport. They were shocked by his appearance. Gaunt and pale, Les looked small and helpless in his wheelchair. He was too weak to walk from the gate to the car. Wally had trouble concealing his horror. "We didn't think Les was going to make it," he said.

After spending nearly six months in the couple's comfortable California home, he felt well enough to return to New Jersey. Piecing his life back together, though, was a slow and difficult process, full of pitfalls that seemed to cast him into spells of depression. Forced to retire from the stage once more, he passed most of his waking hours in his workshop, tinkering with various pickup designs, or trying to upgrade his home studio, which was rarely ever used. Other times he talked for hours on his CB radio. But the onset of pneumonia and a broken ankle made even those solitary pursuits difficult.

"Les had always been a lot of laughs," said Bruce Bolen, then an executive at Gibson. "But after the operation he acted despondent. Once, when I called him at home, he almost cried. He just didn't think he could play anymore. It was hard to get him to do anything after that. He'd get so riled."

A certain amount of Les's testiness was predictable: he was raging against the physical constraints imposed by his precarious heart condition and advancing arthritis. The fact that his relationship with Gibson was rapidly deteriorating only increased his frustration. In December 1969, the guitar manufacturer was bought by a team of investors, who by most accounts had little genuine interest in the musical-instrument business—and even less in Les Paul, who was accustomed to being coddled by the previous owner, M. H. Berlin.

By the mid-1980s, the venerable company, whose stringed instruments were once the standard by which all others were measured, had lost much of its stature in the industry and was up for sale. To make matters worse, as "techno-pop" began its ascent in the 1970s and 1980s, guitar sales began spiraling downward, losing a substantial portion of sales to portable, low-power electronic keyboards. But even within this diminishing market, Les Paul guitars were steadily losing ground to those designed by Les's rival Leo Fender. This only increased Les's disdain for Gibson's profit-oriented executives, whom he publicly referred to as "bozos."

"It's very difficult," he complained at the time, "to tell the president of any outfit or anybody that has any stature that what he should do is to go to a music store for a month and wait on customers to find out what the hell it's all about. They don't do that; they sit in that ivory tower and tell you what it's all about."

Les's hard-boiled aggressiveness did little to bring Gibson's brass around to his way of thinking. In fact, the harder he pressed his ideas on them, the more they backed away from him. They eventually locked him out of the decision-making process altogether, preferring instead to rely upon the younger generation of players for inspiration.

If Les hadn't signed a contract that gave Gibson the use of his name in perpetuity, he might have jumped ship. However, the written agreement didn't prevent him from publicly bad-mouthing the company, which he did with abandon.

Finally Les turned to the one thing that had never let him down: his music. "Playing is my way of expressing myself," he once said, "a way of getting all that anxiety out. It's a great mistress, bartender, psychologist, doctor, and faithful companion. I don't know of anything or anyone who could take its place and do all those things for me." Unfortunately, by the early 1980s, arthritis had severely limited the use of the two outer fingers on his right hand and four on the left. He had to retrain himself to play all over again, just as he had after the 1948 car crash. He crafted "a pick the size of a windshield" to help him strum. Although his technique would never match the speed and agility of his early years, he eventually felt confident enough to get out in front of an audience. First he jammed with friends who had gigs in nearby nightclubs. Then he started showing up nearly every weekend night at Molly's Tavern in Oakland, New Jersey, where he sat in for two or three sets with guitarist Lou Pallo.

Before long, deejay Jazzbo Collins began talking up Les's appearances at Molly's on his New York–based radio show. As Les tells it, the response was overwhelming: "People starting coming to the club from all over—Manhattan, New Jersey, Pennsylvania—so I says, 'It's time to move to New York City.'"

Chapter 22

FAT TUESDAY'S

Les's decision to book a date of his own actually came about with a great deal of prompting from his old friend Wayne Wright, who spent many evenings visiting Mahwah, especially after Les broke his ankle. The two guitarists often hunkered down with a few other musicians and traded licks late into the night. By most accounts, Les never sounded better than during these homespun jam sessions. Unhampered by the need to play to the crowd, he relied less on stock phrases and more on pure musical instinct. "We didn't force anything," recalls Wayne. "We let the music come out naturally and it swung like crazy."

In the winter of 1984, several months after the pair enjoyed a successful performance at a Staten Island jazz concert, Wayne persuaded Les to form a trio and find a club in Manhattan that would offer them a standing engagement. But, Wayne added, "I had to work hard to cajole him into it. After all the arguments, my closing line, and I think the one that finally got him, was 'You need the therapy and I need the gig.'"

They had already found a nimble-fingered bassist named Gary Mazzaroppi. Now all they needed was the right venue. As Les recounts the story, "Everybody said I should go for a room in a nice hotel like the Carlyle. But I said, 'Nah, I want a nice, crummy joint.' "

He and Wayne cruised around Manhattan in Les's old white Lincoln, checking out various clubs on the Upper West Side and in Greenwich Village. Shortly thereafter, Wayne got a call from Scott Alderman, the manager of Fat Tuesday's, a quintessential jazz dive on Third Avenue between 17th and 18th streets. Alderman, who had heard through the grapevine that Les was looking for a place to play, wanted to know what it would take to bring him to Fat Tuesday's. Wayne agreed to arrange a meeting between the two men. Entering the club through a heavy steel door, he and Les padded down a long, narrow corridor limned with smoked-glass mirrors. Then they descended an uneven set of steps to a dark, rectangular room laced with heating ducts and water pipes.

Stuffy in the winter, suffocating in the summer, the subterranean saloon offered seating for more than a hundred patrons in a space that comfortably accommodated fifty. But Les loved it. From the postage-stamp stage, he could easily reach out and touch fans sitting at the front-row tables. Best of all, Alderman agreed to open the place on Monday night, a traditionally slow evening, to give the latest Les Paul Trio a two-week trial run. This was terrific news for Wayne and Gary. "Monday was the one night the two of us usually had trouble getting gigs, but we knew Les would draw any night of the week," says Wayne.

Fat Tuesday's touted Les's March 26, 1984, debut as "The Return of the Legend," and Gibson offered a free Les Paul Studio Standard to help draw a crowd. The additional enticement was probably unnecessary, though. Thanks to Les's *Wizard of Waukesha* documentary and scores of glowing press accounts of his life throughout the 1970s and 1980s, "the Living Legend" had already taken root among young rockers hungry for a durable hero. The house was packed with fans more than willing to shell out $20 for the music charge and minimum.

Les was prepared to play two shows that night, the first beginning at eight-thirty, the second at ten-thirty. Wayne and Gary painstakingly tuned their instruments onstage, while Les remained in the dressing room at the rear of the club, anxiously awaiting his introduction. As soon as he emerged from the closet-sized room, though, the audience welcomed him with a standing ovation. His face flushed with a mixture of pride and relief, he shook a sea of outreached hands as he snaked his way through the tightly packed tables to the wooden stool he'd occupy for the next hour or so. Mounting the tiny, spotlit platform, he leaned over Wayne and pretended to detune the left-handed rhythm player's guitar, evoking a hail of laughter from the house. "I guess they like it so far," he breezily announced.

Indeed. Les still had the power to mesmerize a crowd. Despite his arthritis, sweetly plucked single notes and giddy glissandos flowed from his fingers. When his hands began to ache, he rested them on his hot-rodded six-string—a modified reissue of a '58 Gibson Les Paul—and spun out a few finely honed stories. As usual half were true, half self-aggrandizing myths, but all were highly entertaining. "Les has this charismatic personality that made even the diehard barflies sit up and take notice," Wayne remembered. "He reached everybody that night."

All but one, Les thought. "There was this one gal in the front row and I just couldn't get her," he said. "She kept looking at me and looking at me. But she hardly laughed when everybody else was cracking up and she hardly applauded when I finished a number. So I thought, 'I'm gonna get her if it's the last thing I do.' I knew I could find something in my repertoire that would hook her. Finally I'm down to my last two tunes. My closing song is 'Avalon,' which I know ain't gonna work cause it's too fast. So I do 'Over the Rainbow.' Halfway through I happen to look up and see a tear running down her cheek. After I stopped playing I asked her if she was all right, and she says, 'Oh yeah, I have just been stunned since I came in here. I'm speechless.' I said, 'You know, you made me work so hard all night. Jiminy Christmas, if you had cried in the first number, I could have sat back and rode through the whole set.' "

Les's Monday engagements drew so well that the trio was invited back to Fat Tuesday's for another two months. Then, one night in the middle of the extended run, Scott Alderman stepped into the sound booth and announced: "Ladies and gentlemen, the Les Paul Trio will be here every Monday night—*forever.*"

Turning to Les, he asked, "Is that okay?"

"That suits me just fine," the delighted guitarist replied without hesitation.

To this day, Fat Tuesday's still runs regular ads in several New York City magazines and papers, inviting the uninitiated to come "Experience the Living Legend." Over the years the club has marked each and every one of Les's birthdays and anniversaries with a special celebration, treating customers to free champagne and cake. "It's more like a private party than a nightclub show," the *Daily News* wrote of the guitarist's first anniversary at the club. "He raps, back-chats, and delights his audience with virtuosity on the frets and a razor-sharp wit."

Les's first birthday bash was a little more risqué. Halfway through the second set, a nubile young stripper came hurtling toward the stage with her eyes locked on the stunned guitarist. Wearing little more than a pair of candles on her breasts, she peeled off the rest of her costume as the trio ground out a down-and-dirty blues. In the midst of the number, Les dropped his guitar, exclaiming, "Shit, I can't play anymore!" Regaining his composure a few moments later, he made a determined effort to extinguish the candles he him-self had just lit. "They were trick candles, the kind you can't blow out," remembers Wayne. "But he almost passed out trying."

Paying homage to Les Paul has now become almost a religious rite for every big-name jazz and rock musician who passes through town. In addition to old acquaintances like George Benson, Rick Derringer, and Tal Farlow, the list of Les's Monday night guests has included Larry Coryell, Keith Richards, Barney Kessel, Eddie Van Halen, Al Dimeola, Bob Dylan, Steve Miller, Jeff Beck, Jimmy Page (who per-suaded Les to appear in his 1985 video with the Firm), and Jeff (Skunk) Baxter (who featured Les in his 1991 documentary, *Guitar*). Even Billy Idol, one of the most wigged-out, post-punk rockers of the 1980s, came in one night and proclaimed him "the real king of rock and roll."

The Monday-night gig is the closest Les has ever come to duplicating the freewheeling days of his youth, when he reigned supreme at the Hollywood Rounders Club and was regarded as one of the country's most innovative players. "It's great for your ego," he told a *Washington Post* reporter in 1987, "otherwise you're sitting home and nobody's applauding. You become a TV addict or an isolationist."

During his Fat Tuesday's performances he often speaks lovingly of his late wife and stage partner, painting a picture that obscures the ugliness and pain of their last years together. "Every morning when I wake up," he once told a hushed crowd, "I think of Mary and how she loved to laugh."

The public Les Paul—a warm, effervescent man who embraces his fans with unrestrained affection—bears little resemblance to the private Les Paul, who rarely sees three of his four children. If Les's grinding ambition eventually cost him most of his family, though, he managed to find a new one at Fat Tuesday's. Over the years, he has attracted a dozen or so diehard followers who visit the club nearly every Monday night and often call him at home during the week. They know Les's personal history doesn't always conform to the fairy-tale legends he spins for the public, but they love him anyway. Above all they admire his indefatigable drive to get out there week after week to please a house full of people.

Despite his obvious physical frailties, Les has missed only a few performances since his Fat Tuesday's debut, once in 1986 when a severe spell of vertigo kept him bedridden for several weeks. Even then he returned to the club prematurely, so dizzy one night he nearly fell off his stool in the middle of a set. Too shaky to continue playing, he covered himself by plying the crowd with more stories than usual. But the anxious regulars knew exactly what was happening. He didn't have to tell them.

His well-publicized engagement at Fat Tuesday's eventually extended his professional life in other areas as well. In June 1984, three months after his first gig at the club, Les's trio played the Kool Jazz Festival in Waterloo, New Jersey. The following summer, he was featured on PBS-TV with Bucky Pizzarelli and Tal Farlow in a live hour-long concert at Rutgers University celebrating "Jersey Jazz Guitars." Meanwhile, in his Mahwah studio, he produced a luscious album of jazz standards for noted swing pianist Joe Bushkin, who stopped by Fat Tuesday's one night to ask Les to direct him to the best studio in town.

Although he had devoted most of his career to synthesizing new sounds for his guitar and perfecting multitrack recording techniques, by 1985 Les had become a "back-to-mono man." Today's overproduced disks, he once complained, have the same mushy quality as airline food: "You know that you just ate, but you didn't know what it was." In a radical departure from previous producing efforts, Les swore he'd make the instruments on Bushkin's album "sound live, like they were in the room, not like a phonograph recording." The first thing he did was place a low-impedance, electromechanical pickup of his own design in Joe's piano. Then he recorded all the instruments live, except for the strings, which were dubbed at a later date. Released on Atlantic in 1986, *Play It Again, Joe* lived up to Les's promise: Bushkin's recorded piano strokes had the full, rich sound of a live grand.

While Les was busy rebuilding a career based on performing pre– World War II standards, the rock world held the first of several significant tributes to him. Inducted on November 13, 1985, into the Hollywood Guitar Center's "Rock Walk," which marked the opening of one of the country's largest musical-instrument stores, he placed his signature and hand prints in a sidewalk gallery of autographs that eventually included such industry giants as Eddie Van Halen, Stevie Wonder, Leo Fender, Chuck Berry, Gregg Allman, Jerry Lee Lewis, and Little Richard.

Originating in the Guitar Center's Sunset Boulevard forecourt, the Rock Walk is only a mile from Tinseltown's well-trod Walk of Fame, where Les Paul and Mary Ford already had a star, and only a few blocks from where his house once stood at 1514 North Curson Avenue. A couple of hours before the unveiling ceremony, recalled

Guitar Center manager Dave Weiderman, Les persuaded two other Rock Walk inductees, drum mogul Bill Ludwig and amplifier maker Jim Marshall, to stroll over to the site. The tiny bungalow and garage studio were long gone, replaced by a steel-and-Plexiglas car dealership. But Marshall and Ludwig heard enough stories to visualize Les's ground-breaking recording experiments there forty years earlier.

The half-hour induction ceremony was reminiscent of old-style Hollywood, complete with a red carpet runway, an armada of stretch limos, klieg lights, TV crews, and such celebrities as Martin Mull and Robin Williams. Men in tuxedoes mingled with spike-haired metalheads sporting zebra-skin jackets and Spandex pants. "We had more than fifteen hundred rock-and-rollers here that night, and it seemed like they all just had to have a piece of Les Paul," said Weiderman. "He was eager to talk about his achievements, and everyone wanted to hear about them," including Eddie Van Halen, who was also inducted that night.

During the unveiling, Les and Eddie—the old and new guards of guitar playing—talked intently, their arms wrapped around each other. "I grew up on Cream and Led Zeppelin, so musically, Les and I are from two different worlds," Eddie later said, "but when I met him, I immediately fell in love with him. I looked him straight in the eyes and gave him a big hug and a kiss. He reminded me of my father because my father was also a musician. They had the same sort of sense of humor and openness. Les didn't come off with any attitude, like 'Who's this young punk?' He just treated me great."

The pair chatted for two hours before the Wednesday-night celebration in a small second-floor office in the Guitar Center. As usual, Les shamelessly embellished his past (claiming credit, for instance, for the design of every Les Paul guitar in the Gibson line). Unable to get a word in edgewise, Eddie listened quietly, smoking one cigarette after another. "He just sat there most of the time, soaking up all the stories, like Yoda sitting before the Master," recalled Dave Weiderman.

Reflecting on the unexpected twists and turns of his own show-business career, Les told Eddie, "About the time you think it's over, it's just beginning. You don't dare lay down or smell flowers. Ya just gotta keep moving."

"Too much flowers ain't no good," Eddie replied.

Inevitably, the conversation returned to guitars. Les was more sour than ever on Gibson, which Norlin had sold several months earlier, in January 1985. By most accounts, the new management possessed a better understanding of the music business and its practitioners. However, they were too busy trying to stem the company's financial hemorrhaging to lavish a lot of attention on Les Paul.

So Les found someone who would. Around this time, he became chummy with Dennis Berardi, then the savvy young head of Kramer Music Products. In less than ten years, Dennis had built a small garage operation in Hoboken, New Jersey, into a thriving manufacturing company with up to one hundred employees. At one time or another, his flashy guitars were endorsed by such young rock turks as Eddie Van Halen and Bon Jovi's Richie Sambora. Now it appeared he was courting Les Paul.

Les, in turn, was attracted to Dennis's drive, perhaps seeing a reminder of himself as a young renegade in the guitar business. At one point, Dennis tried to persuade Les to cosponsor music clinics for underprivileged kids. Then he began planning an elaborate music complex he promised would be named after Les Paul. Had the project gone beyond the blueprint stage, it would have contained a twenty-thousand-seat arena and nightclub in Asbury Park, New Jersey, the seedy seaside resort that spawned Bruce Springsteen, "Miami Steve" Van Zandt, and South Side Johnny.

Gibson's new executives were well aware of Les's enduring hostility toward the company—and of Berardi's persistent wooing of one of their main endorsees. But they were positively aghast when they saw Les praising one of Dennis's Kramer guitars on MTV. "This is a very small industry," Gibson president Henry Juszkiewicz later said. "It was devastating to have one of our endorsees do that, even if it was an innocent remark. It would be like if you made Willie Mays baseball gloves and Willie started hanging out with Rawlings and using another glove. Les was associating with Kramer in a way that could be construed as endorsing their product."

The cold war between Les and Gibson reached a climax in the spring of 1987, when Juszkiewicz heard that Dennis was planning to throw a bash for Les's seventy-second birthday. Even though Dennis had already begun arranging invitations, "we just couldn't let it happen," said Juszkiewicz. "But you have to remember, we had just bought a company that had lost millions of dollars. Giving Les an elaborate party is not what I was thinking about at the time."

But that's just what Gibson did. Dreamed up by Paul Jernigan, one of Gibson's most inspired point men, the event was to be a grand fence-mending that would signal a fresh start for both Gibson and Les Paul. The date was set for Tuesday, June 9, 1987; the place, the Hard Rock Café, known as the Smithsonian of Rock and Roll. The trendy midtown Manhattan nightspot agreed to foot a substantial portion of the bill based on Gibson's promise to deliver a star-studded list of guests.

The first batch of invitations went out in the middle of May: "The Hard Rock Café and Gibson Guitars cordially invite you to a party honoring Les Paul on his seventy-second birthday." The response was impressive, but the number of confirmations that poured in during the last forty-eight hours before the Tuesday-night party exceeded Gibson's expectations. "We went from reserving just the balcony area, which seats about one hundred and twenty-five people, to closing the whole club down to accommodate all the RSVPs," says Jernigan. "All of a sudden, we had twice as many guests as we could possibly get in."

The attendance list, drawn from a wide spectrum of music talent, read like a Who's Who of International Pop. It was a fitting tribute to a man whose sixty-year career as an entertainer spanned the country, jazz, and pop fields and whose technical innovations helped reshape the way musicians and recording engineers work in the studio today.

The biggest stars staked out their turf early on. Jimmy Page and Jeff Beck, both in from England for the occasion, commandeered a cordoned-off table next to the stage. Tony Bennett chatted with guitarist Duane Eddy in the balcony. The Lovin' Spoonful's John Sebastian sat nearby with his son, while Bo Diddley, sporting his trademark black derby, gave Les a big hug at the bar below. In the meantime, Rick Derringer, Al Dimeola, the Cars' Eliot Easton, the Doors' Robby Kreiger, *Saturday Night Live* bandleader G. E. Smith, piano maestro Dr. John, and bassist Nile Rodgers grooved to the sound of Paul Shaffer's band.

Not everyone was rich and famous, though. There we e a few of Les's old industry pals and a coterie of friends from Fat Tuesday's. Noticeably absent from this spectacular event, however, were three of Les's four children; his oldest son, Rus, was the only one invited. But then the guest of honor's attendance wasn't entirely assured until he actually stepped out of a black limo in front of the club.

"Les was still so angry at Gibson that he kept telling us to cancel the party the whole time we were planning it," Jernigan recalls. "He wanted out, and I don't blame him. This party was the first time in years he had been shown he was appreciated. It was the first time he had gotten a signal we understood he had been alienated and that we wanted him back."

While uniformed police carefully monitored hundreds of celebrity watchers on Fifty-seventh Street, the two-story club was growing ear-shatteringly loud and suicidally crowded inside. Photographers and TV news crews had a nightmarish time stalking the glitterati. Everybody, it seemed, suspended breathing for a while, lest the walls burst at the seams.

But an open bar and a bountiful buffet of ribs, roast beef, chicken, and shrimp kept things rolling until Henry Juszkiewicz mounted the stage around eleven o'clock to introduce Les Paul to the crowd. The Hard Rock presented the honoree with a Les Paul–style guitar carved from white onyx and marble and a white-frosted cake the size of a card table. Flashing the raunchy humor that has become as much a part of his stage act as his guitar, Les took one look at the blazing candles and proclaimed, "I'm seventy-two, I ain't gonna blow nothin' . . . out."

The high point of the evening, though, was the impromptu—and slightly bizarre—jam session he kicked off with his two sidemen, Gary Mazzaroppi and Lou Pallo. Thin and stoop-shouldered, Les appeared years younger once he mounted the stage and looped his guitar over his left shoulder. The guitarists in the crowd quickly surged to the front of the room, their eyes glued to his fingers as he tore through three jazz-flavored instrumentals. Then Tony Bennett nearly brought the house down with a supercharged version of "On the Sunny Side of the Street."

But the music took a sharp turn from the sunny to the rock side of the street once Jimmy Page leaped onstage and began trading runs with Les on a smoky blues number. Rick Derringer sang the McCoys' "Hang on Sloopy," Dr. John and Paul Shaffer took turns tickling the ivories in the rhythm section, and Robbie Krieger brought the session to a close with the Doors' gritty "Love Me Two Times." Jeff Beck was one of the few stars who didn't sit in that night. He was content to recount his days as a child, huddling by the radio when he was five years old, listening to Les's licks. "You just don't forget that stuff," he said. "It has its impact."

It was three in the morning before the crowd started thinning out, stumbling blurry-eyed and exhausted onto West 57th Street. By then, WNBC-TV had already covered the raucous event on the late-night news. The party was later reported in industry trades and in the entertainment pages of *USA Today,* the *Los Angeles Herald,* and the New York dailies. "I've been to music parties at the Hard Rock before," a *Show Business* columnist wrote, "but this one goes into the history books." "The best jam session I've ever seen!" exclaimed the New York *Daily News. Rolling Stone* ran two photos of Les with Jimmy Page and Jeff Beck, captioned "Saint Paul and disciples," and MTV followed up with multiple airings of the party through the month of June.

With one Olympian birthday bash, fifteen years of battles between Les and Gibson had come to an end. Gibson demonstrated that it was no longer being run by businessmen who couldn't relate to musicians, and Les proved once and for all that he still held powerful sway over the rockers the company so desperately wanted to reach. "Les came home that night," Jernigan later said.

Slowly but surely, Les was becoming part of the national mythology, but 1988 was a banner year. It began on January 20 with his induction into the Rock and Roll Hall of Fame at Manhattan's plush Waldorf-Astoria. That night Les took his place in pop-music history alongside the Beatles, the Beach Boys, the Supremes, the Drifters, Berry Gordy, Jr., Leadbelly, Woody Guthrie, and Bob Dylan. The black-tie crowd, which included such rock luminaries as Bruce Springsteen, Little Richard, Mick Jagger, Billy Joel, Elton John, and Julian Lennon, watched a brief audiovisual overview of Les's career before Jeff Beck stepped up to the podium and presented Les with an eight-inch bronze statuette. "I've copied more licks from Les Paul than I'd like to admit," the lanky British guitarist joked. Atlantic Records' founder Ahmet Ertegun was even more effusive: "Les Paul is an inspiration to a world of guitarists for his playing, for the instrument he created and his multiple-track recording innovations. Without him, it is hard to imagine how rock and roll would be played today."

Les's acceptance speech was uncharacteristically modest—and brief: "I have been credited with inventing a few things you guys are using. . . . About the most I can say is 'Have fun with my toys.' " That they did. Immediately following the presentations, scores of musicians left their ballroom seats and gathered onstage for a rollicking forty-five-minute jam session that produced moments of all-star transcendence.

Les managed to shoulder his way into the crowded front line of entertainers, even though he was decades older than most of them. After George Harrison, Springsteen, and Jagger shared a single mike for a galloping cover of "I Saw Her Standing There," Les exchanged a few sizzling licks with Harrison on Dylan's "All Along the Watchtower." Then Ben E. King and Julian Lennon sang a duet on "Stand by Me," with plenty of help from the Beach Boys.

In truth, the hastily thrown-together session was a cacophony of botched chords and jumbled lyrics. But the excitement of seeing so many big names jamming together on one stage instantly lifted the crowd to its feet. Les's eyes sparkled as he watched hundreds of elegantly attired guests dancing on the Waldorf's upholstered chairs to the pounding beat of the music. "It was one of those once-in-a-lifetime things," he said the next day.

Not quite. The scene was repeated seven months later on the stage of the Brooklyn Academy of Music's Majestic Theater, where Cinemax Sessions staged another major Les Paul tribute. This time, however, Les was the sole honoree. He wanted to appear on the one-hour cable special with some of his personal favorites—Ella Fitzgerald, Oscar Peterson, George Shearing. But the Cinemax producers insisted on inviting younger guest stars, not only those who had benefited from Les's recording innovations, but, more important, those who would appeal to the show's built-in audience.

The final entertainment roster included Eddie Van Halen, B. B. King, Steve Miller, Rita Coolidge, Carly Simon, the Stray Cats, *Miami Vice* theme song composer and keyboardist Jan Hammer, Pink Floyd guitarist David Gilmour, jazz guitarist Stanley Jordan, Waylon Jennings, and Waylon's wife, country singer Jessi Colter. Les had never heard of several of his costars, but he assumed Cinemax knew what it was doing.

On August 18, after three tension-filled days of rehearsal—Les and director Jeb Brien were at each other's throats almost from the moment they met—"Les Paul: He Changed the Music" was filmed before a live audience in the newly refurbished Majestic Theater. Performers and crew alike were more than ready to shake loose at the end of the four-hour show (which began multiple airings on Cinemax two months later). The post-production party at the Hard Rock attracted a long list of star rockers as did the one the club hosted for Les's seventy-second birthday. "It was just one of those magic nights," said Stray Cat Brian Setzer, who played a romping thirty-minute set that evening with his own trio.

The next day, Les was in a reflective mood: "What if Mary was here and the two of us could talk this thing over?" he asked an acquaintance. "This is not something I could have imagined in my time—all these youngsters telling me, 'I wouldn't have a job if it hadn't been for you.' It's difficult to understand, because I wasn't trying to change the industry. I was just trying to create certain sounds I had a craving for, but it drove poor Mary crazy. Too bad she couldn't have seen what has come of all those long, hard nights."

While Les rode to glory on a newly cresting wave of fame, his mother turned one hundred years old. At the time, Evelyn Polfuss was living in LindenGrove Healthcare Center, a sprawling nursing home on the outskirts of Waukesha. Although she hung pictures of him on the wall next to her bed, Evelyn had not seen Les in several years. In the winter of 1988, though, Waukesha decided to combine her March 30 birthday with a salute to her famous son.

Once Les agreed to return for the event, a committee of high-powered locals kicked into gear and put together one of the most elaborate parties the city had seen in years. They rented the Country Inn's newly constructed ballroom in nearby Pewaukee, then persuaded the mayor of Waukesha and the governor of Wisconsin to declare Evelyn's birthday Les Paul Day. As an added flourish, they christened the park bandshell where Les used to entertain as a boy the Les Paul Performance Center. Three giant billboards around town advertised the March 30 celebration, and the *Waukesha Freeman* ran several articles urging readers to attend.

Les arrived at two o'clock in the afternoon on March 29 at Milwaukee's Mitchell Airport, accompanied by his son Rusty, friend Bob Fox, and bandmates Gary Mazzaroppi and Lou Pallo. He visited several old haunts, including the site of his childhood home. But he waited till the following afternoon to stop by the nursing home to see his mother. Evelyn had eagerly anticipated this day for weeks. She had her snowy-white hair set in curls and instructed one of her attendants to buy her a new outfit, a ruffly steel-blue dress with billowing sleeves.

When Les strolled into the LindenGrove dining hall, Evelyn was lunching on her favorite meal—hot dogs, sauerkraut, and Blatz beer. As soon as she spied her son crossing the room, though, she quietly began sobbing. Les knelt down and wept beside her. They talked quietly for a few minutes, but then he disappeared. It was time to return to the hotel to prepare for the main event.

By seven in the evening the ballroom was bursting with more than thirteen hundred celebrants. Though tables and chairs were removed to provide additional standing space, the hall was still uncomfortably crowded. Budding rock stars came to see the man who had just been inducted into the Rock and Roll Hall of Fame, and old-timers in freshly pressed suits showed up to get a look at an old neighbor whose music they would never forget. Several of Les's boyhood chums were there, too, including Claude Schultz, Cullen Casey, Harold Vinger, and Warren Downie, who came all the way from his home in Charlotte, North Carolina.

Les looked years younger than his hometown friends as he raced around the ballroom at a dizzying pace. He pumped hands, signed autographs, and posed for the press with his wheelchair-bound mother. Dressed in a starched white shirt, dark suit, and shiny shoes, he looked like the mayor of Waukesha. But after all the proclamations were read and the honors bestowed, he ripped off his jacket, loosened his tie, and barreled through a couple of forty-minute sets. Between songs, he recalled his school-skipping days with Claude Schultz, and the night Harold Vinger dragged him out of bed to hear Sunny Joe Wolverton perform at a nearby dance hall.

As the party wound down, Les bid farewell to his mother before she was taken back to the nursing home. Then he led a giddy throng of friends and fans into the Country Inn cocktail lounge, which stayed open well past closing time to accommodate the party. Les didn't want this happy night to end. But he flew back to New Jersey the following afternoon and didn't return to Waukesha for a year and a half, just hours before Evelyn's graveside burial service at Prairie Home Cemetery.

Four days after his mother's death, Les was back on the bandstand at Fat Tuesday's. For no matter how many emotional upheavals or enticing opportunities have come his way, one thing has remained constant in Les Paul's life: his commitment to the Manhattan saloon he has called home since 1984. Since then he has stepped up his consulting work for Gibson. "Now Les is easily the most successful endorser of guitars in history," said guitar aficionado Walter Carter. He has also entertained lucrative tour offers and entirely overhauled his home studio to record a new LP for Epic, a Columbia records subsidiary. In the interim, Capitol released a critically acclaimed four-CD retrospective of his work, *Les Paul: The Legend and the Legacy.*

But Fat Tuesday's is the tonic that keeps him going. Every Monday night he sits onstage and invites listeners to "Come in and hear the truth." The prerecorded accompaniment and all the other electronic gimmicks Les previously used have been discarded. It's just the man and his guitar and his music, with a few stories and raunchy remarks thrown in to keep things light.

At least a couple of times a month, broadcast or print journalists, some from as far away as Japan and Australia, drop by the club to interview Les. "To keep your mind from getting old," he once philosophized, "the best thing to do is what you did when you were young, which is to go to a beer joint and play, one-to-one, for someone you can reach out and touch."

Between sets, he swaps small talk and hugs with the regulars, and onstage he performs their requests with relish. "Play 'How High the Moon,' " one suggests.

"Nah, do 'Blue Skies,' " says another.

"Okay," Les answers, " 'Blue Skies' it is. Do you want it pretty? 'Cause if you don't, I'll play it up-tempo for you."

It really doesn't matter which tunes he plays, though. His devotees have heard them all before, dozens of times. "But something is always new," insists Bob Fox, who has barely missed one of Les's performances since 1984. "He plays the song a little differently, tells a different story."

Far from tiring of his rube jokes and recycled stories, the regulars egg Les on, then eagerly watch the unanointed dissolve in laughter. At seventy-seven, he is a wisp of a man with piercing blue eyes and thinning red hair. But on a good night he whips through one old chestnut after another with the vigor of a man half his age. The front-row fans tap their feet in unison with his sneakered foot as he runs through "Avalon," the double-time number that always signals the end of each set. "I'll play until I die," Les told one delighted standing-room-only crowd. "They may have to wheel me out, and I may not be able to hit every note, but I'll go out swinging."

Nobody doubted him.

Source Notes

This book began as a collaborative effort between Les Paul and the author. I met Les soon after writing a *People* magazine review of an exquisite album he had produced in 1985 for swing pianist Joe Bushkin (*Play It Again, Joe,* Atlantic). Initially I called Les at his Mahwah, New Jersey, home simply to get personal information missing from the album's liner notes. What was intended to be a ten-minute interview stretched into a two-hour conversation. Like many others who have met Les Paul, I was immediately captivated by his spellbinding skills as a raconteur. Several months later, I gave him a collection of music articles I had written for *People* magazine and asked if he would allow me to be his biographer. To my surprise, he said he would. Several of his closest friends suggested I would have difficulty getting him to devote the time and attention to detail the project would require. Nevertheless I persisted, attending scores of Les Paul performances at Fat Tuesday's and interviewing him in numerous phone conversations that typically lasted till one or two in the morning. During this period, Les regaled me with expansive tales about his life that were, by turns, hilarious and tragic.

However, he often incorrectly recalled or embellished easily verifiable facts—a biographer's nightmare. (This predilection persists in the biographical information that accompanies his 1991 CD collection.) With little prodding, Les gave me the names and phone numbers of many of his personal and professional associates, and he even encouraged these people to speak with me candidly and honestly. But he became alarmed when I began interviewing the family of Mary Ford, his former wife and longtime stage partner. Unfortunately, in December 1988, Les withdrew his cooperation, despite written assurance that I would honor all reasonable requests for corrections on the final manuscript.

By then I had interviewed more than a hundred people all over the country: members of his family, childhood friends, music-industry associates, and former in-laws, all of whom offered lively memories of Les,

300

ranging from the first time he picked up a guitar in the twenties to the rebirth of the once-forgotten "Legend" as a popular figure in the eighties and nineties. In addition to these interviews—and my own conversations with Les over a thirty-four-month period—dozens of books, articles, and archival sources, which are listed in the bibliography, have yielded information about his life and times.

The notes that follow give me an opportunity to thank all the people who helped me create a portrait of this complex man and the music world in which he thrived. I have identified the sources of all important quotes that I obtained from published stories and interviews. The reader can assume that almost all others are derived from my own interviews.

CHILDHOOD AND YOUTH (CHAPTERS 1–4)

Les's late mother, Evelyn Polfuss, and his cousin Orval Polsfuss shared remembrances of the guitarist's early years. Many more important details were provided by childhood schoolmates and bandmates Cullen Casey, Warren Downie, Larry Knoebel, Fred Rosenmerkel, Claude Schultz, Bill Waschow, and Harold Vinger; Harold also enlisted his daughter, Mary, and son, Donald, to recall their favorite Les Paul stories for later chapters. I owe a special debt of gratitude to "Sunny Joe" Wolverton, who not only gave me hours of his own time but also entrusted me with dozens of papers and photos from his personal archives to document the years he sponsored Les on the midwestern radio circuit. Mayor Paul Vrakas apprised me of Waukesha's political history, and Lorayne Ritt and Isobel Blodgett Wray contributed to the Goerke's Corners background. Teresa Crivello and Terry Becker of the Waukesha County Museum (a magnificent repository of historical and genealogical data) were invaluable in the preparation of the chapters concerning Les's grandparents and parents. Other important sources include the unpublished memoir of Les's boyhood hero Claud "Pie Plant Pete" Moye (courtesy of Nashville's Country Music Foundation) and Waukesha County school and court records.

Page 14 "No one in the history of pop music . . ." *Rolling Stone,* Feb. 13, 1975.

16 "From all over the country . . ." Federal Writers' Project, *Wisconsin,* 1939.

25 "Whatcha wanna hear, kid? . . ." *Capitol News,* April 1951.

26 "Don't *say* you can't . . ." *Reader's Digest,* June 1957.

27 "My teachers saw that I was a dreamer. . . ." *The Wizard of Waukesha* (film).

34 "He bought it with the $5 . . ." *Chicago Herald Examiner,* Nov. 22, 1934.

34 "Was original and the only . . ." Claud Moye, unpublished memoir.

35 "You are a hero to my boy! . . ." Claud Moye, unpublished memoir.

35 "He took that piece of paper home . . ." Ibid.

47 "When we got there, Mother turned around . . ." Yale School of Music oral history archives.

55 "Sally was an unemployed . . ." Emmett Dedmon, *Fabulous Chicago.*
"she had all but pushed into obscurity. . . ." Ibid.

THE CHICAGO YEARS (CHAPTERS 5–6)

Several previously noted individuals were helpful here, particularly Sunny Joe Wolverton, Cullen Casey, and Harold Vinger. I also spoke to a number of musicians who worked or jammed with Les in Chicago during the 1930s and 1940s: accordionist Art Van Damme, bassist Bob Meyer (who also contributed to the chapter covering Les's Hollywood years), and guitarists Doc Parker, George Allen, and Fred Rundquist, as well as the late Harry Zimmerman and Roy Eldridge. Also helpful were Alvino Rey, indisputably one of the country's first electric guitarists; Gibson guitar company veterans Julius Bellson, Walt Fuller, and John Kutilek; former disk jockey Riley Jackson, who used to announce Les's jazz show on WIND; Wilma Atkins, wife of the late Jimmy Atkins, one of Les's first triomates; and the late Fran Allison, who worked with Les at WBBM in the early 1940s. Les's lifelong friend Wally Jones contributed to this and several other chapters of the book. Other valuable sources include Jimmy Atkins's extensive interview with Bill Ivey for *Guitar Player* magazine; Chet Atkins's autobiography, *Country Gentleman;* Chuck Schader's *WBBM: Yesterday and Today;* and Richard Crabb's *Radio's Beautiful Day.*

Page 59 "I didn't do very well . . ." Yale School of Music oral history archives. "Bustin' the bubble . . ." *The Wizard of Waukesha* (film).

59 "Hey, I hate to do this to you . . ." *Guitar,* Nov. 1975.

60 "Harry, what are you trying to do to me?" Ibid.

61 "That was easy . . ." *Guitar Player,* Dec. 1977.

63 "Georgia couldn't do anything . . ." Audio Engineering Society speech, 1987.

64 "They thought I was crazy. . . ." *Guitar Player,* Dec. 1977.

67 "Everybody looked down their noses . . ." *Guitar Player,* Sept. 1976.

68 "As a bullet seeks its target . . ." James Trager, ed., *The People's Chronology.*

68 "Guitar was really put down. . . ." Norman Mongan, *History of the Guitar in Jazz.*

69 "Well, we're ready to go." *Mix,* Feb. 1985.

70 "We'd sit in our room . . ." *Guitar Player,* Sept. 1976.

71-72 "But probably what impressed Fred Waring . . ." *Mix,* Feb. 1985.

THE WARING AND BERNIE YEARS (CHAPTERS 7–8)

Details of Les's involvement with Fred Waring's Pennsylvanians were drawn from personal interviews with former Waring bandmates and from musicians who lived in the same Jackson Heights, New York, apartment building as Les in the late 1930s and early 1940s—Johnny Blowers, Virgil "Stinky" Davis, Bob Haggert, Glen Moore—and from former publicist Jim Moran, who represented Waring during this period. Additional information came from my interviews with Chet Atkins, Wilma Atkins, Milt Gabler, and guitarist Johnny Smith (who professed to have been profoundly influenced by Les's daily performances on the Waring radio show) and guitarist Bucky Pizzarelli (who rarely missed one of Les's performances on Ben Bernie's WBBM radio show). Jimmy Atkins's *Guitar Player* magazine article also informed this chapter. Pete Kiefer, coordinator of The Fred Waring Collection at Penn State, provided background material. Vince Giordano, musician/collector extraordinaire, was a technical expertise on music making of the 1920s and 1930s. Walter Carter of Gruhn's guitar store in Nashville kindly contributed his transcript of an in-depth interview with Les concerning "the Log." Information about New York City was gleaned from several guidebooks and jazz books that examined the music scene in Harlem and on 52nd Street.

Page 84 "the real jive cat . . ." *Down Beat,* Oct. 1, 1940.

87 "I'll never forget it . . ." *The Wizard of Waukesha* (film).

87 "Come on in, Les...." Ibid.

88 "was as proud as ... " Chet Atkins, *Country Gentleman.*

90 "I don't know...." *New York Times,* Jan. 10, 1988.

92 "Turn on your radio...." *Guitar Player,* Sept. 1976.

94 "At four in the morning ..." Ibid.

95 "We enjoyed your music ..." Ibid.

95 "Our professional life ..." *Down Beat,* Oct 1, 1940.

96 "The highly talented ..." *Down Beat,* May 1, 1940.

97-98 "We rehearsed everything ..." Yale School of Music oral history archives.

100 "Where did you meet him?" *Rolling Stone,* Feb. 13, 1975.

101 "Phrasing is one of the toughest ... " *Music and Rhythm,* April 1942.

102-103 "Electric refrigerators ..." *Time,* Jan. 26, 1948.

THE HOLLYWOOD YEARS (CHAPTERS 9–12)

Much of the information concerning this period, perhaps the most productive of Les Paul's life, came from interviews with Maxene Andrews of the Andrews Sisters, who shared the stage with Les in 1946 and 1947; Sue Chadwick, one of Les's colleagues at the Armed Forces Radio Service (1943–44); Lou Levy, the Andrews Sisters' manager and Les's onetime personal business guru; Zeke Manners, former radio personality and lifelong friend of Les Paul's, Murdo McKenzie, Bing Crosby's longtime radio engineer; John "Jack" Mullin, the Ampex engineer who helped Les design his "sound-on-sound" tape recorder; the late Bill Putnam, a fellow audio industry pioneer; Wally Jones; Andrews Sisters' music director Vic Schoen; Les Paul triomates Bob Meyer and Paul Smith; audio engineer Carson Taylor; musical film historian Miles Krueger; collectors Lloyd Rauch and Louis Sarog; former Waukesha deejay Mig Figi; and Sidney Bechet protégé Bob Wilbur. *W. C. Fields: A Life on Film* and *Halliwell's Film Guide* provided helpful descriptions of the movies featuring Les and his trio.

Page 109 "Why should customers pay ..." *Life,* Aug. 3, 1942.

109 "How come you guys have to jam ..." Audio Engineering Society speech, 1977.

112 "They panned the hell ..." R. J. Fields, *W. C. Fields: A Life on Film.*

114 "Play as dumb as you can . . ." Yale School of Music oral history archives.

117 "We needed a benefit to raise money . . ." *Jazz at the Philharmonic* liner notes, by Leonard Feather.

118 "The kids squirmed . . ." *Down Beat,* Aug. 1, 1944.

121 "It has a nice, intimate sound." Audio Engineering Society speech, 1977.

122 "It's a pleasure to welcome . . ." Bing Crosby's *Kraft Music Hall* radio show, Dec. 28, 1944.

123 "The Crosby/Les Paul Trio combination . . ." *Down Beat,* Nov. 1, 1945.

127 "It stinks." *Band Leaders,* Spring 1946.

134 "When the hot spot lights . . ." *Guitar Player,* Dec. 1977.

135 "It packs speed . . ." *Billboard,* Dec. 18, 1946.

136 "America, oui les beeg ranches . . ." *Time,* Nov. 8, 1946.
    "I gave him my guitar . . ." *Down Beat,* August 13, 1952.

136 "only certain audiences . . ." *Metronome,* Nov. 1953.

137 "I heard you on Bob Hope's . . ." *Cosmopolitan,* Jan. 1955.

141 "that overturned his plan . . ." *Washington Post,* Feb. 3, 1963.

143 "As a combined performance . . ." *Down Beat,* March 10, 1948.

143 "Compared to the practice . . ." *Variety,* March 10, 1948.

THE LES PAUL AND MARY FORD YEARS (CHAPTERS 13–19)

I received invaluable assistance for this section from several members of Mary Ford's family—sisters Esther Williams and Carol Corona, and brothers Fletcher and Bob Summers, who kindly lent me pictures and personal correspondence from Mary—and from Colleen Paul, Les and Mary's daughter. My deepest gratitude to them and to Dick Linke, Les and Mary's Capitol PR representative from 1950 to 1955. Additional information about the couple's Capitol tenure was provided by former label executives Jim Conkling, Lloyd Dunn, Tom Morgan, Doreen Lauer, the late Dave Dexter, and Capitol recording engineer Frank Abbey. I also relied on Capitol press releases and newsletters containing Les Paul/Mary Ford bio material. Library of Congress archivists Neil Gladd and Wyn Mathias were invaluable in the formulation of the discography, helping me to tap into a vast computerized national information network. The Oklahoma Historical Society's Scott

Dowell unearthed newspaper clips about Les and Mary's 1948 car accident. Technical and personal information concerning Les's contractual agreement with Gibson during the 1950s and early 1960s was derived from interviews with former Gibson president Ted McCarty, Gibson historian Julius Bellson, chief engineer Walt Fuller, quality control manager Wilbur Marker, and parts department manager Ward Arbanas; additional details are drawn from Tom Wheeler's *American Guitars: An Illustrated History*. Former Ampex museum curator Peter Hammar and Atlantic recording engineers Tom Dowd and Phil Iehle (the first record company engineers to utilize Les's eight-track machine) described Les's leadership in the recording industry. Other sources include guitarist Steve Miller and his mother Bertha, who witnessed Les and Mary's 1949 wedding in Milwaukee; Warren Downie, Les and Mary's first bassist; erstwhile cowboy star Eddie Dean, who introduced Les to Mary in 1945; Dave Palmquist, Mary's first husband; Cliffie Stone, who hired Mary to work on his weekday radio show; Wally Jones, Zeke Manners, and Lou Levy, all of whom spent many hours in Les's garage studio; John Mack, who lived with Les and Mary in 1953 while editing their Listerine TV show; Mitch Miller, who signed the couple to Columbia in 1958; and Bucky Pizzarelli, Don Butterfield, Harold Vinger, Cullen Casey, Bill Putnam, Gwen Ray, Holdie Partridge, Bob Maxwell, Jazzbo Collins, Ernest (Mickey) Knight, Harry Bryant, Shelley Herman, Rosemary Clooney, and Kay Starr.

Page 146 "I wanted something that . . ." *Cosmopolitan,* Jan. 1955.

166 "There was a silence . . ." *Reader's Digest,* June 1957.

174 "Paul and his group . . ." *Down Beat,* Sept. 23, 1949.

175 "Never try to educate people . . ." *Newsweek,* Sept. 5, 1949.

176 "There were times when we . . ." *Cosmopolitan,* Jan. 1955

176 "that used newspapers . . ." *San Gabriel Valley Tribune,* Dec. 20, 1964.

177 "The people you're playing . . ." *Down Beat,* June 15, 1951.

177 "Whadda you guys looking for . . ." George Barnes's personal papers.

178 "We hope to throw a . . ." *Waukesha Freeman,* Dec. 29, 1949.

183 " 'Lover,' the first multi-guitar . . ." *Melody Maker,* May 19, 1952.

187 "It may be a successful gimmick . . ." *Metronome,* March 1951.

187 "Jim, please, . . ." Pacific Pioneers Broadcasters speech.

189 "I'd like to present . . ." *The Bing Crosby Show,* March 21, 1951.

193 "Les Paul was the first . . ." Bill Wyman, *Stone Alone.*

193 "I was intrigued . . ." Joe Smith, *Off the Record.*

193 "This isn't the kind of gimmick . . . " *Metronome,* Feb. 1952.

195 "We grind 'em out . . ." *Time,* Oct. 29, 1951.

195 "I did all the secret work . . ." *San Gabriel Valley Tribune,* April 11, 1989.

196 "They wanted to know . . ." *Down Beat,* June 15, 1951.

197 "The amount of 'extra money' . . ." *Billboard,* Oct. 27, 1951.

198 "I got a better echo . . ." *Time,* Oct. 29, 1951.

199 "I had to stand in . . ." *San Gabriel Valley Tribune,* April 11, 1989.

199 "Laine Falters but Les-Mary . . ." *Billboard,* Oct. 27, 1951.

203 "some sort of pill . . ." *Capitol News,* April 1951.

205 "The powerhouse platter team . . ." *Variety,* June 25, 1952.

206 "Who that is would be . . ." *Down Beat,* Sept. 10, 1952.

207 "And they all told me . . ." *Melody Maker,* Sept. 13, 1952.

208 "But Wally . . ." Ibid.

209 "He sure played guitar . . ." *Melody Maker,* Sept. 20, 1952.

210 "It was obvious that . . ." *Guitar,* Feb. 1975.

210 "I sure like that . . ." *San Gabriel Valley Tribune,* Dec. 20, 1964.

210 "audience reacted . . ." *Vogue,* Feb. 15, 1953.

211 "But if it's a bird . . ." *Radio Electronics,* Oct. 1958.

214 "I'm sitting on top . . ." *Variety,* April 22, 1953.

214 "I was fourteen or fifteen . . ." *International Musician & Recording World,* June 1986.

215 "I told my manager . . ." Yale School of Music oral history archives.

216 "Les Paul and Mary Ford . . ." *Billboard,* July, 1953.

219 "What Benny Goodman did . . ." *Metronome,* Nov. 1953.

219 "she didn't stagnate." *Cosmopolitan,* Jan. 1955.

221 "The fact is . . ." *Melody Maker,* Jan. 22, 1955.

224 "We have to redo . . ." Les to unidentified Boston deejay.

224 "People like me and Crosby . . ." Audio Engineering Society speech, 1977.

229 "You never saw such a . . ." Ibid.

232 "Les Paul, Mary Ford, and eight hundred . . ."

232 "felt that was the wrong way . . . " Yale School of Music oral history archives.

249 " . . . considerable time making . . . " *Bergen Record,* Feb. 23, 1963.

251 "What I mainly want . . ." *San Gabriel Valley Tribune,* Dec. 20, 1964.

252 "Being blond and curvy . . . " *New York Times,* Aug. 9, 1975.

253 "In one of their funniest bits . . . " *Stars and Stripes,* June 1965.

254 "taught me how to play . . . " *Stars and Stripes,* July 3, 1965.

254 "They're playing angry music. . . . " Audio Engineering Society speech, 1977.

THE MID-1960S TO THE PRESENT (CHAPTERS 20–22)

Those who granted interviews for this section include Zeke Manners and George Barnes's wife and daughter, Evelyn and Alexandra, all of whom lived with Les in Mahwah in 1967 and 1968; Bruce Bolen, who worked closely with Les at Gibson from 1967 to the mid 1980s; Wayne Wright, Les's friend and former triomate; Chet Atkins, who recorded two LPs with Les in the late 1970s; and Wally Jones, who, with his wife, Eleanor, nursed Les back to health following his 1980 quintuple bypass surgery. Members of Gibson's management team—President Henry Juszkiewicz, Paul Jernigan, John Hawkins, Tim Shaw, and Kevin Walsh—detailed Les's affiliation with the company. Gibson consultant Bill Lawrence also spoke for the record. Other sources include Eddie Van Halen, Steve Miller, Jeff Beck, B. B. King, Waylon Jennings, Jan Hammer, Brian Setzer, Stanley Jordan, Felix Cavaliere, Dave Weiderman of Hollywood's Guitar Center, Bucky Pizzarelli, Joe Wolverton, Joe Dera, Bob Fox, Mark Joy, Rich Conaty, Mark Dery, Douglas Green, Daniel Kagan, Bob Schwartz, and Timmie Manolis.

In addition to personally witnessing Les's seventy-second birthday party at New York's Hard Rock Café, his induction into the Rock and Roll Hall of Fame, his mother's hundredth birthday party in his native Waukesha, his meeting with Paul McCartney, and the filming of the Cinemax Sessions Les Paul tribute, the author discussed these events with Evelyn Polfuss, Joan Myers, Quince Buteau, Steve Ruthier, and Clark Enselin.

Page 256 "Friends in the . . ." *Bergen Record,* June 13, 1966.

262 "When I toured abroad . . ." *The Wizard of Waukesha* (film).

262 "What drew me . . ." *IM&RW,* June 1986.

267 "The kids went crazy . . ." Yale School of Music oral history archives.

269 "There's an excitement you feel . . ." *Los Angeles Times,* Aug. 30, 1975.

269 "Off they went . . ." *Guitar,* Nov. 1975.

273 "I thought, 'I'm gonna . . ." *Rolling Stone,* Feb. 12, 1976.

275 "It is a vivid, . . ." *Down Beat,* Oct. 1976.

275 "Man, I idolize you," *People,* April 11, 1977.

276 "We were married fourteen years . . . *National Enquirer,* undated.

277 "No, Les, you can't have a . . ." *Guitar Player,* April 1978.

278 "The looseness and intimacy . . ." Ibid.

278 "You talking to me?" Ibid.

278 "Now if that don't grab you . . ." Ibid.

278 "Let's send Les . . ." Ibid.

279 "Paul came out and ripped . . ." New York *Daily News,* April 21, 1985.

279 "Mr. Paul can hardly . . ." *New York Times,* July 9, 1978.

282 "It's very difficult . . ." *Guitar World,* Nov. 1985.

287 "It's more like a private . . ." New York *Daily News,* April 21, 1985.

288 "It's great for your ego . . ." *Washington Post,* May 10, 1987.

288 "Every morning when I wake . . ." New York *Daily News,* April 21, 1985.

289 "sound live, like they were in the room . . ." *Play It Again, Joe* liner notes.

290 "About the time you think . . ." *Guitar World,* Nov. 1985. All Rock and Roll Hall of Fame quotes are from author's personal account of the event.

294 "I've been to music parties . . ." *Show Business,* June 17, 1987.

294 "The best jam session . . ." New York *Daily News,* June 30, 1987.

294 "Saint Paul and disciples . . ." *Rolling Stone,* Aug. 13, 1987.

299 "To keep your mind . . ." *Washington Post,* May 10, 1987.

Bibliography

BOOKS

Atkins, Chet. *Country Gentleman*. Henry Regnery, 1974.

Balliett, Whitney. *New York Notes: A Journal of Jazz, 1972–74*. Houghton Mifflin, 1975.

Baxton, Frank, and Bill Owen. *The Big Broadcast*. Viking, 1972.

Crabb, Richard. *Radio's Beautiful Day*. North Plains Press, 1983.

Dedmon, Emmett. *Fabulous Chicago*. Random House, 1953.

Duchossoir, A. R. *Gibson Electrics*. Hal Leonard, 1981.

Dunning, John. *Tune in Yesterday: The Ultimate Encyclopedia of Old-Time Radio, 1925–1976*. Prentice-Hall, 1976.

Fields, R. J. *W. C. Fields: A Life on Film*. St. Martin's, 1984.

Gillespie, Dizzy, with Al Frazer. *To Be or Not to Bop*. Doubleday, 1979.

Gillet, Charlie. *The Sound of the City*. Pantheon, 1983.

Green, Douglas B. *Country Roots: The Origins of Country Music*. Hawthorn, 1976.

Halliwell, Leslie H. *Halliwell's Film Guide, 7th edition*. Harper & Row, 1980.

Huber, David Miles, and Robert A. Runstein. *Modern Recording Techniques*. Howard W. Sams, 1989.

Keepnews, Orrin, and Bill Grauer. *A Pictorial History of Jazz: People and Places from New Orleans to Modern Jazz*. Crown, 1955.

Kinkle, Roger. *The Complete Encyclopedia of Popular Music and Jazz, 1900–1950*. Arlington House, 1974.

Kozinn, Allan, Pete Welding, Dan Forte, and Gene Santoro. *The Guitar: The History, the Music, the Players*. Quill, 1984.

Langill, Ellen D., and Jean Penn Loerke. *From Farmland to Freeways: A History of Waukesha County, Wisconsin.* Waukesha County Historical Society, 1984.

Malone, Bill C., and Judith McCulloh. *Stars of Country Music.* University of Illinois Press, 1975.

Mongan, Norman, *The History of the Guitar in Jazz.* Oak Publications, 1983.

Moye, Claud. Unpublished memoir.

Sallis, James. *The Guitar Players: One Instrument and Its Masters in American Music,* William Morrow, 1982.

Schaden, Chuck. *WBBM Radio: Yesterday and Today.* WBBM Newsradio 78, 1988.

Simon, George T. *The Big Bands.* Collier Books, 1974.

Smith, Joe. *Off the Record: An Oral History of Popular Music.* Edited by Mitchell Fink. Warner Books, 1988.

Smithsonian Institution. *The History of Music Machines.* Drake, 1975.

Stewart, Rex. *Jazz Masters of the '30s.* Macmillan, 1972.

Thomas, Charles. *Bing.* McKay, 1976.

Trager, James, editor. *The People's Chronology: A Year-by-Year Record of Human Events from Prehistory to the Present.* Holt, Rinehart & Winston, 1979.

Wheeler, Tom. *American Guitars: An Illustrated History.* Harper & Row, 1982.

Whitburn, Joel. *Joel Whitburn's Pop Memories, 1890–1954.* Record Research, 1986.

———. *The Billboard Book of Top 40 Hits.* Billboard Publications, 1987.

WPA Writers Project. *Wisconsin: A Guide to the Badger State.* Duell, Sloan and Pearce, 1941.

Wyman, Bill, with Ray Coleman. *Stone Alone: The Story of a Rock 'N' Roll Band.* Viking, 1990.

PERIODICALS AND PRESS RELEASES

1930s

Chicago Herald Examiner: Nov. 22, 1934, "Behind the Mike with Ulmer Turner."

Waukesha County Commercial: Oct. 21, 1932, "Lester Polfuss, Local Boy, with KMOX St. Louis."

Waukesha Freeman: Feb. 17, 1930, "Local Youth to Give Program Over Air."
Nov. 19, 1938, "Waukesha Boy on Waring Show."

Weekly Variety: May 25, 1938, "Waring Band Signed to Appear on NBC."
Oct. 12, 1938, review, Waring's NBC Bromo show.
July 8, 1939, review, Waring's NBC Chesterfield show.

TIME: June 26, 1939, "Fred Waring, Inc."

1940s

CBS press release about Les Paul, June 19, 1942.

Band Leaders: Spring 1946, Johnny Frazer, "Gitman on the Go."

Billboard: Oct. 12, 1946, disk review, *Rumors Are Flying.*
Dec. 28, 1946, review, Andrews Sisters' concert.

The Billboard 1945–46 Music Year Book: "Transcriptions: They Fill Musical Needs."

The Billboard 1946–47 Encyclopedia of Music: photo essay of Hollywood's small band and cocktail attractions.

Chandler News-Publicist: Jan. 29, 1948, "Entertainer Hurt in Car Accident."

Down Beat: May 15, 1940, disk review, "Out of Nowhere."
Oct. 1, 1940, Leonard Feather, "Waring's Social Club Is Unique in Music Circles."
Aug. 1, 1944, review, Jazz at the Philharmonic.
Nov. 1, 1945, disk review, "It's Been a Long, Long Time."
Nov. 15, 1945, disk review, "Get Happy."
April 22, 1946, disk review, "Baby, What You Do to Me."
June 3, 1946, "Les Give Marilyn [Maxwell] Lesson One."
July 1946, disk review, "Blue Skies."
March 10, 1948, disk review, "Lover."

Sept. 23, 1949, "No, Them Ain't Hillbillies: It's Les Paul and Company."
Oct. 7, 1949, "Les Paul Mugs Way Through Blue Skies."

Life: Aug. 3, 1942, Robert Coughlan, "Petrillo: Little Caesar of Symphony and Swing Wages War on Juke Boxes."

Lincoln County Republican: Jan. 28, 1948, "Les Paul . . . Injured."

Metronome: Dec. 1946, Barry Ulanov, "You Name It—He'll Do It."
April 1948, disk review, "Lover."
June 1948, disk review, "What Is This Thing Called Love."
Aug. 1948, disk review, "On the Street of Regret."
Aug. 1949, disk review, "Until I Hold You Again."

Music and Rhythm: April 1942, "Les Paul on Guitar Playing."
July 1942, Les Paul, "My Twelve Favorite Guitarists."

Newsweek: Sept. 5, 1949, "Paul's Comeback."

New York Times: Oct. 21, 1943, "Ben Bernie Dies."

P.M.: Aug. 5, 1945, Mary Morris on the Andrews Sisters, "The Record-making Daughters of 'Pete the Greek' Talk About How They Live and Work . . ."
Feb. 14, 1947, John S. Wilson, "Band Leaders Mobilize to Beat Jim Crow."

Time: Jan. 26, 1948, "Petrillo: The Pied Piper of Chi."

Variety: Sept. 13, 1944, review, Rudy Vallee's radio show.
    Oct. 2, 1946, review, Gene Autry's Madison Square Garden rodeo.
    Dec. 11, 1946, review, Andrews Sisters' Earle Theater show.
    Dec. 25, 1946, review, Andrews Sisters' Paramount show.
    April 16, 1947, review, Andrews Sisters' Golden Gate show.
    April 30, 1947, review, Andrews Sisters Oriental Theater show.
    March 10, 1948, disk review, "Lover."

Waukesha Freeman: July 4, 1941, Ted Knap, "Les Paul—Red Polfuss to Us—Vacationing with Folks Here Before Taking Big Radio Post."
    Oct. 3, 1949, "Les Paul's Dad Dies Suddenly."
    Dec. 29, 1949, "Les Paul Weds His Vocalist."

1950s

Billboard: Aug. 25, 1951, "Disks by Duo See Four Million."
    Oct. 27, 1951, "Paul & Ford Get 5G for Air Spots"; "Laine Falters But

Les-Mary Pace Strong Para[mount] Bill to Whirl Finish."

Aug. 2, 1952, "The Hits and the Artist Who Made Them."

July 1, 1953, disk review, "Vaya con Dios."

Capitol News: April 1951, "No More Rhubarb for Les."

May 1951, "Capitol's Story of Les Paul."

July 1951, "Les-Mary Under Cap's Dome."

Cosmopolitan: January 1955, Hyman Goldberg, "Les and Mary: Masters of Musical Sleight of Hand."

Down Beat: June 15, 1951, "Want to Get Godfrey Quality," Says Les Paul.

Aug. 24, 1951, "Is Slicked Up Les Still Just Rhubarb Red?"

April 18, 1952, "Les Paul Gets Stiff Multitape Competition."

Aug. 13, 1952, "Beware of Imitations, Says Les Paul"; "Caught in the Act: Les Paul and Mary Ford at Paramount, NYC."

Sept. 10, 1952, Leonard Feather's Blindfold Test, "Les & Mary Vote for Segovia, Ella."

July 1, 1953, disk review, "Vaya con Dios."

Sept. 23, 1953, "Les, Mary Discuss Life, Loves, Sundry Matters."

June 30, 1954, "I Try to Make Perfect Records."

Dec. 15, 1954, Charles Emge, "How Norman Granz' Flourishing Jazz Empire Started, Expanded."

Hit Parade: April 1955, Les Paul and Mary Ford, "Genuine Love."

April 1956, "How Mary Ford Met Les Paul."

Undated, "The Big Switch" (Les and Mary Sign with Columbia).

Life: Dec. 22, 1958, "Rock 'n' Roll Rolls On 'n' On."

Magnetic Film & Tape Recording: Oct. 1954, Mildred Stagg, "The Great Dub."

Melody Maker: May 19, 1952, Laurie Henshaw, "This Twelve-Piece String Section Has a One-Man Line-up!"

Aug. 30, 1952, "Les Paul Reveals His Multi-Dubbing Stage Secrets."

Sept. 13, 1952, "Tony Brown Meets Les Paul and Mary Ford at Southampton."

Sept. 20, 1952, "No Gimmicks—but the Act Is Still Great"; "Les Paul Meets Django: Paris Report from Henry Kahn."

Jan. 22, 1955, "Les Paul Searches for Ideal Guitar."

Metronome: July 1950, disk review, "Jealous"/"Nola."

March, 1951, disk review, "Mockin' Bird Hill"/"Chicken Reel."

June 1951, disk review, "How High the Moon"/"Walkin' & Whistlin' Blues."

Feb. 1952, Barry Ulanov, "All-Star Paul . . . Les, That Is, and Mary . . . "

April 1952, "Metronome 1951 Disc Jockey Poll."

Nov. 1953, "Les and Mary Bring Back the Guitar."

May 1957, "Les Paul and Mary Ford in Hi-Fi."

Music News: March 1952, "Paul-Ford Duel Page in 6M Sales Battle."

Music View: Sept. 1955, TV show announcement.

Newsweek: July 27, 1953, "Polfuses [sic] at Home."

New York *Daily News:* Dec. 5, 1959, "Stars to DA: Dough-Re-Not-Me."

New York Mirror: Dec. 5, 1959, "5 Top Stars Reply on Payola, Back Freed."

New York Post: Nov. 30, 1954, "Operation Fails to Save Mary Ford's Baby."

New York Sunday News: Dec. 2, 1951, Paul/Ford cover story.

Aug. 30, 1953, "Two's a Crowd."

Pathfinder: April 1953, "Mr. and Mrs. Sound."

Radio Electronics: Oct. 1958, "Les Paul: Technician and Musician."

Reader's Digest: June 1957, Les Paul, "Best Advice I Ever Had."

Saturday Evening Post: Jan. 17, 1953, Amy Porter, "Craziest Music You Ever Heard."

Time: Oct. 29, 1951, "The New Sound."

Variety: July 2, 1951, review, Oriental Theater concert.

Aug. 15, 1951, review, Capitol Theater concert.

Oct. 24, 1951, review, Paramount Theater concert.

June, 25, 1952, review, Paramount Theater concert.

Sept. 14, 1952, review, Palladium Theater concert.

April 22, 1953, "Paul-Ford Team Moving at Hot Clip."

Sept. 30, 1953, "Listerine's 2M, 3-Year Deal for Les Paul–Mary Ford Vid Pix."

Nov. 4, 1953, "LaRosa, Les and Mary Cue CBS Radio Shift."

Vogue, Feb. 15, 1953, Les and Mary in star roundup.

1960s

Bergen Record: February, 28, 1963, "Les-Mary Putting Home Up for Sale."

Nov. 8, 1963, "Les Paul Files Suit Against Mary Ford, Says Singing Wife Humiliated Him in Public."

Dec. 17, 1964, "Les Paul Granted Divorce from Mary."

June 13, 1966, Joe Grant, "Les Hopes to Find Talent at Home."

March 11, 1967, Ken Wallace, "The Mahwah Sound."

Herald Tribune: Dec. 17, 1964, "Les Paul Gets Divorce."

Milwaukee Sentinel: Oct. 16, 1961, "Waukesha Welcomes Les Paul."

New York *Daily News:* July 10, 1963, "Mary Ford Sues Les Paul."

Nov. 1963, Alfred Albelli and Lester Abelman, "Les Paul Says His Mary Played Not Only the Guitar but the Field."

Dec. 1, 1963, Francis M. Stephenson, "Guitarist Les Paul Says Mary Fiddled Around, Seeks Divorce."

Dec. 17, 1964, "Les Paul & Mary Ford to Twang Solo Guitar."

New York Post: July 31, 1963, Stan Koven, "Mary Ford Goes Solo—but Les Paul Gets the Bill."

San Gabriel Valley Tribune: July 31, 1963, Charles Mosher, "Mary Ford Wins Alimony Suit."

Nov. 8, 1963, Charles Mosher, "Les Paul Files Suit for Divorce."

Dec. 20, 1964, Renee Dictor, "Valley Profiles: Mary Ford."

Stars and Stripes: June 1965, review, Les's act with Arlene Carroll in Japan.

July 1965, review, Les's act at NCO Club in Japan.

Weekly Variety: Dec. 13, 1961, review, Fairmont Hotel concert.

Waukesha Freeman: Oct 17, 1961, "Les Paul's Homecoming Marks First Appearance in Waukesha Since 1949."

1970s

Audio: Dec. 1978; Paul Laurence and Bob Rypinski, "Interview with Les Paul."

Bergen Record: Sept. 4, 1977, Dave Spengler, "Where's Rhubarb Red?"

Billboard: Aug. 13, 1977, Dave Dexter, "Les Paul Pegged by U.S. Government."

Down Beat: Oct. 1976, review, Mikal Gilmore, *Chester & Lester.*

Guitar: Feb. 1975, Ivor Mairants, "The Original Les Paul."

Nov. 1975, Ivor Mairants, "Les Paul: Living Legend."

Guitar Player: Feb. 1970, "The Wizard of Waukesha."

Sept. 1976, Jim Atkins as told to Bill Ivey, "Jim Atkins: A Life Filled with the Guitar, Chet and Les."

Dec. 1977, John Sievert, "Les Paul."

April 1978, Douglas B. Green, "Chester and Lester Are in the Studio Again."

Los Angeles Times: Aug. 30, 1975, Robert Hilburn, "Catching Up with a Musical Giant."

National Enquirer: undated, Tom Smith, "Whatever Happened to Les Paul and Mary Ford?"

New York *Daily News:* July 17, 1978, William Carlton, "Chet and Les: Great Guitars."

New York Times: July 18, 1971, Dick Adler, "Can Dave [Garroway] Come Back?"

Aug. 9, 1972, "Joi Lansing, Actress, Dies at 37."

July 9, 1978, John Rockwell, "Chet Atkins and Les Paul at Club."

Rolling Stone: Feb. 13, 1975, Chet Flippo, "I Sing the Solid Body Electric."
Feb. 12, 1976, Chet Flippo, "Picker King: The Rolling Stone Interview with Chet Atkins."
Feb. 12, 1976, John Rockwell, "Fender the Founder."

Village Voice: Oct. 10, 1974, Patrick Carr, "Old Farts and Paulverization."

People: April 11, 1972, Jim Jerome, "Somewhere, There's Music, and Les Paul's Influence Is Still as High as the Moon."

1980s

Bergen Record: Sept. 9, 1985, Michael C. Pollak, "Taking It Easy Isn't His Tune."

Down Beat: May 1986, Bill Milkowski (Les at Fat Tuesday's).

Goldmine: Dec. 18, 1987, Stu Fink, "Les Paul: Inventor, Innovator, Hit Musician."

Grammy Magazine: Aug. 1989, Don Meehan, "The Art of the Overdub."

Guitar World: March 1983, Peter Mengaziol, "Les Paul: The Interview, Part 1."
May 1983, Peter Mengaziol, "Les Paul: The Interview, Part 2."
Nov. 1985, Steven Rosen, "Edward and Les" (Eddie Van Halen interviews Les Paul).
June 1988, George Gruhn and Walter Carter, "Log-Jammin'."

Insight: Feb. 22, 1988, Daniel Kagan, "The Master Still Picks Favorites."

International Musician & Recording World (IM&RW): June 1986, Adrian Belew and Gene Santoro, "Happy Birthday Les Paul."

Los Angeles Daily News: Nov. 15, 1985, Jonathan Taylor, "Music World's Famous Leave Their Mark on the 'Rock Walk.'"

Los Angeles Times: Nov. 16, 1985, Jane Greenstein, "Rock Music Greats Win in a Walk."

Mix: Feb. 1985, Mr. Bonsai, "The Godfather of Modern Music."

Newark Star Ledger: May 20, 1984, George Kanzler, "Electric Guitar Inventor Still Strumming."
Aug. 8, 1985, George Kanzler, "Thirteen's 'Jersey Summerfare' Showcases a Concert by Four Giants of the Jazz Guitar."

New York *Daily News:* May 1, 1975, Pat O'Haire, "In Sound, Les Is More."
March 26, 1984, Pat O'Haire, "A Les Paul Giveaway."
April 21, 1985, Douglas Brin, "Starring in New York: Les Paul."
Jan. 15, 1987, Pat O'Haire, "Monday Nights, Les Is More."
June 30, 1987, Pablo Guzmán's "Sounds" column.

May 8, 1988, Marion Collins, "The Plucky Les Paul: Health Woes Fail to Mute a Pioneer Guitarist."

July 28, 1988, Michael Moran, "Paul's Mellow Strings."

New York Post: April 18, 1988, Lee Jeske, "Les Paul, Echoing Legend."

New York Times: April 29, 1984, Kirk Johnson, "The Boom in Electronic Keyboards."

April 17, 1986, John Wilson, "Pop: The Guitarist Les Paul."

Dec. 27, 1987, Evan St. Lifer, "Les Paul: No Stopping the Guitarist."

Jan. 10, 1988, George Simon, "The Night Carnegie Hall Swung."

Record Research: Oct. 1987, "Les Paul with Gene Austin: The '40s Masters."

Rolling Stone: Aug. 13, 1987, "Les Paul's Six-String Salute."

San Gabriel Valley Tribune: April 11, 1989, Frances Young, "Singer Spent Years with Paul, Ford."

Washington Post: May 10, 1987, Paula Span, "The Legend of Les Paul."

Waukesha Freeman: Aug. 7, 1982, Dan Callahan, "Les Paul Wants Museum in Waukesha."

March 4, 1988, editorial, "City Planning Quality Tribute to Les Paul."

June 23, 1988, Larayne Ritt, "A Return Visit to Goerke's Corners."

1990s

Grammy Magazine: April 1990, Miles Kreuger, Letter to the Editor: "Who's on First: The Overdubbing Saga Continues."

Oct. 1990, Ben Sandmel, "Sound Instruments."

Guitar Player: Aug. 1991, Tom Wheeler, "The Legacy of Leo Fender."

New York *Daily News:* June 10, 1990, David Hinkley, "Long Player: Mr. Les Paul Cranks It Up."

New York Newsday: June 6, 1990, John Anderson, "Les Paul, the Thomas Edison of Rock and Roll, Turns 75."

New York Times: Dec. 1, 1991, Mark Dery, "Les Paul: Once a Wunderkind, Still a Wizard."

VIDEOTAPED AND AUDIOTAPED PERFORMANCES, SPEECHES, AND INTERVIEWS

Yale University School of Music oral history archives, interviews by Joan Thomson, Spring 1978.

The Wizard of Waukesha: A Film About Les Paul, produced by Catherine Orentreich, directed by Susan Brockman, 1979.

Audio Engineering Society: Les serves as guest speaker on both May 30, 1977, and Oct. 31, 1987.

Pacific Pioneer Broadcasters: An evening of storytelling by Les Paul, Oct. 30, 1987.

Les Paul interviewed by Ray Briem on KABC radio, Oct. 30, 1987 Cinemax promotional video, Sept. 9, 1988.

Chuck Schadin's Collection of Bing Crosby radio shows: Dec. 28, 1944; Oct. 30, 1946; April 23, 1947; March 21, 1951.

Selected Discography

This discography is an extensive sampling of Les Paul's recorded output. For the most part, it includes only the initial release date of his disks. Omitted are a number of Les Paul/Mary Ford reissues, which have been packaged under a variety of guises and labels, often as greatest-hits collections with other artists. Also omitted are the sixteen-inch transcriptions that Les made during the 1940s for the U.S. military and for radio and transcription libraries. Many of these recordings have been lost or are commercially unavailable, although some can be heard at the Library of Congress. It was impossible to track down every recording on which Les played as a sideman.

SINGLES

LABEL	ARTIST	TITLE	FIRST RELEASE DATE
	Rhubarb Red: vocal, guitar, harmonica; recorded in Decca's Chicago studio on 5/20/36		
Montgomery Ward	Just Because Deep Elm Blues Answer to Just Because Deep Elm Blues, Part 2		1936
	Les Paul Trio, including vocals by Jimmy Atkins; recorded in New York on 10/3/39		
Vocalion	Goodbye, My Lover, Goodbye/Out of Nowhere		4/4/40
OKeh	Where Is Love/Swanee River		2/7/41

Les Paul (g) with Milt Raskin (p), Cal Gooden (rhythm gtr.),
Clint Nordquist (sb); recorded in Hollywood on 12/14/44

Decca	Begin the Beguine/Dream Dust	1946
	Blue Skies/Dark Eyes	5/20/46

Les Paul (g) with Paul Smith (p), Bob Meyer (sb),
Tony Rinaldo (d); recorded in N.Y.C. on 1/23/47

	Steel Guitar Rag/Guitar Boogie	6/1/47

Recording dates for Les Paul/Mary Ford disks are unavailable because Les cut nearly all of them in his home studio or on portable recording equipment while touring. The singles before 1950 were released in 78-RPM format only; others through August 1957 were often released as both 78s and 45s; all subsequent singles were released as 45s unless otherwise noted. Les Paul solo sides are indicated with an asterisk.

Capitol	*Lover/*Brazil	2/23/48
	*Hip-Billy Boogie	4/19/48
	*What Is This Thing Called Love	
	*The Man on the Flying Trapeze	7/19/48
	*By the Light of the Silvery Moon	
	*Caravan/*The Swiss Woodpecker	12/6/48
	Until I Hold You Again	5/49
	You Can't Expect Kisses From Me	
	*Nola/Jealous	5/15/50
	Cryin'/Dry My Tears	6/26/50
	Goofus/Sugar Sweet	9/4/50
	Tennessee Waltz/*Little Rock Getaway	10/20/50
	Mockin' Bird Hill/*Chicken Reel	1/29/51
	How High the Moon	3/26/51
	*Walking & Whistlin' Blues	
	*Josephine	7/2/51
	I Wish I Had Never Seen the Sun Shine	

The World Is Waiting for the Sunrise *Whispering	8/20/51
*Jazz Me Blues/Just One More Chance	10/22/51
*Jungle Bells/Silent Night	11/26/51
Tiger Rag/It's a Lonesome Old Town	1/7/52
*Carioca I'm Confessin' (That I Love You)	5/12/52
In the Good Old Summertime/Smoke Rings	6/16/52
*Meet Mr. Callaghan Take Me In Your Arms and Hold Me	8/18/52
*Lady of Spain My Baby's Comin' Home	11/3/52
Bye, Bye Blues Mammy's Boogie	12/22/52
I'm Sitting on Top of the World *Sleep	3/9/53
Vaya con Dios Johnny (Is the Boy for Me)	6/1/53
*The Kangaroo Doncha Hear Them Bells	10/12/53
White Christmas *Jungle Bells	10/12/53
I Really Don't Want to Know/*South	2/22/54
I'm a Fool to Care/Auctioneer	6/21/54
Whither Thou Goest/*Mandolino	9/27/54
Song in Blue/*Someday Sweetheart	1/3/55
No Letter Today/Genuine Love	5/2/55
Hummingbird/Goodbye, My Love	6/27/55
Amukirki/*Magic Melody	10/3/55

	Texas Lady/Alabamy Road	12/5/55
	Moritat (Theme from Three Penny Opera) Nuevo Laredo	1/23/56
	Send Me Some Money Say the Words I Love to Hear	4/2/56
	Cimarron/*San Antonio Rose	5/28/56
	Runnin' Wild/Blow the Smoke Away	10/56
	Cinco Robles/*Ro-Ro Robinson	12/31/56
	Tuxedos and Flowers/Hummin' and Waltzin'	5/57
	I Don't Want You No More Strollin' Blues	8/19/57
	A Pair of Fools/Fire	10/28/57

Les Paul and Mary Ford, recorded with orchestra at Capitol's New York studio

	Goodnight My Someone *The Night of the Fourth	12/23/57
	More and More Each Day/Small Island	2/58

Les Paul and Mary Ford

Columbia	Put a Ring on My Finger/Fantasy	7/28/58
	*Big Eyed Gal/Jealous Heart	10/13/58
	All I Need is You At the Save-a-Penny Super Store	2/2/59
	*Poor People of Paris/All Night Long	2/29/60
	Wonderful Rain/Take a Warning	4/18/60
	Jura/It's Been a Long, Long Time	4/3/61
	*Mountain Railroad/It's Too Late	9/22/61
	Lonely Guitar/Goodnight Irene	11/24/61
	Your Cheating Heart Another Town, Another Time	4/27/62

	I Just Don't Understand	10/12/62
	Playing Make Believe	
	Gentle Is Your Love/Move Along Baby	3/15/63

45-RPM EXTENDED PLAYS

Capitol	Vaya con Dios	2/22/54
	I'm Sitting on Top of the World	1954
	Christmas Cheer	10/54
	Mister Sandman	11/22/54
	I'm a Fool to Care	11/54
	Whither Thou Goest	1/55
	Songs of Today	1955

TEN-INCH LPs

Decca	Galloping Guitars (Les Paul Trio)	1944
	Hawaiian Paradise (Les Paul Trio)	10/28/46
Capitol	*The New Sound, Vol. 1	7/50
	The New Sound, Vol. 2	8/13/51
	Bye, Bye Blues	11/3/52
	The Hit Makers	5/53

TWELVE-INCH LPs

Capitol	Les and Mary	4/4/55
	The New Sound	4/55
	Bye, Bye Blues	10/3/55
	The Hit Makers	1956

	The New Sound, Vol. 2	1956
	Time to Dream	2/16/57
	The World Is Still Waiting for the Sunrise	8/1/74
	Very Best of Les Paul and Mary Ford	1974
	Johnny (Is the Boy for Me)	1977
	Early Les Paul	9/15/82
	Les Paul and Mary Ford: Their All-Time Greatest Hits (3-LP set distributed by Capitol/Murray Hill)	1980
	Memories Are Made of This	10/26/88

SEVEN-INCH EPs

Columbia	Deed I Do/Makin' Whoopee	3/30/62
	A Cottage for Sale/Chasing Shadows	3/30/62
	It's Been a Long, Long Time After You've Gone	3/30/62
	Am I Blue You Brought a New Kind of Love	3/30/62
	Wrap Your Troubles in Dreams East of East	3/30/62
RCA	Avalon (With Chet Atkins)	1976

TWELVE-INCH LPs

Columbia	Lover's Luau	3/23/59
	Warm and Wonderful	12/18/61
	Bouquet of Roses	7/16/62

	Swingin' South	5/13/63
	The Fabulous Les Paul and Mary Ford	9/27/65
	Guitar Artistry (Les Paul Trio)	1968
	'50s Greatest Love Songs	12/29/71
Decca	*More of Les (Compilation of previously released Les Paul Decca recordings)	1950
London	Les Paul Now! (Rereleased as *The Genius of Les Paul* in 1979)	1968
RCA	Chester and Lester Guitar Monsters (both recorded with Chet Atkins)	2/76 6/78
Glendale	The Les Paul Trio (Radio Transcriptions of '47)	1978
Charly Ltd.	Guitar Genius (Featuring solo recordings by Les Paul, Hank Garland, and Grady Martin)	1985
Circle	Feed Back (The Les Paul Trio, 1944–45)	1986

COMPACT DISKS

RCA/Pair	Masters of Guitar 2-CD/cassette set combining abridged contents of the two previously noted Les Paul/Chet Atkins LPs	1989
Capitol	Les Paul: The Legend and the Legacy (4-CD/cassette set)	11/12/91
LaserLight	Les Paul Trio	1991

PERFORMANCES AS SIDEMAN

LABEL	ARTIST	TITLE	RECORDING DATE
Decca	Georgia White, blues singer: accompanied by Richard M. Jones (p); Les Paul (g); John Lindsay (sb)		
		New Dupree Blues	5/11/36
		Daddy Let Me Lay It on You	
		New Hot Nuts (Get 'em from the Peanut man)	
		I Just Want Your Stingaree	5/12/36
		Black Rider	
		I'll Keep Sittin' on It (If I Can't Sell It)	
		Pigmeat Blues	
		A Trouble in Mind	
		Little Red Wagon	12/7/36
		Dan the Back Door Man	
		Your Hellish Way	
		Marble Stone Blues	
		You Don't Know My Mind	1/28/37
		When My Love Comes Down	
		Walking the Street	
		Grandpa and Grandma	
		I'm So Glad I'm 21 Today	
		Toothache Blues	
Decca	Terry Shand Orchestra with Les Paul		
		Filipino Hombre	1941
		New River Train	
	Bing Crosby accompanied by the Les Paul Trio		
		It's Been a Long, Long Time	7/12/45
		Whose Dream are You?	
		Pretending	5/15/46
		Gotta Get Me Somebody to Love	
		What Am I Gonna Do About You?	2/13/47
		Drifting and Dreaming	
	Helen Forrest accompanied by the Les Paul Trio		
		Baby, What You Do to Me	11/45
		Everybody Knew But Me	

Delta Rhythm Boys accompanied by the LPT

    A One-Sided Affair   5/46
    What Would It Take?

Andrews Sisters and Les Paul with Vic Schoen Orchestra

    Rumors Are Flying   7/20/46

Dick Haymes accompanied by the Les Paul Trio

    What Are You Doing New Years Eve?   7/47
    My Future Just Passed

Evelyn Knight and Foster Carling with instrumental
accompaniment, incl. Les Paul

    Counterfeit Love   7/49
    Play That Barber Shop Chord

Verve   Jazz at the Philharmonic with J. J. Johnson (tb),
Lester Young, Jack McVea, Illinois Jacquet (ts),
Nat Cole (listed as Shorty Nadine) (p), Les Paul (g),
Johnny Miller (b), Lee Young (d), Red Callender on
last two titles (b)

    Lester Leaps In   7/2/44
    Blues
    Body and Soul
    Rosetta
    Bugle Call Rag
    I Found a New Baby
    Tea for Two

(Parts of this live concert have been released over the years on the Clef,
Disc, Mercury, and VSP labels)

Shoestring Art Tatum with the Les Paul Trio

    JaDa   1944
    I've Found a New Baby
    Oh, Lady Be Good to Me
    Somebody Loves Me
    (Above cuts from Tatum's "Piano Mastery" LP)

Sunset	Red Callender Six: Harry Edison (tp), Herbie Haymer (as and ts), Arnold Ross (p), Les Paul (g), Shadow Wilson (drm)	
	These Foolish Things Get Happy	9/12/45
Keynote	Willie Smith and His Orchestra: Billy May (tp), Murray McEachern (tb), Willie Smith (as), Arnold Ross (p), Les Paul (g), Ed Mihelich (b), Nick Fatool (drm)	
	September in the Rain You Ought to Be in Pictures Moten Swing Willie, Weep for Me	11/2/45
Mercury	Clancy Hayes accompanied by the Les Paul Trio	
	My Extraordinary Gal Now Is the Hour Nobody but You On the Street of Regret	1947
	Foster Carling accompanied by "Rhubarb Red"	
	Suspicion	1947
Universal	Gene Austin accompanied by the Les Paul Trio	
	Yearning Cala-California You're Gonna Cause Me Trouble The Lonesome Road Keep-a-Knockin' My Blue Heaven	12/47
Columbia	Al Dimeola accompanied by Les Paul and other instrumentalists.	
	Spanish Eyes (from Dimeola's Splendido Hotel LP)	1980 1980

Atlantic	Janice Siegel accompanied by Les Paul and other instrumentalists	
	How High the Moon (from Siegel's "Experiments in Light" LP)	1982
Hindsight	Uncollected Kay Starr with Les Paul, Joe Venuti, and Billy Butterfield	1986

INDEX